A VERY BRITISH CONSPIRACY

JOHN DEKKER

Copyright © 2014 by John Dekker.

All rights reserved. Printed in the United Kingdom and/or the USA / Australia / Canada / Germany / Spain / Brazil / China or other contracted locations worldwide. No part of this publication may be reproduced, stored in a retrieval system, or transmitted, in any form or by any means, digital, electronic, mechanical, photocopying, recording, or otherwise, without the prior written permission of the publisher or the author(s) [as per CheckPoint Press contract terms]; except in the case of reviewers who may quote brief passages in a review.

A Very British Conspiracy
1st Edition 2014
ISBN-13: 978-1-906628-54-3
Published by CheckPoint Press, Ireland
www.checkpointpress.com

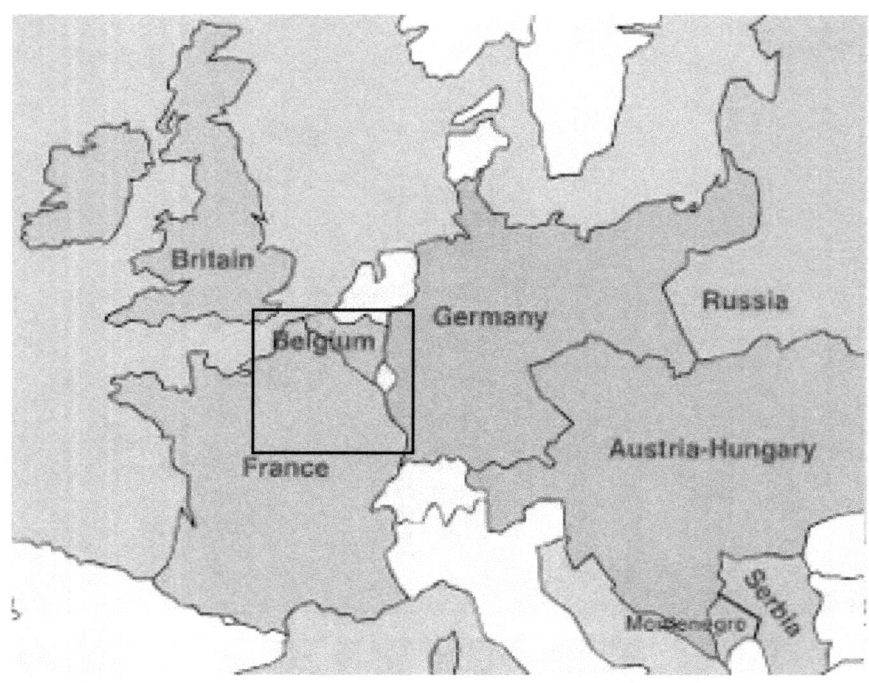

Europe (above) in 1914.   Detail – the Western Front (below)

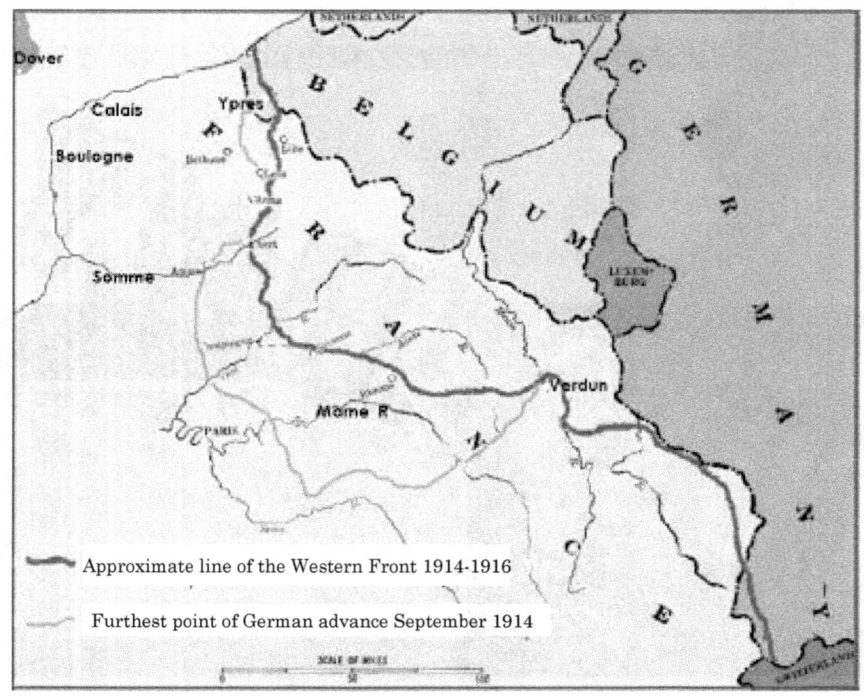

Acknowledgements

I owe a huge (moral) debt to the library of King's College London, the British Library, the National Archives, National Army Museum, National Maritime Museum, Imperial War Museum, the Royal United Services Institute, and Richmond upon Thames public libraries, for everyone's unfailing assistance and advice. I am grateful to The Warden and Scholars of New College Oxford, for permission to quote from the papers of Lord Milner, and to The Trustees of the Liddell Hart Centre for Military Archives for permission to quote from the papers of General Sir Ian Hamilton.

My thanks are due to Aaron Cripps who told me more about the Staff College at Quetta, and Stuart Nourse of the Royal National Lifeboat Institution, for details of George Shee's life, while old friends and colleagues helped hugely – Peter Ceresole steered me through the very accommodating French Military Archives, Peter Hill has been a huge source of encouragement, also Dan van der Vat, and of course, my publisher Dr Stephen Manning who pulled everything together with efficiency and great good humour.

It was my good fortune to be a student, perhaps their oldest, in the Department of War Studies, King's College London, where Brian Bond, Christopher Dandeker, Michael Dockrill, Robert Foley, Beatrice Heuser, Brian Paskins, Brian Holden Reid, and Laughton Professor of Naval History Andrew Lambert, all provided a truly stimulating environment, though of course none of them are remotely responsible for the thrust of my argument or its presentation – perhaps the study of war is too serious a business for journalists.

I recall with affection and gratitude, Ed Cooney at Ruskin College, more than half a century ago, Professor William Mackenzie and colleagues at the Department of Government in the University of Manchester, and the Vice-Chancellor, Sir William Mansfield Cooper, while some of my best friends have been generals (and admirals), notably Field Marshal Sir John Stanier and Admiral of the Fleet Lord Hill-Norton. I remember too, my former comrades - and a long since departed, but not forgotten, host of veterans of the Great War whom it was my privilege to know.

John Dekker, Middlesex, UK, 2014

Contents

Introduction .... *vii*
The Main Players .... *x*

~

One: Council of War 1
Two: The Soldiers and their State 10
Three: Ring of Blue Water 24
Four: Castles by the Seaside 29
Five: Great-great- Granddad's Army 32
Six: The Ghastly Peril 38
Seven: Out of Africa 46
Eight: Flagstaffs in the Persian Gulf 50
Nine: The Man Least Likely To 59
Ten: What They settled I Never Knew 63
Eleven: Poisoned Wells and Beatrice 71
Twelve: The Briton's First Duty 81
Thirteen: Pussy in the Cabbage Patch 88
Fourteen: Last Post for Colonel Trench 97
Fifteen: Dreadnought Gap 100
Sixteen: Two Armies, Two Nations 110
Seventeen: On The Brink 117
Eighteen: The French Connection 124
Nineteen: Agent Orange 130
Twenty: Conspiracy and Confusion 140
Twenty One: The Wrong Kind of War? 149
Twenty Two: The Chief, and the C-in-C 160
Twenty Three: Never again? 167
Conclusion 177
References & Further Reading 178

I GREW UP IN THE SHADOW OF THAT WAR.

I LISTENED TO VETERANS OF THE WESTERN FRONT, I LIVED THROUGH THE SECOND GREAT WAR, AND WAS OLD ENOUGH TO PLAY A SMALL PART IN IT; FRIENDS DIED IN BATTLE; ONE OF MY COMRADES FELL BESIDE ME; I CAN STILL HEAR HIS DYING SCREAMS.

THAT 'CONSPIRACY' OF LONG AGO IS UNCANNILY REPLICATED TODAY. THE PROFESSION, AND THE 'MILITARY-INDUSTRIAL COMPLEX' ARE WITH US STILL – AND AGENTS OF THE STATE ARE DECEIVING US – AS ALWAYS.

John Dekker, Middlesex, UK, 2014

INTRODUCTION

"We have to suppress the truth and resort to subterfuge at times to meet hostile public opinion."

*Sir Charles Hardinge,
Permanent Under Secretary,
British Foreign Office 1908.*

Taking the nation into a foreign war is a doubtful, dangerous act – especially if the government has not been truthful about it. To the very last moment the Prime Minister denied there was any undertaking to fight in Europe, yet in August 1914 he sent the army to do just that.

The bloodiest war in British history? More died in the Civil Wars of the 1640's when the population of the British Isles was far smaller, but it is widely believed the 'Great War' of 1914-18 wiped out an entire generation – young lives squandered by incompetent generals. Others say the generals weren't that stupid and the sacrifice was regrettable but necessary – a matter of honour. For all that, the Great War *was* a profound shock to a people conditioned by a century of peace – not counting the Boer War, the Crimean War and seventy two colonial 'wars' in Queen Victoria's reign. And although Britain emerged triumphant, her enemy defeated, disarmed and demoralised, a war that began as a holy crusade ended as a national tragedy. It left an open wound that will not heal, a memory that tugs at the public conscience – images of men in muddy trenches, their letters home, their memoirs, the haunting verse of the soldier-poets, while every year another generation visits the battlefields in France and Flanders and the vast cemeteries where so many of their kinsmen lie. The Great War cast a very long shadow.

When the fighting was done and close on a million names of soldiers from Britain and her Empire were engraved on headstones and monuments, the statesmen began to set the record straight, recalling how they did their utmost to avoid this war, how surprised and dismayed they were when it came - and why *they* were not to blame. The generals too left *their* memoirs – or their much more interesting letters and diaries – to give some idea of what the principal characters said and did, or thought they were doing, in those critical years before August 1914.

One thing is certain. The men in Whitehall had long expected war with Germany – albeit a very brief war. The Navy would sink the Kaiser's fleet while the French and the Russians did the serious fighting on land, perhaps with a little help from the Army, but the generals had a *different* idea – to fight on the continent of Europe. Yet in all the years of agitation and hysteria—of frantic scaremongering by newspaper barons and attention-seeking busybodies peddling lurid fears of invasion and clamouring for conscription—the British people could never imagine what they were committed to; their rulers were afraid to tell them.

Oddly, it was a Liberal government that took the nation into this war, a 'radical' government that set itself against wealth and privilege and laid the foundations of a welfare state. But in 1914 that government was clinging to power, beset by adversity, scandal and sleaze, with Ireland on the brink of rebellion and the army's loyalty in doubt. The Great War was the climax to years of confusion, intrigue and deception – altogether a 'conspiracy' of statesmen, generals, diplomats and hangers-on who to the last moment and beyond, contrived to deceive the nation – and themselves. But this was a very *British* conspiracy.

'Conspiracy': gentlemen with well-trimmed beards, lace collars and funny hats. Gunpowder, treason and plot. We are wiser now. England never had a monopoly of ineptitude and self-deception, and everywhere in this distracted world states conspire against their own citizens to hide an inconvenient truth – which is what the agents of the British state were doing in their own cynical, slipshod way during those confused and fevered times, long before August 1914.

The Main Players

Foremost among the men who led their country into this war, **Sir Edward Grey**, baronet, born on 25th April, 1862, was from a wealthy Northumbrian 'dynasty' with strong political and military antecedents; but he was himself an unlikely 'warmonger.' A country gentleman and nature-lover, he was a keen angler and wrote a text book on 'dry-fly fishing.' When he was very young, his father, an equerry to the Prince of Wales (the future King Edward VII) died suddenly. Grey was sent to a leading 'public school,' Winchester, and went to Oxford, where he showed little sign of the 'effortless superiority' of the typical Balliol College student. Expelled for his 'idleness and ignorance,' he was allowed to return, and obtained a third-class degree in jurisprudence.

However, he soon entered politics as MP for the border town of Berwick-upon-Tweed, a safe Liberal seat. He married a local girl, Dorothy Widrington, but she too preferred country life. She found London a 'horrid place' but her husband was also a director of the North Eastern railway, which made it easier for them to keep in touch with their beloved Northumbria. It also provided a modest income, for, until 1911 members of parliament were paid nothing.

SIR EDWARD GREY.

Grey quickly earned a reputation in his Party as 'a high-minded man' and was soon in a Liberal administration as Under Secretary for Foreign Affairs. Ten years later, at forty three, he would be Foreign Secretary. It was the start of a nine–year conspiracy that ended in war, and it was Grey who, along with his close friend Haldane and with Asquith's consent, authorised the secret military 'conversations' with France. However, he quickly distanced himself from all responsibility, preferring not to know what the generals were up to. He was diligent, but like so many of the nation's ruling elite, arrogant. He discouraged the curiosity of his fellow ministers, and he certainly deceived his countrymen, but his capacity for self-deception was limitless, and his career ended in failure.

The Main Players

Richard Burdon Haldane was born in Edinburgh on 30th July 1852. The family seat was at Cloan in Perthshire, and many of his forebears were naval or army officers, but his own upbringing directed him to Edinburgh Academy and the University itself, where he gained First Class honours in philosophy. He studied briefly at Gottingen university, and became a fluent German speaker. He was a lonely young man. Spurned by his only girlfriend, he never married, but remained close to his mother and his sister all his life.

A barrister, he successfully contested the East Lothian Haddingtonshire constituency as a Liberal, and was a member of parliament for sixteen years, until he became Lord Chancellor. His speeches were long, and often hard to understand, but he did not scruple to jockey for position and in 1905 was rewarded with one of the most important jobs in government; the War Department. He was the best war minister the army ever had. Defying noisy opposition, he raised a reserve army of part-time volunteers, but he also fashioned a 'striking force,' a secret army to fight in a European war. It was the wrong kind of war, as things turned out, but he must share the blame with his fellow conspirators.

Herbert Henry Asquith, born on the 12th of September 1852, was a grammar school boy whose thoroughly 'middle class' family was in the Yorkshire woollen trade. He too got into Balliol College, that Oxford hothouse for future leaders. A not very successful barrister, he wrote for the Spectator magazine, and turned to politics. With help from Haldane, he was elected as Member of Parliament for East Fife, safe Liberal seats being easier to find in Scotland. Thereafter he progressed rapidly, and began to earn rather more at the Bar. Home Secretary in the

Liberal government of 1892-95, he took a hard line during industrial disputes, even using troops to fire on striking miners. In 1905, he was Chancellor of the Exchequer, but three years later Sir Henry Campbell-Bannerman died, and Asquith was Prime Minister, stoutly denying there was any commitment to send the Army to fight in a European war. But the Liberals' huge majority of 1906 was shrinking fast, and soon he was only staying in Downing Street by courtesy of a handful of Labour MPs and eighty-four Irish nationalists. The Conservatives and their supporters made the most of his discomfort, but he did take on that built-in Conservative majority in the House of Lords, and he won. But by 1914, his grip on power was flimsy. He had lost control of events, and was little more than a helpless spectator.

In striking contrast, **Mr Winston Leonard Spencer Churchill** was at just thirty nine, the youngest of those ministers at the War Council. His father Randolph was third son of of the Seventh Duke of Marlborough, and the young Winston was sent to Eton's rival, Harrow School, which he found rather boring; but he enjoyed Sandhurst, the training school for army officers. After a brief spell in someone else's war in Cuba, he saw action with the Malakand Field Force, and the Tirah Expeditionary Force. Now serving in a crack cavalry regiment, the 21st Lancers, he was at Khartoum, where General Gordon had died long ago. Oddly, he was correspondent for the Morning Post, and in between, serving in the South African Light Horse. Captured by the Boers, he managed to escape, but the army never liked this brash adventurer.

Back home, now the Conservative Member of Parliament for Oldham in Lancashire, Winston, with an eye to the future adroitly changed sides, 'crossing the floor' of the House of Commons to be the Liberal MP for North West Manchester after the great victory of 1906, and later, for Dundee. Thought to be a dangerous radical, he was sent to the Colonial Office for a couple of years; and then, the Board of Trade. He worked hard and took everything seriously. Then Asquith made him Home Secretary and, in a further shake-up, First Lord of the Admiralty – his most absorbing task. Until recently, he'd opposed higher naval spending, but in a quick U-turn he gave the admirals even more

The Main Players

battleships. The admirals found him a hard master, though, a boss determined always to be in the front seat. Unlike his fellow ministers, he welcomed 'this glorious, delicious war.'

Blenhein Palace, the Churchill family home

John Arbuthnot Fisher, born 25th January 1841 in Ceylon (Sri Lanka), saw little of his army officer father turned coffee-planter, but patronage and the 'nomination' of Nelson's last surviving Captain got him into the Navy. He fought in the China wars, he was gunnery lieutenant in Britain's first 'ironclad' *HMS Warrior*, and later, in the invasion of Egypt (1882) he bombarded the forts of Alexandria. 'Jackie' Fisher was a pioneer of technology, especially torpedo warfare and modern gunnery. He introduced the 'revolutionary' Dreadnought battleship but favoured the swifter 'battle cruiser' and the submarine. And like the generals he so distrusted, he saw Germany, not France, as the enemy. As First Sea Lord – head of the Navy – he concentrated British naval power in the North Sea. 'Ruthless, relentless, remorseless,' he even proposed a surprise attack on the Kaiser's new fleet in harbour at Kiel. Tactless, abrasive in manner, he was difficult to work with, but he handled the press with skill. No respecter of rank, he listened to subordinates, and was a refreshingly different leader. Brought out of retirement in 1914, and back in his old job, he clashed with Churchill, now First Lord of Admiralty, over the ill-fated attempt to force the Dardanelles Straits, but failure obliged both men to resign. Fisher died in 1920.

Reginald Balliol Brett, born in London on 30th June 1852 to a wealthy family, was sent to Eton and Cambridge, was a Liberal MP for five years, but renounced party politics, 'preferring power to responsibility.' His clandestine role in the Navy Scare of 1884 had brought him useful press contacts, but he was already at home among the 'establishment.' His appointment as 'permanent secretary' of public works, which included royal palaces, gave him ready access to Queen Victoria and the heir apparent, the future King Edward VII. The second Viscount Esher (his father died in 1899) had a flair for organising state occasions, especially the Queen's funeral and Edward's coronation, and after the Boer War he conducted sweeping reforms of the Army's high command. A 'permanent member' of the Imperial Defence Committee, he used his position to further the undercover talks between French and British staff officers – and the secret commitment for the British Army to fight on the side of France in a war with Germany. As the King's favourite courtier, Esher held his own court with his cronies, seeking to 'eclipse' the cabinet, he was much disliked. Vain, pompous, arrogant and capricious, he contrived always to distance himself from accountability, but with the death of the king he fawned upon and flattered, Reginald Brett's back stage influence diminished altogether. As Governor of Windsor Castle, he died in 1930.

Herbert Horatio Kitchener, 1850-1916, was the nearest thing to a military dictator in Britain since Oliver Cromwell, but this war lord spent most of his career in the Empire: Sudan, India, South Africa for the Boer War, and in Egypt. Hastily appointed War Minister in August 1914, he forecast a long war, and quickly raised a 'New Army' of a million enthusiastic volunteers. But he was out of touch with developments at home, and colleagues found him difficult to work with. Dispatched on a mission to Russia, he drowned when the cruiser Hampshire struck a mine.

The Main Players

General Douglas Haig: Not blue blood, but whiskey, nurtured the first Earl of a Scottish border family. His ancestors had been making whiskey for two centuries at least – in 1655 Robert Haig was caught distilling on the Sabbath. Whiskey made the fortune that enabled Douglas Haig, born in Edinburgh on the 19th of June 1861, to be sent to Clifton College in Bristol. He was one of eleven children. At Brasenose College, Oxford, he enjoyed the sport and social life and did just  enough work to obtain a 'pass' degree. A prize-winning student of the Royal Military College Sandhurst, though aloof and sparing of words, he excelled too on the polo field, a useful accomplishment for a cavalry officer. His regiment, the 7th Hussars, was stationed at Poona in a 'quiet' part of India, but Haig was soon on the staff at Army HQ and found a patron in general Sir Evelyn Wood.

Haig served under Kitchener in the re-conquest of the Sudan, and in the Boer War under Sir John French, a cavalryman like himself – Haig lent him money. Invited to Windsor Castle, he met his future wife Dorothy, a maid of honour to the Queen. Haig now had the ear of King Edward VII, and George V. The courtier Viscount Esher persuaded Haldane to put Haig in the War Office where he helped create the secret 'striking force' that was to fight in Europe as the ally of France. In 1914 Haig commanded an army corps under the BEF Commander-in-Chief Sir John French, whose job he coveted, and eventually secured, making use of his influence at Court. Inspired by a strong sense of duty and commanding the largest army Britain had ever seen, his understanding of modern warfare was slight; he dreamed of a great cavalry break out that never came. But he had a talented staff and an army of heroes, to bring victory.

Sir Henry Campbell-Bannerman, British Liberal Party politician and British Prime Minister from 1905 to 1908, referred to as 'Britain's first, and only, radical Prime Minister.' During his tenure legislation was passed favourable to the working classes and trade unions. In defiance of Kind Edward, Campbell-Bannerman would also take two 'radical extremists' (Winston Churchill and David Lloyd George) into his government.

xv

Of this most unconventional pair, **David Lloyd George** really *was* the odd man out – peering in. A small-town lawyer from 'Welsh Wales' and a vociferous nationalist, he was a passionate Liberal who'd been Caermarthen's MP since 1890, and he was very ambitious. Nine years in government, by 1914 he was on the threshold of supreme power. No pacifist, but labelled 'Little Englander' for his pro-Boer stance, and later, for opposing naval rearmament, he could swiftly change his views to further his own career. He was widely thought to be involved in financial scandal, but he *was* an efficient minister, and he laid the sure foundations of the modern welfare state.

William Henry Smith (1825-1891) successful newsagent and Methodist, was an able politician, sneered at for his tradesman's background, lampooned by Gilbert and Sullivan as 'Ruler of the Queen's Navee' when First Lord of the Admiralty. Smith was the architect of the 1884 Navy Scare that unseated the Liberals (and gave the young Reginald Brett a chance to meddle behind the scenes). Despised by Gladstone, of course, but recognised by Disraeli as a 'new kind of Conservative,' and respected for his industry, tact and patience, 'Old Morality Smith' was one of the best prime ministers Britain never had.

1   2   3

The Main Players

Also featured in this book:

British Generals
1. Henry Wilson
2. Frederick Roberts
3. William Robertson
4. Sir John French
5. Sir James Grierson

4

5

British Admirals
6. Charles Beresford

7

8

9

French Generals
7. Joseph Joffre
8. Ferdinand Foch
9. Robert Nivelle
10. Philippe Petain

10

11

11

French Politicians
11. Georges Clemenceau
12. Major Victoire Huguet (no image)
13. Captain Antione de Tarlé (no image)

Others
14. Arthur Balfour
15. King Edward VII
16. Charles Repington
17. Sir George Clarke
18. Maurice Hankey
19. George Shee (no image)
20. Major John Seely

14

15

16

17

18

20

FOR MY FAMILY

~ 1 ~

Council of War

No one starts a war – or rather, no one in his senses ought to do so – without first being clear in his mind what he intends to achieve by that war and how he intends to conduct it.

Carl von Clausewitz, On War *

This was not his finest hour. The Right Honourable Herbert Henry Asquith Esquire, Member of Parliament, First Lord of the Treasury and Prime Minister of Great Britain and Ireland, had just declared war on Germany. But that was the easy bit. The next day – August 5th 1914 – the King's first minister summoned his advisers to a 'War Council.' This hastily-convened assembly was a roll call of martial talent; three field-marshals, nine generals and one admiral arrived at Number Ten Downing Street under the gaze of curious bystanders. The night before, crowds had gathered outside Buckingham Palace as if drawn by instinct to the notional seat of power, for this was a deferential society. As protocol required, one junior minister was dispatched to the Palace for a late-night session of the King's Privy Council, for only the Sovereign, as Head of State, could actually declare war. This was a polite fiction since the decision had already been taken by the Prime Minister—in the King's name of course. Last week the monarch spoke out of turn, assuring his cousin Prince Henry of Prussia (the Kaiser's young brother and one of Queen Victoria's many grandchildren) that Britain would keep out of a European war, but his chief minister—who a few days earlier had been in much the same mind—swiftly made him recant.† Mr Asquith and his Foreign Secretary might talk about the importance of 'public

---
* Clausewitz *On War* (Ed & Trans Howard M & Paret P) 1976 p 579
† Fergusson *The Pity of War* p 167

opinion,' but the House of Commons represented less than a third of the British public, while only sixty percent of men over twenty-one had the vote—and no women at all. In 1914 Britain was *not* a true democracy, nevertheless that same parliament would soon be asked to find the money to pay for the war – and it did.

The Prime Minister had invited just three of his colleagues; all Privy Counsellors like himself: the Viscount Haldane of Cloan, sometime Secretary of State for War and now Lord Chancellor; Sir Edward Grey, Baronet, Knight of the Order of the Garter, Member of Parliament and Secretary of State for Foreign Affairs; and Mr. Winston Leonard Spencer Churchill, M.P., First Lord of the Admiralty. A 'little local difficulty' – a mutiny of army officers in Ireland – had obliged the Prime Minister to double up as war minister, but Haldane had returned to the War Office the day before to ease the burden on his chief. Mr Asquith could do without the rest of his cabinet that afternoon. Most of them – fifteen out of twenty – had deep misgivings about going to war at all, but only two ministers resigned, and though the Foreign Secretary's 'explanation' to the House of Commons two days earlier was angrily challenged by some members—Liberal and Labour—the opposition was more friendly. The crisis had brought Asquith's beleaguered administration an unexpected though brief political truce, and a welcome respite from domestic discord.

Of the three field-marshals, the first; the Right Honourable Earl Herbert Horatio Kitchener of Khartoum, hero of Omdurman, Minister Plenipotentiary and Privy Counsellor, Agent and Consul-General in Egypt, was on his way back to Cairo when the summons came. The second; the Right Hon Earl Roberts of Kandahar, Pretoria and Waterford, who earned his Victoria Cross suppressing the Indian Mutiny, had fought the Afghans and defeated the Boers, while the third man, Field Marshal Sir John Denton Pinkstone French, KCMG, GCB, had recently been Chief of the Imperial General Staff – the army's top soldier. Of the nine generals present, two would be assured of fame; Sir Douglas Haig and a very junior major-general, Henry Wilson. The world's largest and most powerful navy was represented by a solitary admiral, the First Sea Lord His Serene Highness Prince Louis Alexander of Battenberg – whose German-sounding name would swiftly unseat him despite his royal lineage.

Mr Asquith—'Squiff' to denizens of the Whitehall-Westminster village where his drink problem was no secret—set the tone. The situation, he said, was 'not unlike one which had constantly been considered' but on which 'no decision had ever been reached'. This was an astonishing statement, and quite untrue. It was not that Britain was unprepared for war. There were plans for a maritime blockade of Germany; arrangements to seize German ships in every port in the British Empire; for censoring mail and telegrams; locking up 'enemy aliens' and confiscating German property. The Fleet was on a war footing and the generals had mobilised the army, yet the larger matter, the over-arching question as to *how* the war was to be fought, and *where*, had never been resolved – well, at least not by the Cabinet. *That* was all decided years ago, by Sir Edward Grey in the Foreign Office and Mr Haldane in the War Office—with Mr Asquith's full knowledge and consent. They didn't inform the Prime Minister for several weeks, and when they did, old Sir Henry Campbell-Bannerman was not at all pleased. Other ministers had to wait another five years before they, or some of them, learned that in the event of a European war the British Army was committed to fight in France. It was a detail Mr Asquith preferred to forget – indeed he repeatedly told parliament there was no such undertaking.

Britain had a huge navy, but her army was very small and a lot of it was deployed in the Empire. A hasty recall of reservists had beefed up a small 'Expeditionary Force' of trained soldiers, but where should these men be sent, and what should they do when they got there? It seemed there was no obligation for them to go anywhere or do anything – Mr Asquith himself had said so on many occasions. Just four days ago his Cabinet decided—or thought it had decided—that this little army should stay at home. Britain was a maritime power, so any war would be fought at sea, and Sir Edward Grey had generously offered France the protection of the Royal Navy should the Germans threaten the French coast—even if Britain stayed out of the conflict. Perhaps Asquith, Grey, Haldane and Churchill too, were hoping to allay the fears of the majority in cabinet who balked at sending the Army to the continent, because in response to German ambitions the Mediterranean Fleet was already stripped of its most powerful ships. France now ruled in waters where Britain had long been supreme, while the Royal Navy guarded the Channel and stared across the North Sea to where the Kaiser's battle fleet lay. A quiet 'arrangement' between the British and French navies—they even shared code books—worried some ministers when they got wind of it,* and though it had since lapsed, the French saw it as a continuing alliance, despite British denials. There was a similar 'understanding' too, with the Russian navy.

But as the Foreign Secretary said in the same breath, well almost, Britain *did* have 'obligations of honour and interest' to safeguard the independence of Belgium, and his doubting colleagues in Cabinet

---

* *The Cabinet not told – Fergusson p 481, nor the Foreign Office – Steiner Z Britain and the Origins of the First World War p 101*

agreed that a 'substantial violation' of Belgian territory would be sufficient to justify 'intervention.' It would have been awkward, of course, if the Belgians had chosen to side with Germany – and that was not impossible, for until a very late hour the Belgian government hesitated to commit itself either way. But now their army was resisting the Germans, so a relieved Asquith could declare war to defend Belgium—never mind the coast of France, and *now* he could dispatch the 'British Expeditionary Force.'

Its commander-in-chief was Field-Marshal Sir John French, a distinguished cavalry leader who straightaway admitted there *was* a 'prearranged plan' for his men to go to Maubeuge in northern France 'to act on the left of the French Army against the German right flank,' but because we hadn't mobilised when the French did, that was no longer a safe place to be, so instead the BEF should assemble at Amiens – closer to the Channel ports. Sir John, however, would much rather take his army to Antwerp 'with a view to co-operation with the Belgians and the Dutch.' No one listening to this eminent soldier seems to have been bothered by his casual assumption that the Dutch would willingly risk everything by 'co-operating' with their next door neighbour, and nor were they worried by Sir John's ignorance of geography, for both sides of the Scheldt estuary lie in Dutch territory and the approaches to the Belgian port of Antwerp were fortified. So if the Dutch remained neutral (as they did) and refused to allow the BEF a safe passage, the British would have to use brute force to get through – as the Germans were now doing in Belgium. The task would not have been too difficult, for the defences were obsolete and Messrs Krupp of Essen had failed to deliver some new guns*, but the British Government would have been in the odd position of hastening to the rescue of one small nation while invading its next-door neighbour. Happily, this hypothetical embarrassment was avoided. The Navy thought the voyage to Antwerp would be too dangerous, and the Army's Chief of Staff confirmed the destination of the BEF – it was scheduled for *France* because if the troopships went to Antwerp the railway timetables would be 'dislocated,' as he tactfully explained. It was 'war by timetable' for everyone now.

So if not Antwerp, where else could the BEF go? Belgium remained the clear favourite – after all, the German invasion of that small country was the reason why Britain had gone to war, or so the British people were told, and besides, the generals in the War Office had long believed that in a war against Germany the Low Countries would side with Britain, so it was no surprise when one of Sir John's corps commanders, Sir Douglas Haig – another cavalryman – produced a list

---

* Kossman E H *The Low Countries 1780-1940* p 435

of questions suggesting that he too had not been paying attention of late. Was there 'time to organise,' would the BEF be big enough to 'turn the tables,' could it go to Antwerp or Ostend—and what did the French want? Incredibly, two of Britain's most senior military commanders appeared as ignorant of their own army's war plans as their civilian masters pretended to be, for they now proposed to scrap the 'pre-arranged plan' in favour of an entirely separate war in Belgium, even though that old favourite, the 'Belgian Option,' had long been shelved, as this pair ought to have known.*

So perhaps the army should go to France after all, but somewhere safe, and in their hesitation Sir John and Sir Douglas were not alone. Mr Churchill suggested the BEF could 'join up with' the French reserve army, if there was one, and *that* could go to the front instead. Even the Foreign Secretary saw disaster looming. Just two days ago he assured Parliament that Britain would 'suffer little more' by entering the war than by staying out, but now Britain *had* joined in, Sir Edward wanted to know if we could 'extricate the BEF should the French be overcome. His ally had yet to fight the frontier battles in which so many Frenchmen would die, but the smell of defeat was already in the English air.

It was now the turn of Henry Wilson, Director of Military Operations at the War Office, the man who'd spent four years fine-tuning that 'prearranged plan' for the BEF to be dispatched to northern France in accordance with the wishes of the French High Command, the man who now gave a breezy assurance that the best place for the Expeditionary Force was...Amiens. According to his personal diary, written perhaps with an eye to his place in the history books, *he* was the one who put the War Council right, but the record kept by that ever-tactful and upwardly mobile Royal Marine Captain Maurice Hankey, secretary to the Committee of Imperial Defence, shows it was not Henry Wilson but the Army's Chief of Staff who explained the impossibility of sending the BEF anywhere but France.†

Wilson's contribution was more subtle. He explained how 'a month ago,' shortly after the Austrian archduke's assassination at Sarajevo, and with what must have seemed remarkable foresight on his part (though his diary suggests otherwise) he sent some of his staff officers to France to prepare 'an alternative scheme' whereby the troops could go to Amiens, an important rail centre, and 'very easily be dispatched in any direction.' Certainly, officers from his logistics team in the War Office *were* in France in late June for a French Army 'Staff Ride,' a

---
* Tyler J E *The British Army and the Continent 1904-14* pp62-65, and 'War with Germany for Belgian neutrality' WO106/46/E2/8, CAB16/5 4 January 1907
† War Council minutes, 5 August 1914 CAB 22/1 TNA

routine exercise on paper—by coincidence held this time at Amiens—where 'the railway movement as planned was tested very thoroughly,' a subordinate later recalled.* Those officers did *not* change the existing arrangements and there never was an 'alternative scheme,' but in assuring his distinguished audience that the BEF could now go to Amiens, the 'safer' destination a hundred miles short of Maubeuge, Henry Wilson made it easier for everyone to agree that five of the BEF's six infantry divisions should be sent to France. The sixth division was to stay at home, though the ageing Field-Marshal Lord Roberts—who for years had been warning the British public that a German invasion was not only possible but highly probable—could now state with full authority, that it was neither.

The War Council met next day in the same pusillanimous spirit. The Cabinet had decided 'in principle' to dispatch the Expeditionary Force to France, but it was Kitchener (now appointed War Secretary, thus ending Haldane's one-day stand-in), Kitchener the legendary imperial conqueror who had spent much of his life outside England, who explained to his civilian colleagues it would be 'hardly politic' to send more than *four* divisions. Asquith, his own finger on the pulse of 'public opinion' as he liked to think, agreed with the Field-Marshal. Indeed, ministers perturbed by recent industrial strife were afraid the war would bring mass unemployment, a food shortage and widespread unrest. So just four divisions it was, plus the cavalry—about 100,000 men—and Sir Edward Grey's task it was, to inform the Belgian Government that the BEF was going to France instead 'to act in concert with the French army for the assistance of Belgium.' So the BEF went to Amiens but, completely ignoring the Cabinet, Wilson ordered the troop trains to continue *a hundred miles beyond,* to Maubeuge, the 'pre-arranged' destination, so the British could still take their appointed place on the left flank of the French army.

As an afterthought the War Council noted Lord Roberts' advice that it was 'most undesirable' for 'native' troops to be employed in a European war—although they would be very soon. A few thousand (white) soldiers could be spared from garrison duty in South Africa, but the British-officered Indian Army would now have to capture Dar-es-Salaam in Germany's East African colony with no help from England.

In all the years of 'staff conversations' no one in the War Office seems to have shown much curiosity about their ally's war plan, and nor had the French done more than pencil-in a place for the BEF (they could never be sure the perfidious English would actually show up). The French had little respect for their junior partner's military talent (old habits die hard) and they could manage very well without the

* Gen Sir Percy Radcliffe: lecture 1925 WO/106/49A/1 TNA

BEF. When the BEF *did* arrive, though, it would not be under French command,* though Marshal Joffre seemed to think otherwise. Sir John French had been told by his British superiors to 'co-operate' with his ally 'without actually fighting'† and anyway, he wasn't to join battle with a more numerous foe without authority from another Field Marshal, Lord Kitchener. But this approach was soon to be tested when the BEF encountered a very large German army. Vastly outnumbered and in retreat, Sir John wanted to pull out of France altogether until Kitchener 'persuaded' him to stay. Britain was now on the way to becoming a 'continental' military power but by Christmas almost half the Expeditionary Force were dead, wounded or missing. In the next four years more than five million men would serve in the British Army and three quarters of a million would die – most of them in France and Flanders. The Prime Minister's son Raymond would be among the fallen.

On that historic Wednesday afternoon in Whitehall a centuries-old tradition; 'the British way in warfare'—using maritime power to place the minimum of military force at a chosen point on the continent—was given the last rites – or so it seemed. In a remarkable turn of fortune, as the Navy was being modernised and virtually rebuilt in response to the perceived challenge from Germany (it was now getting nearly twice the Army's budget) its influence on strategy had inevitably diminished as the Anglo-French *Entente* metamorphosed into a secret military 'commitment' – an alliance in all but name. The admirals had long since lost the initiative, and when the long-expected war with Germany did come they found themselves relegated to second place in support of the Army, the 'junior service,' escorting the troopships to wherever the Army wanted, while the Grand Fleet waited for its 'decisive' encounter, that great battle in the North Sea – a second Trafalgar. The sailors were confident they would keep Germany short of food and war material, but a maritime blockade would take months, even years, to have any real effect, while on dry land the war could be won – or lost – in just a few weeks. This was just as well really, because the Governor of the Bank of England had warned the Chancellor of the Exchequer, Lloyd George, that a long war would wreck the British economy.

It was natural the generals should welcome the greater influence and adopt the enhanced status to be gained by taking the leading rôle in a short sharp conflict. Especially eager was the garrulous, ambitious, ardently-Francophile Henry Wilson whose calamitous error of judgement had placed the British army in the path of almost certain

---
* French, D *British Strategy and War Aims* p27
† Woodward D *Field Marshal Sir William Robertson* p 15

destruction. But if the generals had found their true purpose, to fight in a continental war, they lacked the essential ingredient – an army to match. To back up their 'Expeditionary Force' they could of course bring troops home from the colonies, but once that resource was tapped there remained only a 'territorial force' of half-trained civilian volunteers, 'weekend soldiers' for home defence, with no statutory obligation to fight in foreign wars. It was this manpower deficiency—and the perpetual myth of foreign invasion—that in peacetime fuelled the agitation for every male to undergo military instruction; a cause for which Field-Marshal Lord Roberts—now eighty-two—had spent nine strenuous years campaigning for—to no real effect. For most people 'compulsory training' meant conscription, which hardly anyone would vote for, so in their strident propaganda Roberts and his National Service League were careful not to mention the 'c' word. Critics pointed out that an army of national conscripts wasn't needed to stop a foreign invasion—(after all, what was the Navy for?)—so *that* sort of army could have only *one* purpose; to fight on the continent of Europe in someone *else's* war.

That kind of war was imagined in 1905 when staff officers played a 'War Game' simulating a German invasion of France. This 'showed' that a successful defence of France would require the support of 120,000 British troops—a very small addition by continental standards—as much as could then be put in the field; though happily, just enough to tip the scales in a battle between two evenly-matched continental armies. But what if the Germans—who were playing their own War Games around this time—what if they destroyed this little expeditionary force before Britain could raise a larger army? Those paltry six divisions would be 'fifty too few' as Henry Wilson privately conceded, so even this modest contribution could be a hostage to fortune. When Henry asked his hero Ferdinand Foch, commandant of the French War College, how many British soldiers France would need in time of war, the reply was, 'One – and we would make sure he was killed!'* When war came, that 'one' British soldier was duly killed—and many more—as Britain's leaders found themselves continually reinforcing an army that soon became the largest in the nation's history; an army that would eventually *win* a continental war, albeit with great sacrifice of blood and treasure.

But Wilson and his seniors, most of whom despised *all* politicians, had powerful patrons inside the Liberal Government, ministers who encouraged the soldiers in an act of breathtaking irresponsibility and never enquired of them; what if our little army is not enough, and the French make further demands on us? Astonishingly, no thought had

---

* Callwell, CE *Field Marshal Sir Henry Wilson: Life and Diaries* Vol I p76

been given to that, for everyone had assumed the big battles would be fought by France and Russia, while Britain made a token military contribution; a 'limited liability.' But this time the liability would be unlimited and Mr Asquith's 'Council of War' had really been a waste of everyone's time, for the fate of millions of British citizens was now entrusted to the generals; 'the Profession.'

~ 2 ~

The Soldiers and Their State

> *"The profession, either army or navy, is its own justification. It has everything in its favour: heroism, danger, bustle, fashion. Soldiers and sailors are always acceptable in society. Nobody can wonder that men are soldiers and sailors."*
>
> *- Jane Austen, Mansfield Park*

'Bedroom Slippers for the Knight'

If Sir William Edmund Garstin had not been so determined to punish his wife Mary for her longstanding adultery he would not have resorted to the old ruse of dispatching a telegram to his house on the Suffolk coast, asking his wife to send by the next train to London, the bedroom slippers he'd forgotten to pack. And if the 5.30 pm from Liverpool Street had not been 'Wednesdays only' Lady Mary Garstin would not perhaps have dallied in London and, as a result, become obliged to leave the marital home in disgrace. Major Charles à Court (who took the name of Repington on his father's death) could then have stayed in the army and the Times would *not* have hired him as their Military Correspondent. But the telegram *was* sent, and Mary was *not* at home to receive it, for her train did *not* run. Stranded in London, she sought refuge in the Great Eastern Hotel with only her gallant admirer for comfort, but 'Mr and Mrs Goodwin' were instantly recognised by the private detective her husband had engaged, and in due course Major à Court was cited as co-respondent in divorce proceedings.*

---
* Ryan, WM Lt Col Charles a Court Repington p 41

The affair had begun three years earlier in Egypt where Sir William, a Knight Commander of the Order of St. Michael and St. George and Under-Secretary of State in the Ministry of Public Works, was easily the most useful functionary in a land so heavily dependent on one great river. As Inspector-General of Irrigation—and *the* civil engineer who built the first Aswan Dam—he was acclaimed by fellow hydrologists for his bold scheme to divert the Nile round 12,000 square miles of crocodile-infested Sudanese swamp by persuading the locals to dig a 175 mile bypass, the imaginatively-styled though unconsummated 'Garstin's Cut.' Meanwhile, Major Charles à Court was serving his country in the 'Army of Occupation' as it was tactfully named.

Egypt was the lynchpin of the British Empire, though never actually part of it. Conquered by the Turks in 1517 it was now the Sultan's fiefdom—in name only. The overriding importance of the Suez Canal as Britain's passage to India (completed 1869) persuaded a dithering British Prime Minister to annexe the country by force in 1882. A nationalist uprising against a puppet ruler and a 'massacre' of Christians provided Prime Minister Gladstone (himself a shareholder in the canal company) sufficient justification for a noisy though ineffectual Anglo-French naval bombardment of Alexandria's defences. Most of the shells were dud, the sailors complained, but the mission was accomplished by General Wolseley's thorough destruction of the Egyptian army. With polite concern for Turkish susceptibilities the British had arranged a communications blackout, secretly landing two officers on the Palestine coast to sever the wires between Cairo and Constantinople, the actual work done by a local manager who was promptly dismissed. Meanwhile the noted orientalist Professor Edward Palmer ventured into the Sinai desert with a hefty bribe to keep the Bedouin tribesmen quiet, but he and his companions were waylaid, robbed and murdered.*

With Colonel Arabi's revolt suppressed and French influence greatly diminished, Egypt became 'the Veiled Protectorate' reigned over by the Khedive but ruled by Lord Cromer. Cromer was one of the Baring family of bankers, a despot who restructured the finances of this debt-ridden country so skilfully that the British occupation would henceforth be entirely paid for by the Egyptian peasantry—and as a bonus, the Royal Navy now had a base in the eastern Mediterranean to guard the Canal and keep the Russians bottled up in the Black Sea. In 1914 Egypt's 'Veil' was removed but the British stayed another forty years.

Imperial strategy notwithstanding, Major à Court's romance blossomed in England as in Egypt, only to attract widespread attention

---
* Blunt W S *The Secret Occupation of Egypt*

when, in 1901, the embarrassing details of Lady Garstin's inconstancy were revealed in court and published in the newspapers, as the law then allowed. Her lover's career was effectively ruined. Hitherto the accused philanderer had served his country with distinction on the fringes of Empire and in Afghanistan. He was present at Kitchener's bloody victories of Atbara and Omdurman, he was Military Attaché in Brussels and The Hague as well as 'technical adviser' to the Conference on Arms Limitation, so he might reasonably expect further promotion. If practised with discretion, adultery was no bar to advancement in the British Army. Sir John French was a serial womaniser whose own career was imperilled until his superiors forgave him. But the offence occasioned by à Court's irregular liaison with a respectable married woman was aggravated by the matter of his earlier undertaking to end the affair. This written pledge* was entrusted to his old comrade and friend Henry Wilson, who may have formed a dislike for a possible rival, and who now turned upon him. Exposed as having broken his word—behaviour amounting to 'dishonourable conduct'—à Court appealed in vain to his former commander in chief, Kitchener, but informal pressure quietly exerted by his brother officers—Wilson was one—ensured his premature retirement from the army on half-pay.

Spurning the invitation to live out his days in obscurity the disgraced officer embarked forthwith upon a career in journalism; briefly for the Liberal-leaning *Westminster Gazette* and then as Military Correspondent of the *Times*, a newspaper so noted for its partiality to the Conservative-Unionist Party and its closeness to the ruling élite, that foreigners thought it 'semi-official.' The post at the *Times* offered him every opportunity to display his considerable talent for intrigue, and moreover it brought in the additional income he urgently needed, for he had forsaken wife and children for the fragrance of Mary, and his mode of living was hardly frugal. He enjoyed smart society—and he was often in debt.

Á Court-Repington's influence was never as great as he wanted everyone to think, but he energetically exploited his position at the *Times* to agitate for increased military spending and conscription, as well as by more recondite means. In his spare time he managed to edit the official *Army Review*, to the considerable annoyance of his employer, Lord Northcliffe. Repington was a clever man of great personal charm, a snob whose family claimed kinship with the Earls of Pembroke, a sycophant who excelled in dissembling and mischief-making. In his constant desire to be seen as a man of importance—proffering gratuitous advice and posing as honest broker—he sought always to

---
* Ryan, p 40

insinuate himself into high places; 'never in the way and never out of it.' His style of journalism often suggested an urge to curry favour with powerful patrons, quite apart from his professional need to be seen frequently in print, however puerile some of his efforts might appear. Perhaps his abrupt departure from the army, and the years of watching enviously as his erstwhile contemporaries (and in his opinion less deserving ones) were steadily advancing to the highest rank – had embittered him. Fallen from grace, his reputation almost gone, he was a meddler and a mountebank with few cards to play, but in the dozen or so years before August 1914 he had a finger in every pie.

French Lessons

If the infant Henry Wilson had been reared by a *German* nanny he might have gained at her knee a more favourable impression of her homeland – and who knows, he might have formed early in life those habits of industry and application that would have enabled him to satisfy the examiners at the Royal Military College. Unfortunately the boy's upbringing, while not wholly devoid of domestic comfort, was entrusted to a succession of *French* governesses. These young ladies imparted a tolerable fluency in their own tongue—and a love of France—but were insufficiently rigorous in their general mode of instruction, with the deplorable consequence that despite expensive remedial tuition at Marlborough College, Henry contrived to fail the examination for Sandhurst on *three* occasions—but only twice for the Woolwich artillery and engineer academy. Undismayed by such minor setbacks, the youth promptly obtained a lieutenant's commission in the 6th Battalion of the Longford Militia, but soon found himself in the Royal Irish Regiment—a regular army unit—whence by great good fortune he speedily secured a transfer to that élite corps, the Rifle Brigade. The purchase of commissions, one of many abuses in the old Army, had long been abolished, to be smoothly replaced by a respectable black market operated by a sort of dating agency which, for a modest fee undertook to match an officer with the means to 'exchange' his commission in a less fashionable corps, with another who could not afford the expensive life style of his own regiment and was glad to 'trade down' for a couple of thousand pounds or so.* However it was managed, the twenty-year-old Lieutenant Wilson lost no time in placing his feet on the first rungs of the ladder to the highest rank. One day his hand would clasp a Field-Marshal's baton, but not before he had stepped upon other men's fingers.

The importance of being Henry lies in his career.† Brief tours of

---

* Trading commissions – in Baynes *Far from a Donkey: the Life of General Sir Ivor Maxse*
† Jeffery, K *Field Marshal Sir Henry Wilson: A Political Soldier*

imperial service—his face bore the mark of wounds inflicted by an unwelcoming resident of Burma—and a spell in the War Office Intelligence Section, thanks in part to his friend and brother officer Charles à Court (Repington); then to South Africa for the Boer War with Lord Roberts; and after that, the required twelve months' command of a battalion before another desk job, again, under Roberts. Thereafter came two dream postings: firstly, as Commandant of the Staff College he could and did indoctrinate impressionable young majors and captains in the 'continental strategy,' personally conducting them round the battlefields of 1870, preaching the coming of war against Germany—with England the staunch ally of France. Then the jewel: when, as Director of Military Operations at the War Office from 1910 to August 1914 Wilson and his staff worked in strict secrecy to perfect the arrangements for moving the British Expeditionary Force to France.

Wilson had played no part in the earlier 'staff conversations,' but he would later claim (as several others did) that he had done more than any other man to get Britain into the war. Certainly, Wilson—like Repington—sought always to present himself as more important and influential than his actual rank would justify, but his pivotal position in the War Office during those four fretful years afforded him every opportunity—which he was quick to seize—for dissimulation and intrigue.

It was only to be expected that young Henry Wilson should entertain a high esteem for French institutions, and the military in particular. But his was an emotional attachment that survived infancy and certainly coloured his outlook, even warping his professional judgment. Especially, his unrequited hero-worship of General Ferdinand Foch, the some-time Commandant of the French War College, was unwise to say the least. Another mistake was to keep a diary.

Most public figures have been content to produce their memoirs long after the notable events in which they had some part, but since it would require courage and candour to belittle their own contribution to the ordering of things or to admit to errors of judgement, the reader should not be disappointed by an occasional lack of objectivity and self-criticism on their part. Perhaps to compensate for this deficiency, Henry Wilson always took care to write his own version of history at bedtime. This meticulous, near-obsessive habit may have served to relieve his feelings at the end of a trying day on the rare occasions when his advice had gone unheeded, or possibly to reinforce an inner conviction of his own superior intellect. The diary was secret, but had he survived to compose his autobiography, had his life not been cut short by the bullets of an assassin, he could scarcely have resisted the urge to quarry from his journal whatever material he might find useful in hindsight to justify his conduct, and it is hard to believe he intended that no one should ever read his colourful observations on powerful personages encountered, or on debates in which his was ever the sole voice of reason. Moreover, these contemporaneous entries are a valuable guide to the author's state of mind. They suggest not only vanity but a deep-seated anxiety, a somewhat infantile need for the praise of important people, an inability to distinguish a genuine compliment from the small change of social intercourse and meaningless flattery. They indicate too, a fear that he might not be taken seriously – and worse, an unworthy desire to impress his hearers. The biographies of famous men are commonly close to hero worship, but Henry Wilson's widow rendered a priceless service in making his journal public. Even so, his idiosyncratic version of events is often accepted without question, and in some historical accounts he is depicted as wielding greater influence than was the case, or, he is prematurely promoted to high rank and honour as 'General Sir Henry Wilson' – not that he would have complained. At first a mere colonel acting one rank up, this Director of Military Operations was for most of his time 'Brigadier-General Wilson' (the rank has been 'Brigadier' since 1921) until his promotion to Major-General in November 1913—and it was plain *Mrs* Wilson until July 1915 when her husband got his knighthood. A *Temporary* Lieutenant-General three years later, a full (four-star) General by 1918 and a year after that, Lloyd George made him a Field-Marshal.

Of Henry Wilson it might truly be remarked, as it was uncharitably said of another general (Haig), that with the publication of his diaries* he 'committed suicide *after* his own death.' Witty, garrulous, mischievous, a master of conspiracy who throughout his very public career belittled his colleagues and schemed against them, Henry Wilson defies approbation. In his journal, in his correspondence and in the official record, he cuts a ruthless, unscrupulous, irresponsible and even treasonous figure. Mentor and speech writer to Field-Marshal Roberts in the campaign for conscription—as well as the denigration of the new volunteer Territorial Force—Wilson privately counselled the Leader of the Opposition, he fostered armed resistance to Irish Home Rule and encouraged a mutiny of British officers.

It is odd, to say the least, that such a man should be raised to the highest rank and chosen to exercise supreme authority over the British Army, for he betrayed his oath of allegiance by undermining military discipline, and conspired against the elected government. Yet in his own estimation he was a man of honour, and certainly the cleverest in

---

* Callwell CE, *Field Marshal Sir Henry Wilson: His Life and Diaries*

the army – a title hotly contested in an age noted for self-advertisement. Both he and Repington would separately conspire with another military paragon, one with very similar attributes.

Nora and Fred

If Nora Henrietta, daughter of Captain Bews, 73rd Regiment of Foot, had not chosen the son of Abraham to be her lawful wedded husband, life in Edwardian 'Middle England' would not have been quite so noisy. Certainly, fortune smiled upon her spouse and favoured him above all other men. As the first Earl of Kandahar, Pretoria and Waterford, and Viscount St Pierre, Knight of the Order of St Patrick, Knight Grand Cross of the Order of the Bath, Knight Grand Commander of the Order of the Star of India, Knight Grand Commander of the Order of the Indian Empire, Knight of the Order of the Garter and Member of the Order of Merit, Honorary Colonel of the Irish Guards, Privy Councillor, Old Etonian and Protestant, Frederick Sleigh Roberts was surely blessed in his union with Nora Bews. Nora was a woman of strong character, a genuinely supportive wife who took a keen interest in her husband's career, unstinting of advice even on trivial matters such as the professional advancement of his subordinates—so much so that during the war in South Africa the couple were disrespectfully known as 'Lord Bobs and Lady Jobs.' Truly, in all things great and small, Nora was for more than half a century Fred's constant helpmeet and companion, the woman who loyally sustained him to the very end of his long and busy life.

Born in Cawnpore (Kanpur) in North India but educated at Eton and Sandhurst, the young Frederick followed his father Abraham, an Indian Army general, and attained distinction in the ruthless quelling of the Great Mutiny, being one of the very first to win the highest decoration 'for valour' – the newly instituted Victoria Cross. Twenty years later, he earned greater fame by his astute handling of the press corps in Afghanistan. A further twenty years' imperial service, crowned by the supreme command in Ireland, and Roberts would be just in time to get the credit for redeeming the British Army from humiliation in South Africa.

The newspapers, especially the ones whose owners were friendly to the Conservative-Unionist Party, had taken a fancy to this excitable little man of Anglo-Irish descent—his mother Isabella, daughter of Major Bunbury of the 62nd Foot, came from Kileacle, Tipperary. Unlike the Army whose Commander-in-Chief he would soon become, 'Bobs' was hugely popular – 'Kipling's General.' His chest glittering with medals, clasps, bars and other military decorations, he was twice rewarded generously by a grateful parliament. Bobs boasted honorary degrees from half a dozen universities as well as the freedom of fourteen cities and royal boroughs. For many years he had only one serious rival to share the fame and the honours; Sir Garnet Wolseley. Wolseley was immortalised in *The Pirates of Penzance* as 'the very model of a modern major-general.' Much amused and greatly flattered, Wolseley would sometimes enliven dinner parties with his own spirited rendition.

Rivals certainly, but the British Empire was large enough for both, and growing larger. Wolseley had his own power base in the United Kingdom, and Roberts held his fiefdom in India, the land of his birth, but they shared the spoils of political patronage, Wolseley flirting with the Liberals, Roberts favouring the Conservatives, though both supported the Anglo-Irish Union. And while serving the government of the day as soldiers must, neither had the slightest scruple in denouncing that government in the House of Lords. But the war in South Africa had eclipsed Wolseley's reputation – and done Roberts a power of good.

Old soldiers never die, and technically Field-Marshals never retire, though the last marshal received his baton in 1994* and the species will eventually become extinct. When his post as Commander in Chief of the Army was abolished in that great cleansing of the War Office stables after the South African (Boer) War, Roberts was quickly found a place on the high level Committee of Imperial Defence, but he took against his colleagues on matters of strategy. Nor would they heed his call for compulsory military training for boys, so he began to make resignation noises and stepped down for higher things, having already accepted the presidency of the National Service League. Roberts was no decorative figurehead, though Wilson and Repington, each persuaded of his own superior intellectual powers, sought to manipulate the Field Marshal—Repington especially despised him, but Bobs had a well-developed political sense. These three were united though, in their contempt for politicians and democratic institutions, and their cynical lack of scruples in furthering their own aims.

"I've 'eard different"

If William Robert Robertson, one of seven children of a Lincolnshire village postmaster, had remained in domestic service—first with the Cardigan family of Deene Park in Northamptonshire, thereafter polishing the silverware at Hanbury Hall, Worcestershire—Henry Wilson's diary would have been much less interesting. A generation earlier, William Robertson would surely have merited a chapter in that

---

* Except for Sir Charles Guthrie and Prince Charles

odious little book by Samuel Smiles, *Self Help*, for by hard work, application, self-discipline, a fortuitous marriage and a generous helping of royal patronage, the youth who so upset his mother by enlisting in the 16th Lancers, 'Wully' Robertson was the first, and only, private soldier to rise to the very highest rank in the Army, but his long-standing, most dangerous rival was Henry Wilson.

In background and in character they were a world apart. The widely accepted picture is of Henry Wilson; the witty urbane intriguer, near-genius, the 'political soldier' – and Wully; the gruff stolid, honest plodder somewhat lacking in imagination and sadly deficient in the social graces. It is an image reinforced by Wilson's private journal in which his colourful personality emerges, while Robertson, in his correspondence, his memoranda and his stiflingly dull memoirs achieves a wooden style that belies the intellect behind it. Yet it was Wully, the 'desk general' who never commanded troops but headed the entire British Army for most of the Great War, Wully whose stock response to fools, 'I've 'eard different,' would resound in the corridors of Whitehall, and it was Wully who served his country—and the Profession—more faithfully than the man who engineered his downfall.

The Joker in the Pack

The Profession had several cards to play; the Press Card, the Court Card, the Party Card, the Orange Card, the Business Card and the Masonic Card. Many naval officers—and soldiers too like Haig—were freemasons, their Sovereign Lord Edward the Seventh was Grand Master of the Order, and his son George was Grand Patron of the three Masonic institutions.

The Business Card was handy for the retired admiral angling for a directorship of one of the big naval shipbuilding firms; but several high-ranking army men remained in the public sector, some as chief constables, notably Sir Charles Warren the 'irascible, eccentric' freemason, archaeologist and regular churchgoer who was briefly Metropolitan Police Commissioner. He presided over the 1887 'Bloody Sunday' demonstration in Trafalgar Square, but incurred Queen Victoria's displeasure when during a rabies scare a lady's pet dog was savagely beaten to death in the street by his truncheon-wielding policemen.

The Orange Card was especially useful to the soldier, for the Conservative and Unionist Party was committed to preserving the Union of Great Britain and *all* of Ireland – including the province of Ulster, and most army officers were not only 'conservative' in outlook but broadly sympathetic to the Protestant cause. In the Irish 'Home Rule' crisis of 1914 some quite senior figures, aided and abetted by Henry Wilson and Field Marshal Roberts, played the Orange Card against the government – and effectively demolished the cosy belief that the British Army never got itself involved in politics.

For Bernard Shaw, *all* professions were 'conspiracies against the laity.' Powerful, self-governing and exclusive, self-regulating and self-protective, the doctors, clergy, lawyers, policemen, and soldiers too, sought always to show their acceptable face: selfless, impartial, trustworthy, incorruptible, infallible. The military were the perfect fit, and generals like Roberts in Afghanistan or Wolseley in Africa played the Press Card adroitly – a 'family' newspaper like the *Daily Mail* sold more than the *Times, Daily Telegraph, Morning Post* and *Manchester Guardian* put together. Kitchener excelled in the art of 'disinformation' and that most eccentric of admirals, Jacky Fisher, was advised by the courtier Viscount Esher to 'play upon the delicate instruments of public opinion with your fingers and not your feet.' But the soldier who really knew how to use Fleet Street to his advantage was the man with the poker face and the Press Card up his sleeve – Wully Robertson*.

The Court Card was just as important. Soldiers professed allegiance to the monarch they had sworn to obey and studied to flatter, though invasion and regime change in 1688 showed that if it suited their professional interest they would not bother to save their king, and nor would they resist an invading army, but ever since, the military had enjoyed a 'special relationship' with the Crown. Every officer prized his licence to manage lawful violence—the sovereign's commission—and Queen Victoria signed each one personally. She took a keen interest in 'her' army, insisted *her* name should head the Army List, and whenever a new regiment was raised Her Majesty had to be consulted on every detail of their uniform. Generals at the War Office complained they spent more time discussing Highlanders' tartan kilt patterns than anything else. Her son and heir Edward VII liked to keep the royal finger in the military pie, as did George the Fifth, for above all, the King, *every* king, needed 'his' army quite as much as the soldiers needed 'their' sovereign. The monarch was the 'natural head' of the army, and Queen Victoria liked to keep the job in the family. The Duke of Cambridge, who boasted he never obeyed orders from civilians, was Commander-in-Chief for nigh on forty years, time enough for the other generals to grow tired of him. The ambitious officer would take care to marry within – or as Wully Robertson did – *into* the upper echelons of society, for a well-adjusted, well–connected spouse was a precious possession, just as the rifle was to the private soldier. A

---
* Woodward, D *Field Marshal Sir William Robertson* p51

dutiful wife could be a useful spy for her husband, his ever-present agent, a handy letter-drop whereby selected pieces of gossip could be directed to the highest level, and nor did the Monarch discourage his favourite generals from writing to him in private, especially on matters concerning the fitness of other generals for high command. Douglas Haig, whose good fortune it was to wed one of the Queen's Ladies in Waiting, played the Court Card against his superior Sir John French, the BEF's first commander, until French was replaced – by Haig. Not only did such communications bypass the military chain of command, but whichever politician might temporarily sit in the War Office was not privy to them either. There were exceptions. One general, Henry Wilson, who privately rated the Russian Tsar as 'devoid of character and purpose as our poor miserable King,'* never enjoyed such ready access to his sovereign's ear. But it was rare for a Prime Minister to put the Monarch in his place – as happened when Wully, whose humble origins made him a favourite of King George V, was sacked by Lloyd George.

What stuck in the throat of many an officer was the inescapable reality that the army—the ultimate political instrument of the state—was just another public institution funded by Parliament and controlled by ministers appointed by the sovereign, on the prime minister's advice. This sensible, indeed comfortable arrangement, whereby the blame for mismanagement could usually be laid at the politicians' door, was never fully appreciated by the likes of Henry Wilson. The idea of an army run by a politician was 'vicious in theory and hopeless in practice.'† He improved considerably on that statement in a lecture to impressionable young officers at the Staff College, with the dangerously misleading advice that their 'maximum allegiance' was to King, not Cabinet.‡ His time in Whitehall had not mellowed Henry's distaste for politicians, 'those ignorant men,' forgetting there might also be ignorant men in uniform – some well versed in 'political expediency.'

In this, the most politicised of professions, the Party Card – Liberal or Conservative – was essential, and despite their ingrained contempt for parliamentary democracy, the generals soon learned how to manage ministers of either hue. In a bygone age any admiral or general, Whig or Tory, might hope for some notional but well-paid public office – a nice little earner requiring no actual work so as to reward him for loyalty to the government, or to keep him quiet. But in more enlightened times, and reflecting the Profession's institutional mindset, the Conservatives were generally rated as 'sound' on defence, while the Liberals—who believed in free trade and even downright

* Wilson *Diary* 21 December 1916
† *Diary* 31 December 1901 – Callwell Vol I p47
‡ *Lecture* 14 March 1907 Wilson Papers HHW3/3/4 in Jeffery, p 125

pacifism—were considered an untrustworthy lot. Field Marshal Wolseley yearned for the time when 'the licence of democracy and socialism' would be 'conquered by the sword, and succeeded by cruel military despotism,' but the Conservatives thought him a dangerous radical for siding briefly with the Liberals, despite his loathing for Mr. Gladstone and his 'socialists.'

Whichever party governed, the generals (and the admirals) were obliged to justify their continued subsidy from the public purse, and Britain's frequent colonial wars served the purpose well, being relatively cheap while bringing fame and fortune to theatre commanders like Wolseley and Roberts, and credit to the Profession. As a bonus, any addition to the empire could be economically governed by the man who had seized it – and thus absorbed with colonial stewardship, building highways, barracks, courthouses and prisons, he could be kept well away from London and political intrigue* (though there were ways round that, as Kitchener found). Likewise, a naval officer was the embodiment of imperial authority, the warship he commanded a floating consulate and police station. But lest the heady thrill of delegated power should induce some warriors to step out of line and try their hand at statesmanship, it was Palmerston who sternly reminded them not to take 'important steps' without 'Instructions.' His spell at the War Office had taught him a lot about the Profession.

Every high ranking officer had served his apprenticeship in the colonies, fighting in little wars with courage and skill, but some generals were gazing enviously at their near neighbours and dreaming of war on the grand scale with an army of 'continental' size – and as an unavoidable by-product, the enlargement and aggrandisement of the military establishment. Accordingly they would not scruple to frighten, shame, bully or blackmail their stingy civilian paymasters for the means to prepare for whatever 'mission' *they (*the generals) deemed essential for the safety of the nation and the empire. Only the foolhardy statesman dared shut his ears to their importuning, for the Generals had allies at Court, in Fleet Street, among the 'chattering classes' and in both Houses of Parliament where many army officers sat. Some of those officers were still on the 'active' list, though Sir Charles Warren put his career at risk when he stood for parliament as an 'independent liberal' in Sheffield – without success.† More fortunate was Arthur Wesley (Wellesley), barely out of his teens when he inherited the 'family seat' in the old Irish Parliament before his army career took off so spectacularly on the plains of India. A Westminster MP with three different seats in as many years, he was Chief Secretary for

* Hilton B *A Mad, Bad and Dangerous People? New Oxford History of England 1783-1846* p 567
† The same seat was won by a Liberal Democrat, Nick Clegg, in 2005

Ireland until the war in Spain, and then, as Duke of Wellington, an 'unwilling' cabinet minister, taking time off to fight the battle of Waterloo, with lengthy stints in between as Commander in Chief of the Army, and as Prime Minister (twice). At a humbler level, one officer with a seat at Westminster and a regiment in India managed to hold down both jobs until he was killed on the North West Frontier.

With Britain's little army busy extending the empire with help from Indian troops, the country was, without realising it, in a state of near perpetual war. Indeed, it would not have been too surprising if, in a time of 'crisis,' some victorious soldier had returned to sweep away the squabbling politicians and 'save the nation.' But while the Iron Duke was no democrat he knew there were limits to his own decidedly authoritarian rule. Despite Field Marshal Wolseley's talk of 'cruel military despotism'; or Henry Wilson's quixotic but sinister definition of the soldier's 'duty of allegiance'; or Wully's thoughtless remark that, 'practically anything may happen to our boasted British Constitution before this war ends';* or, Lloyd George's nightmarish fears of 'a military clique' or 'cabal'; there was in fact no generals' plot. England was not Prussia – 'an army with a state'; Douglas Haig was no Hindenberg; Wully Robertson no Falkenhayn; and Henry Wilson was no Ludendorff, although he and Field Marshal Roberts had been quite prepared to take the Army to the brink of civil war in Ireland.

British generals had no need to 'seize power' – they had it anyway. Snugly embedded in the political establishment they affected to despise, they were content to preserve the fiction of unswerving loyalty to their constitutional masters, while demonstrating their absolute indispensability by finding a *mission*. Often it was *they* who determined not only the shape and size of that mission but its purpose too, for above all else it was the institution, the *profession*, that must continue to exist *as an end in itself* – ' we do it because we *can*, and because we *are*.'

Jane Austen – two of her brothers became admirals – was right. The Profession *was,* as always, its own justification. It was essentially *theatrical,* for a successful general must have something of an actor in him – just like the politicians he so despised. The uniform, the gold braid, the ribbons and medals, the parades and the pageantry, the curt speech and autocratic manner – all commanded respect and awe, and set the officer corps above ordinary men. With their muscular Christianity and the comforting embrace of an extended family, 'The Regiment' was a sort of institutionalised Arthurian Round Table. They were fortified too with a rigid caste system and a set of beliefs rooted in a bygone age when war was the employment of kings and the

* Robertson to Haig 8 March 1916 MS 1/22/30, and Lloyd George *War Memoirs* Vol II p 1669

nobility – another blood sport with its own brand of institutional freemasonry.* This clannish, near-exclusive band of brothers, now increasingly recruited from the moneyed middle class seemed to exist chiefly to keep itself in being – a self-perpetuating job-creation scheme for the privileged elite.

Intelligent, diligent, courageous, accustomed to the unquestioning obedience of subordinates, untroubled by self doubt and listened to with respectful attention in matters well beyond their narrow speciality, men like these would soon be entrusted with the fate of millions of their countrymen. But it was a deferential society that served the likes of Charles a Court Repington, Henry Wilson, Frederick Roberts, Kitchener, Wully Robertson, Douglas Haig, and their brothers in the Profession.

---

* Gordon A *Rules of the Game – Jutland and British Naval Command* pp 180-1, 301

~ 3 ~

Ring of Blue Water

Her dauntless army scatter'd, and so small,
Her island-myriads fed from alien lands –
The fleet of England is her all-in-all;
Her fleet is in your hands,
And in her fleet her Fate.

– Lord Alfred Tennyson, 1886

Queen Victoria wondered why naval officers always smelled of mothballs. Someone should have told her they spent rather more time on board Her Majesty's ships than at Court, and so had fewer occasions to wear full dress uniform. Of necessity they lived 'above the shop' amidst complex weapons and machinery, and were more concerned with the technicalities of their profession than, say, their brethren in the Foot Guards or the Household Cavalry, but while the Navy was not ungenerously endowed with talent, its higher ranks did sometimes appear a touch less sophisticated, less practised in the 'political' arts, less familiar with the ways of Whitehall, Westminster and the Court, than the military. Few naval officers sat in parliament. Lord Charles Beresford, an Irish peer, was a colourful rarity. The soldiers, urbane and worldly-wise, were perhaps better placed to argue their case with ministers and civil servants, more attuned to politics and more at home in the lobby than those honest sailors basking complacently in the sunshine of the 'long Victorian afternoon,' confident the 'Silent Service' would always be the Senior Service. Besides, they had friends in high places. A berth in the Royal Yacht brought a naval officer close friendship with young princes, future admirals, and future kings too.

As one of the more outspoken (and seldom silent) admirals, Sir John (Jackie) Fisher said that Britain had a 'Court Army' and a 'People's Navy.' The vast organisation he headed made no extravagant claim on the nation's manpower. Warships were crewed by relatively small numbers of highly-trained technicians who were long-service volunteers. The fleet was 'capital-intensive,' but not intrusive. Beyond the confines of the dockyard and nearby towns a naval uniform was a rare sight, and those who wore it enjoyed the approval and respect attaching to a mysterious fraternity, since for an island race most Britons seemed to know very little of the sea.

What they *did* know, hazily, was that Britain was a maritime nation with a huge volume of seaborne trade. At the start of the twentieth century the British merchant fleet was the world's largest, and the Red Ensign could be seen in every port of any consequence. British ships carried the coal, the textiles and the machinery from British mines, mills and factories to every continent, and as every schoolchild was constantly reminded, much of Britain's food now came from overseas – in British ships. Few people questioned the need for a navy to protect those ships, and most were persuaded that while their country menaced no-one, the British Isles and the Colonies were under constant threat from envious or revengeful foreign powers. The Royal Navy was Britain's first line of defence, a shield against invasion and a guarantee of cheap food in the shops.

A well-regarded institution, the Navy was a reminder that Britain really *was* a great power. Taxpayers could see where their money went, and though warships and naval bases were costly to build and maintain – two and a half million for the first *Dreadnought* – the burden was not too heavy given the huge industrial legacy of Victorian Britain. There was a welcome spin-off, too. A third of the world's merchant fleet had been built in British yards, much of it insured by Lloyds of London, and there was a thriving bespoke trade in battleships, cruisers and gunboats for discerning customers from Turkey to Chile. Ships complete with guns, armour plate, engines, machinery, boilers, pumps and electric motors were all made by highly-paid craftsmen – *British* craftsmen in the nation's shipyards, foundries and factories. Moreover, when times were hard the Admiralty could be relied upon to fill empty order books. As one First Lord observed, 'the wage-earning classes are very fond of the Navy.'

The purpose of the 'sea service' was never in doubt, however imperfectly understood by landsmen, whereas a standing army was regarded with suspicion. Redcoats were traditionally seen as policemen, as agents of overbearing authority, but bluejackets had a reputation for being friendly and helpful. The Navy was the acceptable face of imperial power. The legalised piracy of Drake, Hawkins and Frobisher, the epic voyages of Anson and Cook, the brilliant victories of Rodney and Nelson, the fortunes to be made from 'prize money,' were celebrated in penny pamphlets, in song, in theatre, reflected too in the novels of Jane Austen, although in her eyes the naval profession was 'more distinguished in its domestic virtues than in its national importance.'* Certainly, the Victorian Navy interfered very little with the rest of society and functioned with quiet efficiency, engaging in 'precision warfare' at minimum risk to human life – (on its own side of course) – and in the century after Trafalgar more navy men died of tropical fever than in battle.

The Navy was there – everywhere – to safeguard British trade, show the flag and keep interlopers out of British-held territory. Under the protection of that distant fleet of battleships, Britain's mastery of the seas was upheld every day by the cruisers, sloops and gunboats. The Navy held together the colonies and the vast territories once governed by the Hudson's Bay Company or the East India Company. No Navy; no Empire. The Navy also watched over Britain's 'informal empire' of protectorates and client states of the City of London, and it was the Navy that charted the seas and pioneered scientific exploration, often at great sacrifice, as in Franklin's ill-fated search for the 'Northwest Passage.' It was the Navy that put down piracy, policed the fishing grounds and patrolled the fever-ridden coasts of West Africa to suppress the slave trade – a truly selfless task. It was the Navy too, that brought swift aid to remote communities struck by natural calamity, the Navy that dealt a firm hand to avenge insult to British subjects, anywhere; and it was the Navy that 'persuaded' the Chinese to open their ports to 'free trade' – in British opium. As Palmerston explained, 'these half civilised governments such as those of China, Portugal, Spanish America, require a dressing every eight or ten years to keep them in order'† – the nineteenth century gunboat diplomacy of the *Pax Britannica*.

It was all done without great difficulty. Two centuries of war had left Britain a global support system of bases, dockyards and coaling stations in all the right places; Gibraltar, Malta, Aden, Bombay, Capetown, Singapore, Trincomalee, Hamilton (Bermuda), Hong Kong, Port Stanley in the Falkland Islands, Esquimault on Canada's Pacific coast, Halifax on the Atlantic – an infrastructure no one else could match.

* *The final sentence of Persuasion*
† Lynn, M "Policy, Trade and Informal Empte" *Oxford History of the British Empire* Vol III p108

3 - Ring of Blue Water

Given the size of the Royal Navy and its moral superiority, no other nation could seriously challenge British sea power for a hundred years after Trafalgar – not even the French, whose not inconsiderable fleet joined the British in a coalition of the willing against Russia in the Baltic and the Black Sea, 1853-56; in the second 'Opium War,' 1856-60; and in Mr Gladstone's assault on Egypt in 1882. Meanwhile France acquired an extensive empire in Africa, Asia and the South Seas without much objection from the British. With no navy at all, King Leopold of the Belgians managed to grab a very large piece of central Africa for his personal enrichment. The rest of Europe was busy re-arranging land frontiers and creating new nation-states; while in the western hemisphere the Americans were consolidating their hold on the huge land mass between Atlantic and Pacific, and using their modest flotilla in colonial ventures in the Caribbean and the South China Sea, chiefly at the expense of the Spanish Empire.

The great battles so vividly portrayed; men of war cannonading each other at hailing distance, and cutlass-wielding sailors boarding enemy vessels, belonged to the past. 'Wooden walls' of the age of sail gave way to ships of iron and steel, coal-burning, steam-powered. The old-fashioned muzzle-loading guns, each separately aimed by its crew, had gone to the scrap yard, and now the torpedo and the moored mine – a lot cheaper than ironclads – threatened to change everything.

Yet the world's biggest fleet seemed to be losing its way. Unlike other navies it didn't stimulate much original thinking about 'strategy,' but British admirals weren't unduly bothered. The senior service had no need of a 'mission statement' – its fighting record was enough. It was 'there because it was there.' That was how it had always been, and always would be. Theory—'intellectual underpinning'—was for foreigners, but there was some home-grown talent. John Knox Laughton,* sailor-turned-academic, was that odd mixture of practical mariner and thinker who belied the notion of the bluff sea-dog for whom good seamanship, smart drill and physical courage were enough. Laughton did not lack courage – as a 'schoolie' (instructor to junior officers) he fought beside his pupils in the China wars – but it was he and the earnestly long-winded Admiral Philip Colomb—'Column and a Half'—who combed through Britain's maritime history, not to glory in victories long ago but to analyse events and formulate underlying principles for warfare at sea, just as thoughtful soldiers like Clausewitz had done for war on land, but it would take a while for the intellectual approach to become respectable in England.

Besides, there was another distraction for the admirals, the inva-

---

* Lambert AD *The Foundations of Naval History: John Knox Laughton, the Royal Navy and the Histrical Profession*

sion bogey, that constant fear of a foreign army, usually French, descending upon a defenceless people when the Royal Navy was looking the other way – a regular fright for the credulous, a useful tool for the unscrupulous, and the sailors were forever impaled on the invasion hook.

~ 4 ~

Castles by the Seaside

> *"No one really thought that the Prussians and French combined would invade our shores and devastate our fields and plunder London, and carry our daughters away into captivity."*
>
> – Anthony Trollope, The Prime Minister (1876)

In just a few years Queen Victoria built a hundred and nineteen of them. They weren't so forbidding as the traditional sort favoured by Norman and Plantagenet rulers, but hers were more powerful – especially the half dozen huge red brick fortresses commanding a stretch of Hampshire countryside, built not to intimidate her subjects, but to protect her chief naval base at Portsmouth. Five of them squat on the heights above the town and harbour, but they faced *inland*. The last word in military engineering, these massive citadels were designed to be mutually supporting, and impregnable, with artillery and a close-range weapons system. As the besiegers formed up in open country stripped of trees and all cover, they would come under fire from batteries of cannon and mortars. Then they would have to jump thirty feet down into a wide ditch – an easy target for riflemen safe behind a thick shield of brick – before the survivors could think about scaling the vertical walls of the fortress.

'The last English castles' were built because the world's biggest and best Navy couldn't be trusted to stop an invasion, or more likely because Palmerston's foreign policy required 'public opinion' to agree with him that a resurgent France, eager to avenge the defeat of Napoleon, had to be kept in her place. An attempt on the life of the third Emperor with a bomb quite possibly made in England, and completion of the world's first ironclad warship, undeniably made in France, revived the age-old mutual dislike and suspicion, especially when England followed with HMS *Warrior*.

The official line was that if the Fleet could be lured away down the English Channel, the French would emerge from their new base of Cherbourg in fast modern steamships on a dark foggy night, to deposit an army on the beaches of West Sussex.* The soldiers would then drag their heavy artillery twenty miles across country to Portsdown Hill, overlooking Portsmouth dockyard, and those guns would quickly pulverise the naval base. With much of the British Army unavoidably detained in Ireland, India and a score of imperial outposts, the invaders would then march on London. The City would take fright, a run on the pound would cause the collapse of Britain's finances and the ruin of her trade. Trafalgar and Waterloo would be suitably avenged.

This latest invasion scare triggered more spending on armaments – and a massive building programme. 'Palmerston's Follies' took ten years to complete, but weren't that expensive despite complaints by Mr Gladstone at the Treasury and there was no lack of skilled labour when the first railway construction boom ended. These forts were out of date long before they were finished and few were ever fitted with cannon, but just in case those new French ironclads did come with an army, yet more forts were deemed essential for Portsmouth, Spithead, the Solent, Chatham and the Thames Estuary, not forgetting Devonport, Milford Haven, Barrow-in-Furness, Hartlepool and Weston-super Mare. Even the ones built for Henry VIII and Charles II were modernised.† The scale of armament was impressive – close on a thousand cannon for Portsmouth alone, to hurl 'armour-shattering' projectiles at the attacking ships, and pour 'hot shell' on the unfortunate troops wading ashore. It would have been hard to find the men to handle all that artillery, and less than half was installed despite a further cash injection; but technology was moving so fast that by 1914 Portsmouth was reckoned safe with just fifty-five modern guns. Years later, in another invasion scare, King George VI fairly oudid his great-grandmother with 'sea forts' in the Thames Estuary and hundreds of miniature concrete 'pill-boxes' to guard almost every square mile of his realm. His distant ancestor George III defied Napoleon with 'Martello Towers'‡ built on the coast and trenches hastily dug around London – even that traditional early warning system, the chain of hilltop beacons, was renovated.

---
* West Wittering on Sea, perhaps, or Bognor Regis
† Hogg I *Coast Dfences of England and Wales1856-1956*, Longmate N *Island Fortess: Defnce of Great Britain 1603-1945*
‡ Ireland got some too – one near Dublin immortalised by Jammes Joyce in *Ulysses*

Palmerston's Follies were never tested in war, but forts were in fashion everywhere. America's Atlantic harbours were guarded against a repeat of 1812 and another burning of the White House. The Civil War made forts famous, and the British came up against some hefty Russian masonry in the Baltic. During the 'Fashoda crisis' of 1898 the French were much afraid their Cherbourg naval base would be pounded to rubble – the fate dreamed up for Portsmouth forty years earlier. In Britain, thinking the unthinkable pointed to her second line of defence, heavy artillery behind bricks and mortar, and the sailors would be safe in their dockyards. Moreover, forts being essentially defensive, they were more acceptable than an expensive standing army, but England now had a new 'army' of unpaid civilians.- the Volunteers.

~ 5 ~

Great-Great-Granddad's Army

V is for the unobtrusive Volunteer
Who fills the Armies of the World with fear
Moral: Seek with the Volunteer to put aside
The empty Pomp of Military Pride.

- Hilaire Belloc 'Moral Alphabet' 1899

The acceptable face of soldiering, they arrived before the first load of concrete, and in twenty years, eight hundred thousand had signed up, including a hundred and thirty Members of Parliament. With a quarter of a million joining *every year* there were seldom fewer than two hundred thousand Volunteers actually on the muster rolls. In the half century this Victorian Home Guard existed, nearly two million civilians learned something of the soldier's trade without ever seeing an enemy – except a few who went off to the Boer War. Whether the Volunteer really did fill the Armies of the World with Fear will never be known, but he deserves a place in British military history[*] along with the guardsmen at Inkerman and Waterloo, for in this astonishing 'people's army' can be seen the idea of a 'Nation in Arms.' An almost forgotten strand of British society, the Volunteer movement did much to make militarism respectable – and conscription well-nigh impossible.

'There is nothing new under the son' a courtier is said to have observed of Prince Frederick of Hanover's dalliance with the same lady who'd been intimate with his father, George II *and* his grandfather George I – the pun probably sounded better in German. Alarmed by

---
[*] Cunningham H *The Volunteer Force: a Social and Political History*

widespread sympathy for the French Revolution, and 'intelligence' of terrorist plots to destroy the Bank of England and the Tower of London, militiamen and patriotic citizens were mobilised to quell rioters *and* repel invaders, an imaginary threat until Napoleon assembled his army, or some of it, just across the Channel for a while. That set off a series of panics, and an almost forgotten prime minister, Henry Addington (Viscount Sidmouth) raised 400,000 Volunteers in the southern counties of England – fifty per cent of all men from 17 to 55. He followed that with a 'Levy en Masse' to conscript the fainthearted remainder, thus netting one in five of *all* males of military age, until one way or another 800,000 were enrolled – when the population of England was scarcely nine million. Napoleon soon moved his troops from Boulogne to face the Austrians – *before* his defeat at Trafalgar – but Volunteers, 'fencibles,' did help to round up a raiding party the French had carelessly unloaded near Fishguard in west Wales, instead of Ireland where they were supposed to go.

Half a century later, another invasion scare, but the new forts for Portsmouth existed only on paper, and there were never enough soldiers. Germans were hired for the Seven Years War, the American rebellion, and the Napoleonic wars, and 'foreign' mercenaries in the Crimean War.* but in the 1850s the Chartists were still a recent memory, and it might have been risky to put weapons in the hands of the lower orders, yet the middle classes, the ones more likely to join, did so – in great numbers and with great enthusiasm.

Of course, they could never be like the Militia, *conscripts* chosen by lottery (the ballot) to meet the quota for each parish. Only the disabled were exempt, but draft dodgers could always join their local Volunteer Corps instead. Otherwise ten pounds bought a year's deferment, and a paid substitute could be found for the obligatory three to five years' service – in practice three weeks' annual training – so the ranks were largely filled by the poor. Numbers fell after Waterloo and with the end of the draft, the 'Constitutional Militia' was just a reservoir for the 'regular' army, and from the same class of unemployables the recruiting sergeant had his eye on. Their officers got favourable notice from Jane Austen, and a militia commission was a useful back door into the regular army – as the young Henry Wilson found – but it was very much a separate 'army,' run by county grandees with a power base in both houses of Parliament – and an obstacle to any politician seeking to alter the military landscape.

Militiamen were never much use for quelling popular unrest, so without a professional police force this was a job for the Yeomanry, a

---

* Beckett IF *The Amateur Military Tradition*, and *Riflemen Form: A Study of the Rifle Voluntteeer Movement, 1859-1908*

part-time 'cavalry' also under semi-feudal control. Mostly the sons of farmers and landed gentry, with property to defend as well as their country, the Yeomanry were socially superior and politically 'sound,' but their methods of crowd control aroused disquiet, especially after the 'Peterloo Massacre' in Manchester, where they used their swords unwisely and inexpertly to disperse a large and peaceable gathering, killing several people and wounding many more.

The mid-Victorian Volunteer movement was an immediate and resounding success, as professional men, shopkeepers and skilled artisans hastened to join their local rifle corps. Hailed by the intelligentsia, notably the poet Matthew Arnold, and by Samuel Smiles whose phenomenally best-selling little book *Self Help* had just appeared, the movement basked in the approval of the Queen and her Consort Prince Albert. A royal review of several thousand Volunteers was enthusiastically reported by the corps of journalists – and by the Manchester cotton merchant and part-time ideologue Friedrich Engels, whose unfailing generosity kept his friend Karl Marx in respectable comfort. 'Although a foreigner, I am ready to join with spirit in this noble cause,' he rhapsodized in hopes there would soon be 'an English National Guard.'[*] Ever since his own conscript days in the Prussian artillery Engels had been fascinated by all things military, and he was now a self-appointed defence pundit who would however conspicuously fail to pick the winner in the Seven Weeks War between Austria and Prussia. He was on safer ground with the Volunteers, and in distinguished company. One of the earliest to detect 'a sound of thunder afar' was the Poet Laureate Alfred Tennyson who dutifully composed a fresh piece of intoxicating doggerel now best forgotten save for its third verse which neatly caught the patriotic mood:

> *Let your reforms for a moment go!*
> *Look to your butts and take good aims!*
> *Better a rotten borough or so,*
> *Than a rotten fleet or a city in flames!*
> *Storm, Storm, Riflemen form!*
> *Ready, be ready against the storm!*
> *Riflemen, Riflemen, Riflemen form!*

All the publicity was free, and in less than fifty years this imitation army put down enduring roots. In their distinctive uniform, grey or green – *red* coats came in 1900 when the Army itself donned khaki – the Volunteers were more acceptable in society than the regular soldiery. But if never turned away from public houses – some of which

---
[*] Letter to *Manchester Guardian* 10 May 1859

were named 'The Rifle Volunteer' – they were never taken seriously by the public, or the military. The Poet Laureate urged them to form, but no one really expected them to *fight*. Ready to meet the storm, perhaps, but *was* there a storm? Could it be that patriotic amateurs were not really needed to defend England? Was this merely a political gesture to impress the foreigners and quieten the middle classes? Or was all the fuss about invasion a pretext for the creation of a large army of *conscripts* to fight in foreign wars? But the Volunteers couldn't reinforce the regular army and they couldn't be sent overseas. Real soldiers viewed them with amused contempt – lesser creatures to man the new forts, whenever they were finished, but no use on the battlefield – the Duke of Cambridge, the Army's near-perpetual Commander-in-Chief, grumbled about all this 'playing at soldiers.'

It is unfair to portray the Victorian 'regular' army as an institution officered exclusively by the none-too-bright sons of aristocracy, its ranks filled by dull-witted drifters, but the impression was widespread and the army was seldom the thinking man's chosen career. A quantum leap in firepower had to be met by the 'moral superiority of the offensive,' so the soldier was taught the virtue of unthinking obedience, but the Volunteer thrived on intelligent self-discipline. He might be mocked in the streets and on the parade ground, but he made up for his lack of soldierly bearing with enthusiasm and brains, or so his officers claimed, and with reason – future Prime Ministers Sir Henry Campbell-Bannerman and David Lloyd George were keen Volunteers, as was the 'pre-Raphaelite' Sir John Millais.

A respected local figure in business or one of the learned professions, the Volunteer officer lacked the social standing of the Sandhurst product. Often, when a unit was formed around an industrial enterprise, the management provided the officers and the foremen were sergeants, though sometimes the men elected their officers – a practice firmly discouraged by the War Office. Patriotic employers 'persuaded' their workers to enlist, but elsewhere the mere act of joining, let alone going to summer camp, could cost a man his job.

Being a Volunteer wasn't cheap – twelve pounds, a month's wage for a skilled worker, for uniform and equipment, and the commanding officer had to dip into his own pocket to buy rifles because the government provided so few – one colonel even bought machine-guns at his own expense without troubling the War Office. Some units specialised in artillery, field engineering, and 'submarine mining' (in harbours), but most volunteers were riflemen. The rifle was to mid-Victorian society what the longbow was in the late middle ages – weapon and status symbol. Shooting competitions were popular, wealthy patrons distributed the prizes and prosperity attended the manufacturers of small arms ammunition.

Some men joined to please their employer, or because it made them 'respectable,' but over the years more seem to have signed on for the sport and recreation. Parliament had slashed the working day to a mere ten hours, 'the hands' had Saturday afternoon free, and their bosses gave them seven days annual vacation – unpaid. So with more time and energy for leisure, a young man might prefer to spend an evening with his mates in close-order drill or at target practice, and if the first recruits endured insult and injury from hooligans and street urchins, the movement was now a familiar part of the urban scenery, a remarkable though unintended piece of social engineering. Though part time soldiering might be a burden for professional men, employers or skilled tradesmen, the trend was briefly halted during the Boer War when Volunteer postal, telegraph and railway specialists went to South Africa, but one Yeomanry formation – which included some Irish 'masters of foxhounds' – suffered heavily.*

Though the shores of England were heavily fortified; her fields guarded by amateur warriors and the surrounding sea swept clear of foreign warships, the ghost of invasion could never be completely laid to rest. Rather, it was eagerly exhumed by the publishers of cheap novels. Invasion thrillers were as popular as detective stories and science fiction – overlapping and intermingling – since most yarns feature a secret weapon or a dastardly foreigner, often both. Wherein a Frenchman, a Russian aristocrat, even a Prussian, tricks the honest, gullible and sadly-effete Anglo-Saxon long enfeebled by years of peace and prosperity – 'a nation of shopkeepers' who believe Free Trade brings harmony and good will, making armies and navies unnecessary.

Sometimes England is overcome by agents smuggled in years before and posing as waiters, but in *The Taking of Dover* (1888) entire English-speaking regiments infiltrate the town in the guise of tourists. With guns in their luggage these latter-day Trojan Horsemen check in to hotels and boarding houses, to emerge as the advance guard of the French and Russian armies.† Elsewhere the slow-thinking natives are defeated by superior technology – submarines, or flying machines bombing their cities; and in a short story by H G Wells an entire army is routed by a few technicians in armoured vehicles with something uncannily like a laser-guided weapon.

For readers who preferred to fight their wars by proxy *The Battle of Dorking‡* has the ideal story line, but the author was no Grub Street

* Jeeffery K *Field Marshal Sir Henry Wilson* p 47
† Clarke I F (ed) *The T\ale of the Next Great War, 1871-1914*
‡ *Blackwood's Magazine*, M\ay 1871

hack. Sir George Tomkyns Chesney, Army engineer, hero of the Great Mutiny, one of the men who ruled India, and briefly Member of Parliament (Conservative), described a near-future invasion – not by the French this time, but a German Army advancing on London through the 'Dorking Gap' in the Surrey hills. It was a runaway publishing success, despite the response, *The Battle off Worthing: Why The Invaders Never Got To Dorking,* hastily written by a 'Captain of the Royal Navy.' Mr Gladstone cautioned everyone against 'alarmism,' but Chesney's fantasy generated yet another invasion scare; another twenty years of public debate, and eventually a line of 'mini-forts' along the North Downs to guard the 'Dorking gap' and other likely routes to the metropolis. But these very modest hillside emplacements, of doubtful value even for their time, were never armed or occupied – a forlorn relic can be inspected on Fort Lane, near Reigate just off the M 25 London Orbital Highway. To make quite sure, a few trenches were dug for a last-ditch defence at Croydon in Surrey and Chiselhurst in Kent.

The change in the real world was soon noticed. A Volunteer who went to fight the Boers, the maverick Anglo-Irish Erskine Childers, wrote the best-known of all invasion thrillers, *The Riddle of the Sands* (1903). Set on the mud flats and sand banks off the North German coast, the story is complete with a renegade Englishman whose comely daughter falls for the hero, and national honour is saved. Less happy is the native son who comes home to find his countrymen chafing helplessly under German occupation and widespread collaboration—especially by the police—in *When William Came*, though it does end on a hopeful note. The author, H. H Munro – 'Saki' – wrote in 1914 'I have always looked forward to the romance of a European war.' Two years later a sniper killed him on the Somme.

And if the fear of invasion could sell militarism wrapped in fiction to a patriotic but credulous citizenry, Queen Victoria's Volunteers had served the purpose longer than anyone could expect, but too long perhaps for generals dreaming of a continental-size army – and conscription. But for most Englishmen, their frontier was not the English Channel, but the wide ocean.

~ 6 ~

The Ghastly Peril

You, <u>you</u>, that have the ordering of her fleet,
If you should only compass her disgrace,
When all men starve, the wild mob's million feet
Will kick you from your place,
But then too late, too late.

- Alfred Lord Tennyson *The Fleet, Verse IV 1886*

The middle classes were always good for a panic and they shuddered when the Poet Laureate put his oar in. The spectre of a rotting fleet, ever a comfort to the Opposition Party, would haunt the public mind for a generation and more. Mr Gladstone thought the world's finest navy 'almost valueless for any purpose than defence of home waters'* and with engaging candour the admirals agreed they might just manage to fend off a new Armada, though the real danger was not invasion, but *starvation*, because they were not at all sure how to protect British ships from the marauding cruisers of a weaker naval power. Convoy was ruled out – steamship captains could never keep together† – though the battle fleet routinely moved 'in convoy' screened by smaller craft, and anyway, the ports would be congested if everyone arrived at once. It was to be 'every ship for herself' unless the entire British merchant fleet was 'transferred' to the flag of an obliging neutral state on the outbreak of war.

---

* Marder AJ *Anatomy of British Sea Power* p 45
† Offer A *The First World War: an Agrarian Interpretation* p 221

If that wasn't enough, there was more bad news for the British Public. Their all-powerful Navy would soon be outnumbered by the competition. Everyone was building or buying battleships; France, Russia, Italy, Austria, Japan, Turkey, Chile, Brazil. Of course, league tables gave only half the picture; the French navy was not that dangerous; the Russians were compelled obliged by geography to keep *three* navies, Baltic, Black Sea, Pacific; and the Germans had barely dipped their toes in the water. The big players might be strong on land – the Franco-Prussian war had shown that – but for most nations a navy was more of a fashion statement, except where Austrians and Italians glared at each other across the Adriatic. The Royal Navy might be 'technologically backward, reactionary in outlook and organisationally confused' but there was no serious opposition, no one to call its bluff. In England though, what really mattered was 'public opinion' as shaped by newspaper proprietors, 'defence' pundits, admirals, politicians – and public opinion could *not* be ignored.

The contemporary novelist Anthony Trollope was less impressed, one of his larger-than-life statesmen demanding 'four bigger ships of war than had ever been built before, with larger guns, and more men, and thicker iron plates, and above all, with a greater expenditure of money.'* Without them Britain would be invaded by France and Germany, India seized by the Russians, Canada annexed by the USA, and worse. Fact, or fabrication, followed fiction with the usual time lag, but as former defence official Lord Sydenham recalled, the public had to be 'enlightened,' and the press, 'wisely using its great teaching powers,' would oblige with a 'popular demand.'†

That popular demand emerged in the carefully managed Navy Scare of 1884, led by the youthful 'Liberal Unionist' Hugh Oakley Arnold-Forster, with back-room assistance from a wealthy young man with close connections to royalty, Reginald Baliol Brett, briefly a Liberal MP, but preferring 'influence' to open accountability. They approached William Thomas Stead, the crusading journalist who championed every 'liberal' cause but didn't mind if he upset Mr Gladstone now and then. Spiritualist, Salvation Army supporter, campaigner for 'social purity' in politics. Now editing the 'Liberal' *Pall Mall Gazette*, W T Stead was handed a scoop; 'The Truth about the Navy' based on 'information from naval officers.' One of those officers was Captain John Arbuthnot Fisher, a torpedo specialist now running the Naval gunnery school at Whale Island, Portsmouth, but the most eminent Victorian admiral, Sir Geoffrey Phipps-Hornby, had also gone public on this one. It was scary stuff; 'ships without speed, guns

---
* Trollope A *The Prime Minister* Vol 1 p 297, 344
† Sydenham (Sir George Clarke) *My Working Life* p 142

without range, boilers with only a few months of life in them.' Certainly, Mr Gladstone halved naval spending, to the discomfiture of the armaments industry and the distress of shipyard workers and their children, so the disclosure of apparent negligence in the administration of the Fleet caused a useful commotion that jolted the Liberals into a hasty construction programme, and Arnold-Forster would eventually get something out of it – a seat in parliament. One day a Conservative government would reward him with a junior place at the Admiralty, *and* the 'poisoned chalice' of the War Office, which did his health no good – intellectuals seldom flourish in English politics. The campaigning journalist who triggered a naval spending spree turned to more good causes like arms limitation and Anglo-German friendship, while Reginald Brett had quietly eased himself into the Office of Works as 'permanent secretary' in charge of public buildings, including the upkeep of Royal Palaces, a not very demanding task that unavoidably necessitated close contact with the occupants, especially the ageing Queen Victoria *and* the Heir to the Throne, Edward Prince of Wales who generously gave him rooms in Windsor Castle – a sort of tied cottage for the caretaker who just happened to own a large house practically next door.

But the prime mover in this Navy Scare was not W T Stead or Arnold-Forster, nor even Reginald Brett. They served that well-known bookseller and Conservative politician William Henry Smith, so cruelly lampooned as 'Sir Joseph Porter' in Gilbert and Sullivan's *HMS Pinafore*. As a recent 'ruler of the Queen's Navee' and First Lord of the Admiralty, 'Old Morality' Smith, knew his admirals, and he knew who mattered in the 'square mile' and in particular the City of London Conservative Association. A staunch Non-Conformist, it didn't take Smith long to get everyone into line, so when Lloyds of London were asked if the Navy was now too weak to protect British ships and their cargo, a spokesman dutifully nodded in agreement.*

W. H. Smith had formed a pressure group which he guessed would disconcert Gladstone's government, and it did. Smith had the timely aid of another 'Russian scare' and the usual knee-jerk reaction in the City with a run on the Funds to frighten the British Public. Then a botched colonial expedition with Crimean hero Wolseley failing to rescue another legendary institution, leaving General Gordon besieged in Khartoum. Wolseley came home, used Queen Victoria's shoulder to cry on, blamed Gladstone for everything and turned his back on the Liberal Party. The Poet Laureate weighed in with another rhyming rant, this one aimed at the hapless Lord Northbrook, now Admiralty

---

* Smith R B 'Public Opinion,the Navy and the City of London:The drive for British Naval Expansion in the Late 19th Century' *War and Society* Vol 9, No 1 May 1991 University of New South Wales

First Lord, on whom would fall 'the curse of all the land' should he 'fail to understand' what was required of him. His lordship did not fail and hurriedly topped up the navy estimates with a five-year, five and a half million pound life jacket, too late to save his floundering comrades.

With the Liberals out of office, the City continued its shrill demand for a bigger navy, to the embarrassment of the briefly resurgent Conservatives. In vain did W H Smith endeavour to stifle his love-child —he was a cabinet minister again—but the London Chamber of Commerce adopted the creature, sponsoring public meetings of ship owners, underwriters, naval officers and political luminaries. At one such event in May 1888—another depressing year for shipbuilders, and hence time for another Navy Scare—the organisers paraded an impressive phalanx of sixteen admirals. Some had yet to retire from the Silent Service, but to a man they bore witness to their functional impotence.

Swords might be rusty, but pens were sharpened in Fleet Street, the Press 'wisely using its great teaching powers.' Model pupils all, Lord Salisbury's ministers fair outdid the Liberals with the Naval Defence Act of 1889, a multi-million pound package for a born-again navy; ten new battleships, thirty eight cruisers and twenty two smaller craft.

The Naval Defence Act did more than rebuild the British navy. It started an arms race by encouraging everyone else to order more warships, though in part compensation, some of those would be built in the United Kingdom and British armaments manufacturers weren't fussy about their customers. Britain's fiscal landscape was permanently altered too, because upgrading the Fleet came at a price. Thirteen million pounds in 1886; approaching twenty two million ten years later; more than 27 million by 1900; and the Navy Estimates would ratchet up to 51 million by 1914 – when the army, now the poor relation, had to manage on less than 30 million.

Not since the wars against France had the Treasury been so busy looking for new sources of revenue. Direct taxation of land and inherited wealth was never in favour, and Mr Gladstone thought income tax was on the road to Communism. The Victorian State preferred indirect taxes, especially on tobacco and beer – the working man's beverage – but henceforth the gentry and the great landowners would have to pay more for their navy.

They'd been grumbling about the tax on legacies – 'succession duties' dated from 1853 – but now the Conservatives had no qualms about a one per cent slice off anyone's estate worth more than £10,000.

The Liberals improved considerably on that with 'death duties'- now 'inheritance tax' for the squeamish. Juggling figures at the Treasury to fund more battleships as well as the fledgling but relatively expensive Edwardian welfare state, David Lloyd George willingly embraced death as a convenient opportunity for the wealthy, or their descendants unaware of the possibilities of creative accounting, to pay the price of Admiralty.

Significantly, naval rearmament on such a grand scale shifted the balance of power from the shires to the City of London with its worldwide grip on trade, banking, insurance, the 'invisible' exports – and overseas investment. For good measure, large tracts of late Victorian and Edwardian suburbia emerged as private estates were sold off to speculative builders in London and other great cities, to pay death duties.

For all that, the Silent Service needed a louder voice – said the Big Navy lobby. That voice was soon heard at the Royal Naval Exhibition, a carefully-crafted piece of showmanship that toured all the great cities, bringing in two million visitors, and that same voice echoed noisily throughout the depression of 1893 when times were hard for shipbuilding firms and their workmen – until trade picked up after a timely warning from Admiral Beresford about swarms of French torpedo boats in the English Channel. As an Irish peer, Lord Charles William de la Poer Beresford was a Member of Parliament for twenty years on and off, representing the people of Waterford, Marylebone East, York, Woolwich and Portsmouth, while contriving to be a naval officer in between – and briefly, Fourth Sea Lord at the Admiralty. He opposed the abolition of flogging, but was said to be popular on the lower deck.

The ever-helpful press, or most of it, obliged once more, with a few exceptions. 'The panic mongers are abroad' cried the *Daily News*, with 'admirals joining juvenile politicians.' The 1893 Navy Scare certainly frightened Gladstone's fourth cabinet. Alarmed by word of French construction and some supposedly powerful new Russian cruisers, the 'juvenile politicians' heartlessly dumped their venerable chief who shuffled out of public life muttering 'it is the admirals who have got their knife into me.' His comrades picked a new leader and gave way to the Profession in a way the old man had refused to do. Blithely ordering another seven 'first class' battleships, six cruisers, three dozen destroyers and a brace of sloops, they took an option to buy extra battleships if the foreigners were thought to be getting more. Public Opinion – and the Profession – must *not* be ignored.

Three scares in ten years and there was a powerful head of steam behind naval rearmament. The Conservative *Morning Post* defence correspondent Spenser Wilkinson urged voters to back only 'Big Navy' men for Parliament, and in 1895 the Navy League emerged on the frothy crest of a wave of manufactured excitement, declaring itself 'absolutely distinct from all party politics.'

If this new pressure group was expected to provide a forum for debate, i.e. a sounding board for naval officers, marine architects, engineers and scientists; well, that already existed in the nation's oldest military 'think tank,' the Royal United Service Institution. In an age of technical advance and continual shifts in design, the shape and size of the battleship was in question, even its purpose, but the Navy League just wanted more of them, albeit with better guns. Pressure groups like this, and the London Chamber of Commerce, would always endorse the Admiralty's shopping list,* and could always be kept at arm's length. Less impressed by the League's alarmist language and notably absent from its councils were the naval historian John Knox Laughton.† Another dissenter was Spenser Wilkinson who joined believing its aim was to give the Navy a General Staff, a 'brain.' He promptly quit when the idea was dropped.

Undismayed, Navy League scriptwriters found new threats to 'national security.' The latest French cruisers were apparently ready to 'plunder, burn and sink English shipping on the distant seas' while nightly bombarding 'defenceless towns, such as Brighton and Hastings' – and there was more. Some disaffected French officers had given the League details of their country's secret plan for the long-awaited resumption of The Great War – the one against Napoleon. This time the victors would be the French, and the vanquished would have to pay a huge fine. The port of Dover would be ceded to France 'in perpetuity,' as well as two dozen or so British possessions including future problematic ones like Cyprus, Hong Kong, Fiji, Sierra Leone – and Ireland, north and south, would be for ever a *French* responsibility. Cruellest humiliation of all, the British Museum would lose its Elgin Marbles – to the Louvre.

The lunatic fringe of the navalists' perhaps, and inside the Admiralty their lordships' toes might curl in embarrassment, but the League's table of patrons and supporters is an impressive list of the Great and the Good. Field-Marshal Lord Roberts was 'honorary vice president'; Rudyard Kipling was an 'officer'; Henry Wilson a card-carrying member; and there was no lack of retired army and navy officers, gentry and nobility. The Countess de la Warr presided over the all-female South Kensington committee, assisted by seven other

---
* Marder, p 59
† Lambert A D *The Foundations of Naval Hisstory* pp 115-6

titled ladies, including two admirals' wives and the widow of Admiral Sir George Tryon; whose careless handling of his battleships in a fleet exercise had recently occasioned great loss of life, including his own.

In this fertile soil League membership grew to 100,000 by 1914, though it never quite matched its German counterpart – more than a million, not counting the German Women's Navy League. But the British had the solid backing of the City of London and the London Chamber of Commerce, while the big shipbuilding firms could expect more business – after all, the Admiralty was their 'fairy godmother.'*

Navy League organisation was thorough, with specialist sub-committeees; Finance, Colonial, Provincial and Lectures, Publications and Parliamentary, and Ladies (Provisional). Local branches were advised on public relations while 'remoter parts of the Empire' – Malta, Toronto, Hong Kong and Georgetown in Guyana – were welcomed into membership.

From the start the message was aimed at the young and impressionable. A little book...'dedicated to the British Schoolboy' explained how the Navy had protected the East India Company's 'very profitable' trade in opium. When Chinese customs officials seized large quantities of the drug and 'molested' British merchants importing it, a 'powerful naval squadron' was promptly dispatched to 'enforce freedom of trade for British subjects.'† For the less historically minded, League propaganda went straight to the stomach. In time of war, *these* children were told a weak navy meant food would be so expensive, they would be crying for their supper

The League's conference on 'Food Supply' attracted the usual heavyweights like Admiral Phillip's brother Sir John Colomb, Sir Charles Dilke and Hugh Arnold-Forster, now a 'Liberal-Unionist' MP. Major Henry Wilson showed up too. Speakers who probably knew what they were talking about – grain merchants and importers – wanted 'state granaries.' But if the world's biggest and best navy could do nothing about 'the ghastly peril of starvation' well, that was really beside the point, for the world's granaries would soon be emptied when demand for fertiliser outstripped supply. The 'deadly peril of not having enough to eat' was already on the menu for the British Association for the Advancement of Science, but fortunately the German chemist Fritz Haber discovered in the nick of time how to produce unlimited quantities of artificial fertiliser by 'capturing' nitrogen in the atmosphere. He won a Nobel Prize for that. When war came 'the Kaiser's chemist' would use his skill to foil the British naval blockade

---

* Marder p 24
† Navy League *Britain Beyond the Sea* 1898 pp 61-62

by making nitrogen for explosives. He also pioneered a 'higher form of warfare'– poison gas – but his attempt to extract gold from seawater to pay Germany's postwar debt did not succeed.

Heedless of chemistry, the admirals were not too concerned by the ghastly peril, even if much of Britain's food was now imported. The protection of trade was somehow beneath their dignity. They spoke vaguely of sending cruisers to 'patrol the sea lanes,' though of all people *they* knew no other navy could keep steam-powered raiders on the high seas for very long. Only the British had a worldwide network of coaling stations and dockyards to keep their ships on station, and though the French excelled in warship design, their new cruisers so much feared by Navy League propagandists were tied to their home ports for servicing. The dreaded 'guerre de course' by marauding warships on the high seas would count for little – until the long-range diesel-powered submarine brought further terrors.

British admirals believed in the offensive. *Their* cruisers were the eyes of the fleet and their battleships were built to sink the French or the Russians in a stand up fight – or the German navy, when that became a nuisance. Moreover, an unshakeable belief in 'sea power' was rooted in the mind of every British statesman, for whom the Royal Navy had always been Britain's sword as well as her shield; an instrument of power-projection that entitled her to Great Power status not only on the wide ocean but across the continental land mass of Europe as well. It was this faith, routinely expressed in Foreign Office memoranda, that influenced every British government right up to August 1914, an assurance that Britons could sleep safely in their beds, they would never go hungry – *and* they would never have to fight on the continent of Europe.

~ 7 ~

Out of Africa

"South Africa is now a manly and high minded society."

- Canon Hensley Hemson in St Margaret's Westminster 1st June 1902

'No end of a lesson' cried Rudyard Kipling when it was over – a colonial campaign lasting two and a half years that sucked in four hundred and fifty thousand soldiers. Twenty thousand died, most from typhoid fever, with a hundred thousand sick or wounded – on the British side alone. Way over a budget of £10 million – at two hundred and thirty million the second Boer War was Britain's most expensive conflict since the 'Great War,' that twenty year struggle with France still being paid for a century after Waterloo. The *next* Great War, with Germany, would cost rather more.*

Greater than the expense was the shock to a people accustomed to a seemingly boundless imperial enterprise; a succession of vast territories won by brave soldiers and sailors vanquishing heathen enemies. Suddenly the onward march of the British Empire had faltered in South Africa, but not everyone was chastened. The admirals and the Big Navy lobby could boast how British sea power ensured the safe passage of tens of thousands of soldiers from the colonies as well as the homeland – 'force projection' on the grand scale, as in earlier times. In the war for America, sea power – actually *wind* power – sustained an army of fifty thousand on the far side of the Atlantic, until the French interfered. Eighty years later British sea power reached out to hammer at the gates of Imperial Russia in the Baltic and the Black Sea – even

---
* Hurst & Allen *British War Budgets* OUP 1926 p11

reaching across the Pacific. This time, sea power – now *steam* power – had shrunk the sprawling empire to manageable proportions. Under the Navy's watchful eye fast troopships summoned by the electric telegraph and the submarine cable had conquered space, pulling together dominions, colonies and motherland. There would be no seafights with the Boers or anyone, but the imperial purpose was served. A dozen years later, the value of speedy and secure maritime communication would again be proved as armies from Canada, Australia, New Zealand, India, North America and South Africa were swiftly and safely ferried across the oceans to fight in Europe and the Middle East.

Yes, the Royal Navy 'deterred' other Europeans from interfering, but nobody wanted to fight England for the independence of a few farmers of Dutch descent six thousand miles away, and the navy that *could* have sunk the troopships did not exist. There was righteous anger in the Netherlands once they got over their distaste for the 'coarseness' of their Afrikaner cousins – and forgot about their own imperialist war in the East Indies, still dragging on after thirty years, and that was it. Britain had few friends abroad, but when the Navy League seized upon every shred of 'evidence' that—while her cruisers guarded the route to the Cape—England lay wide open to assault by a French armada, yet no one seemed to worry.

Kipling was right, though. It *was* no end of a lesson – on dry land. The British army had a wealth of combat experience, but this was its first 'European' war since the Crimea. Except in the Transvaal and briefly in Canada, they had always fought non-European 'natives'- the strong against the weak, modern versus primitive. As Hilaire Belloc rhymed, 'whatever happens, we have got the Maxim Gun, and they have not.' But these Boer farmers had modern weapons and used them well, they were ably led and at first they seemed to be winning, but then few armies would have done better than the ill-prepared, badly positioned and under strength Britsh army. When a new commander, Roberts, arrived with reinforcements and a flair for public relations, the Boers were defeated in battle, then crushed in a lengthy 'counter-insurgency' campaign conducted by Kitchener of Khartoum, who took over when 'Bobs' went home to a hero's welcome and £100,000 from a grateful Parliament.

The rest of Europe's press saw a British army poorly trained and ineptly led; an army that need not be taken seriously. The Germans, who displayed no great military talent in their own colonial adventures, were particularly disdainful, a team of observers from the Great General Staff finding the British had 'no mental grasp of the requirements of a modern battle.' The Prussians came down hard on the 'supine' Sir John French – a verdict undeserved, for the Boers on their little ponies were no match for his splendid cavalry. They did have kind words for one regiment that had 'a definite plan' and showed 'unity of command,' but such graceful compliments were rare.*

But it was Roberts himself who acknowledged that the British soldier 'did not know how to act for himself.' Too much importance was attached to 'order and regularity' and far too little to 'individuality.' The official German narrative – quoting Roberts – commends the Boers for their 'healthy common sense.' It was just as well the Prussians never saw the diary kept by a young brigade-major, Henry Wilson, who– before Roberts arrived – recorded his own unflattering assessment of his superiors.†

In a somewhat opaque appraisal worthy of General Carl Philipp Gottlieb von Clausewitz himself, his countrymen fairly put the boot into a British officer corps 'governed by vicious ideas,' and blaming 'the superiority of the Enemy's armament' for their failure. This magisterial rebuke might have given the impression that the British had actually *lost* this war, but the conclusion drawn by other armies was that cavalry still had a future in modern combat, if handled well‡

The most serious defect lay beyond South Africa and outside the province of the military. The Boers had unwittingly furnished a window into the condition of the British Army, and another into the state of the nation's health, for three out of every five volunteers were found physically unfit, so how would Britain fare in a war with a continental European power if the ranks were filled by under-sized weaklings with rotten teeth? Soldiers, politicians, journalists and 'opinion-formers' all agreed that while something must be done about the army, something should also be done about the physique of its recruits if the imperial super-power could hope to stay in the top league.

Something *was* done about the Army.§ The usual response was an official inquiry, and the Conservatives set up several – into how the Boer war was fought, how the army was organised, and the state of Britain's reserves. Even before the ceasefire, one high-powered team led by a City banker was crawling all over the War Office and condemning everything in sight. A Royal Commission under Lord Elgin denounced the commanders in the field (though not Sir John French himself) for slackness and incompetence, while the Duke of Norfolk's

---

* *The German Official Account of the War in South Africa, prepared for the Great General Staff, Berlin*, translated by Colo H du Cane 1906
† Jeffery K *Field Marshal Sir Henry Wilson* p 36
‡ Echevarria A J "Combining Firepower and Versatility: Remaking the 'Arm of Decision' before the Great War" RUSI *Journal* June 2002
§ Adams RJQ, Poirier PP *The Conscription Controversy in Great Britain 1900-18* p 8

Commission found the army's back-up – Militia, Yeomanry and Volunteers – quite beyond aid unless completely remodelled, and the ever-present Spenser Wilkinson recommended conscription for home defence, but he was in a minority of one.

The Great Purge of the War Office that followed was overseen by that wealthy dilettante, courtier and backstairs manipulator extraordinary, Reginald Balliol Brett, sometime militia officer, now second Viscount Esher and Deputy Governor of Windsor Castle. At his behest eight generals were sacked and Field-Marshal Lord Roberts of Kandahar, Pretoria and Waterford found himself the very last Commander in Chief – though for Esher, the 'natural head' of the Army could only be the King. There'd be a new board of management; an 'Army Council' of soldiers and a few civilians *and* a General Staff—of sorts—would see to the training and equipment of the troops; the 'military education ' of the officers; their postings and promotions; 'intelligence' about possible enemies; and plans to wage war on them. The government's sole adviser on military affairs was to be the Chief of General Staff, though of course the other generals would still use their own private back door to the Palace, and the monarch did not dissuade them – it *was* 'his' army after all, and they were always grateful for royal encouragement and support against their constitutional 'masters' the politicians, or, in their feuding with other generals.

Those few thousand Dutch farmers could not have known they were the catalyst of change. But for that disagreeable experience in South Africa the War Office might have escaped the inquisition, there would have been no shake-up, no cull of senior management, and the Profession would have reverted to type, retreating to the North West Frontier in Asia. Instead, Britain was to get a new model army by stealth, for North West Europe. Ironically, it had taken an expensive colonial war to set that army on the road to Flanders and Picardy; its ranks swollen by millions who had never thought of soldiering – with or without bad teeth.

~ 8 ~

Flagstaffs in the Persian Gulf

A narrow strip of water separates the Arab world from a very different branch of Islam. Mariners pick their way carefully through the Strait of Hormuz—just thirty four miles wide—past the lofty Jabal Karim, a knobbly finger protruding into the sea as if warning them not to enter the Gulf. The Musandam peninsular in Oman with its lovely fiords—'Arabia's Norway'—bears reminders of the old East India Company. One inlet is named after the Honourable Mountstuart Elphinstone, soldier-governor of Bombay renowned for his method of collecting taxes; flogging and torture for late payers.* The nearby Malcolm Inlet brings to mind another of the Company's hard men, a despot who ruled a vast tract of India by armed force.

The Portuguese came this way and stayed 150 years. Then the British arrived; naval officers, soldiers, explorers and farsighted pro-consuls descending upon this corner of Arabia, so close to Persia and so near the western flank of Britain's prize domain, India. They made treaties with local sheiks, and then a 'perpetual maritime truce' under the protection of Queen Victoria whose navy patrolled the 'Pirate Coast,' earning the gratitude of the pearl fishers, though not the slave traders. British officials—'Residents'—dispensed 'advice' to the sheikhs for another seventy years until this patchwork of fiefdoms; the 'Trucial States' which included Dubai and Abu Dhabi, were merged into the 'United Arab Emirates.' After a secret ten-year 'war' a slice of Oman overlooking the Strait of Hormuz was also added. Long before though, the sea had been charted and lighthouses erected, as the narrows between Arabia and Persia became as important as the

---

* He would rather have had them 'blown from guns' Washbrook D A "India 1818-1860 The Two Faces of Colonialism" *Oxford History of the British Empire* Vol III p405

Straits of Dover and Gibraltar; the Suez Canal; the Malacca Strait; or Bab al Mandab in the Red Sea – the veritable 'keys of the world.' Conveniently for Great Britain, all these strategic locations were held by His Majesty King Edward VII, and with this 'choke point' at the entrance to the Gulf now also under British control, the flow of imperial lifeblood was assured.

'Sword and shield of empire,' the Royal Navy was going through a revolution in technology – not only firepower and communications, but also a switch from Welsh steam-coal to a more efficient fuel. Soon, much of this black, sticky, smelly crude oil would come from the ancient kingdom of Persia, which had never been a part of the British Empire. Drilling began in 1901 and seven years later the Anglo-Persian Oil Company was in business. At the head of the Gulf lay Mesopotamia (now Iraq), cradle of civilisation and fount of riches still awaiting the oil men. Mesopotamia at the time 'belonged' to the Turkish Ottoman Empire as did much of the vast Arabian Peninsula. Here too the foreigners would discover more oil. The British were already nibbling at the edges and in 1913 Kuwait emerged as an 'independent' state with the blessing of Britain and Turkey; while Persia was already being parcelled into British and Russian 'spheres of influence' with a neutral zone in-between – for in these parts, the Russians were as unwelcome as the French, at least in British eyes.

The Flagstaffs *

They were put there, not to mark the annexation of yet more real estate for the British Empire, but to 'show the flag' as the Navy had been doing in every corner of the globe until very recently. Not the White Ensign this time, but the Union Jack, because this was on dry land – albeit someone else's land. The Hon. Mountstuart Elphinstone and Sir John Malcolm would surely have approved. It was the modestly named 'Telegraph Island'; a lonely waystation along the submarine cable linking London with Bombay, that had the honour to receive the first flagstaff of the twentieth century. They were massive structures. Iron tubes 38 feet high with 'wooden yards and signal halyards.' The proudly fluttering Union flag would proclaim the *Pax Britannica* to all who passed through the Strait – but therein lay a difficulty. Foreigners would certainly be impressed by this reminder of Britain's imperial might if they could actually *see* the Meteor Flag of England, but having gone to all that expense His Majesty's ministers now had cold feet, their man on the ground prissily acknowledging their desire that these flagstaffs should not be be ' too prominent.' So they had to be where passing seafarers were less likely to notice them – lest they

* TNA Cab 6/276D, and 63rd Meeting CID, Cab 2/1 23 February 1905

take offence.

Union Jacks being hard to come by in these parts, someone found a few 'blue ensigns' which might pass for the real thing – at a distance. Then came a fresh snag. Protocol required each flag to be hoisted at breakfast time and hauled down at sunset, but no one lived nearby to perform this ceremony. The pace of mid-Victorian technology had closed the manager's office on Telegraph Island, and even the local fishermen found life unbearable in the summer heat. But, as realists pointed out, flags left fluttering all day and all night would be 'blown to rags in a very short time.'

Now the Admiralty weighed in, complaining that despite the Navy's considerable experience of hoisting, showing and waving flags, their Lordships hadn't actually been consulted, and anyway, they (the flagstaffs) were 'practically meaningless.' Wary perhaps of zealots (and possibly concerned for their own career prospects) officials began to distance themselves from the Flagstaff project. Minutes and memoranda were shuffled about until at last everyone could extricate himself with honour as a decision was reached; to keep just *one* flagstaff – on Telegraph Island. The others were quietly abandoned.

The fluttering of near-invisible flags on a foreign shore was not so much a demonstration of confidence but more of a distress signal from an élite corps of governors, viceroys, and officials. They were anxious that some region just beyond their grasp – now so important to British trade – should fall under the sway of another great power. This explains why the flag staff project got onto the agenda of the Committee of Imperial Defence in Whitehall in the first place. This was the Cabinet's 'Defence Committee' all smartened up and stretched to include not just top brass but anyone else the Prime Minister fancied. Other bits of Whitehall machinery—a 'Military and Naval' committee and another for 'colonial defence'—were scooped up. With the Prime Minister in the chair the 'CID' was – or should have been – the most impressive piece of joined-up government thinking Edwardian England could muster, albeit originally conceived by a pair of marines in Queen Victoria's time.

The Secretary of the CID was that 'bouncing, coarse fellow' Sir George Sydenham Clarke,* a true Victorian all-rounder; military engineer; fortifications expert; Superintendent of the Royal Carriage Factory (for gun mountings); instructor in geometry, and an all-round busybody who'd been Secretary to the Colonial Defence Committee *and* a Royal Commission on Army and Navy administration. Sent to govern the Australian State of Victoria, briefly and without much enthusiasm,

---
* Fraser P Lord Esher: *A Political Biography* p 96

he was called back to assist Lord Esher and Admiral Fisher in the cleansing of the War Office stables, a task he relished, for he'd long been upset by admirals and generals not speaking to each other and, more importantly, ignoring *him* altogether.

The Committee of Imperial Defence was an impressive collection of martial, political and bureaucratic talent whose job was to co-ordinate the plans of Army and Navy for the defence of Britain and the British Empire.* It soon became a resting place for retired or redundant warriors put there to humour their conceit and keep them quiet, but the odd man out was its 'Permanent Associate Member,' the capricious courtier Viscount Esher, that 'occasionally meddlesome member' who instantly took charge and gave it a secretariat; an elementary piece of organisation the Cabinet itself had to manage without until the Great War.

Flagstaffs could vanish from the Persian Gulf, but the Defence Committee was stuck with another permanent fixture, Lord Roberts, the Army's very last 'Commander in Chief.' But the redundant field marshal made a speech too far, calling in public for the 'military education' of young men and boys.† He sought to use the Committee as a sounding board for conscription, or 'compulsion,' whereupon after a little seemly hesitation – his arm firmly twisted by his adviser and speech writer Henry Wilson – he walked the CID plank in a well-rehearsed huff, having hugely embarrassed the Conservative government. Even his resignation letter was published before the Prime Minister was shown the contents, because 'the King had approved it.' But the British Public had not heard the last of Frederick Sleigh Roberts.

Imperial Sunset

It was an extraordinary predicament for the world's first and *only* super-power to be so afraid of its enemies and so uncertain as to how to protect itself, despite spending rather more on 'defence' than the Russians or the Germans. Not even a hundred years since the British tried to burn down the White House, who could be sure the western provinces of Canada were safe? Half a world away, Japan had emerged as an assertive regional power with a formidable navy, though Germany was uncomfortably closer to home. It seemed the 'weary Titan' was beset with foes, unless diplomacy could come to the rescue – and the diplomats had done just that. By 1902 Japan was an ally, and two years later England's historic enemy France suddenly became her

---

* See d'Ombrain N *War Machinery and High Policy: Defence Administration in Peacetime Britain 1902-1914* p 8-11
† Fraser p 159 and Pall Mall Gazette 2 August 1905

very good friend – an achievement attributed to Edward VII whose erratic interventions in foreign affairs served little purpose, despite his liking for Paris society and his understandable distrust of his excitable nephew Wilhelm. One day even the Russian Empire—already the ally of republican France—might be England's friend too, and the years of 'splendid isolation' would end.

The Anglo-French *Entente* brought a truce in a century of Cold War. But an agreement about colonial frontiers and fishing rights was a long way from a military alliance, even if there was a clause tacked on—a bland agreement to 'consult' as to the appropriate diplomatic steps should either party feel threatened by someone else—and *that* had given some people the hint of a new dimension to British foreign policy – and a new mission for the British Army.

Britain's maritime empire had some very long land frontiers, especially Canada's border with America, but the one that grabbed the headlines was in Asia – the 'North West Frontier.' Keystone of Empire and Britain's most profitable possession, India was buttressed by colonies in East Africa and South East Asia, with military power thrust up the Nile valley and the Irrawaddy, while the Indian Ocean was patrolled by warships using the dockyards and coaling stations at Aden, Bombay, Trincomalee, Simonstown and Singapore.

The men who ruled India were obsessed by fears of a Russian army sweeping through Afghanistan, that unforgiving land where in the winter of 1842 another Elphinstone (not Mountstuart) perished with his little army in retreat from Kabul. Only one man survived. It was *'a terrible, perhaps useful lesson to those rulers who think that a territory may be gained by ..... blowing open a few gates, storming a few forts, and shooting down a few hundred wild Afghans.'* Sadly, the lesson was forgotten thirty years later when *three* armies were sent in.

It was not a good time for Britain's military reputation. In 1880 General George Burrows, outnumbered ten to one, was very much defeated at Maiwand in Afghanistan. He would be avenged by another general, Frederick Roberts, who conducted a 'reign of terror' in Kabul. Roberts made his famous march to Kandahar – with a modest victory on the way – and earned himself some useful publicity back home. But not everyone was impressed: 'In Afghanistan hopeful anticipations are apt to prove baseless,' the *Boys' Own Paper* informed its readers. *

Years later, the Field Marshal reminded himself—and the Defence Committee too—of 'a principle of far reaching importance'; the proper way for the cavalry to carry their rifles. Citing an incident long ago when the 9th Lancers had unwisely left their carbines attached to their

---
* *Boy's Own Paaper* 6 October 1880

horses (this being the regulation at the time) and several of said horses had then shown 'good horse-sense' and departed the battlefield. The Earl of Kandahar, Pretoria and Waterford gave a harrowing account of dismounted soldiers *'without firearms, helpless against the Afghans [and] vainly endeavouring to defend themselves with their lances, being further impeded by their long boots, and by their swords dangling between their legs.'* Recollection of this unhappy episode stirred earlier memories of the Indian Mutiny, though he couldn't explain why he failed to remedy this organisational defect when he'd been Commander-in-Chief of the entire British Army. *

The Russians were probably more worried about their own southern underbelly and the dubious loyalty of their numerous Muslim subjects, than the prospect of gaining several millions more in Afghanistan and India. Nevertheless, British governors, viceroys and generals—all gentlemen-players of the 'Great Game'—persisted with their 'forward policy' to forestall the Bear, though by the twentieth century it was reckoned that to move an army of any consequence through Afghanistan would require a baggage train of two million camels. A hasty hump count revealed just 200,000 of these useful creatures in the entire sub continent – and the Bear would need at least *five million* for a similar enterprise, unless he built himself a railway. †

The real threat to India was not from Russia – though Kitchener thought otherwise – nor from Afghanistan and the fierce tribesmen on either side of the ill-defined frontier. The British Army was in India to spare the Viceroy the horrors of another mutiny, and it was the mute hostility of 'the natives' that kept a sizeable garrison there. India was in effect a huge imperial barracks,‡ a vast training-ground where troops could be tested in manoeuvres and blooded in skirmishes along the border. Their equipment might not be up to European standards, but 75,000 British soldiers—white men—plus a 'native' Britishofficered Indian Army twice as large, made a respectable fighting force with its own command structure. There was even a staff college. The rest of the British Army was scattered across the globe or in regimental depots at home, but with her extended land frontier in Asia (longer than that between France and Germany) Britain possessed a continental army by default, and though no one consciously used India as a rehearsal room for Europe,§ a force like that could have a mind of its own. India might be governed by the Viceroy, George Nathaniel Curzon, but the overbearing Commander in Chief had *his own* power base in the Army, and Kitchener engineered the downfall of Curzon

---
* 19 January 1905 and TNA CID 82rc Meeting 4/1/48 B 25 November 1905
† Gooch J *The Prospect of War: Studies in British Defence Policy 1847-1942* p 225
‡ Washbrook D A p 419
§ Allison M *The National Service Issue 1899-1914* PhD Thesis Universssity of London pp 04-95

without putting a single battalion onto the streets. Using his talent for intrigue and his personal contacts in London (one was Colonel Repington of the *Times),* Kitchener left no doubt as to who was in charge; *he* was, and Curzon soon departed. India was now a Soldier's State.

More to the point – as far as the Indians were concerned – was the fact that they had long been keeping Britain's finances out of the red. India had a flourishing export trade in opium, and much of the expense of Britain's colonial wars consisted of charges on the Indian taxpayer – about half the Viceroy's budget. Of course, native troops were also cheaper than 'real' Englishmen. Long after the 'Mutiny,' or Rebellion, British-officered Indian troops were in Abyssinia, Afghanistan, Baluchistan, Burma, China, Cyprus, Egypt, Malta, the Sudan (twice), Uganda, Nyasa and South Africa. As the cynics would say; *'We don't want to fight, but by Jingo if we do, we won't go ourselves – we'll send the mild Hindoo.'*

Thus India figured prominently on the agenda of the Committee of Imperial Defence. Important questions were raised: In a war with Russia how many extra soldiers would have to be sent out from England? A hundred thousand, said Kitchener. How many horses and mules, how many British 'white' officers for the 'native' Indian Army, and what about India's outermost defences from Aden to Singapore? And if they weren't used, then a hundred thousand British troops earmarked for the North West Frontier could make for a very useful 'Striking Force' for somewhere else – North West Europe perhaps? But only if the Bear was looking the other way – as Sir Edward Grey hoped he would. So, the Defence Committee was now looking closer to home – an imaginative scheme to defend Canada with submarines on the Great Lakes was jettisoned.

From the start, the Committee's inbuilt bias was in favour of the *'traditional maritime, colonial, strategy. Too big for a little war and too little for a big war,'* the Army was *'a projectile to be fired by the Navy,'* said First Sea Lord Sir John Fisher, *and besides, the CID was merely an adjunct of Admiralty as far as he was concerned. Another 'permanent member' of the CID was Sir John French, who began his career in the senior service and was said to be keen on 'amphibious' warfare, though he now held the Army's prime field command at Aldershot, where Esher's son Maurice was on his staff. Esher himself was supposedly 'blue water,' as was the (non-voting) secretary George Clarke, while in the War Office itself one intelligence colonel was still arguing *'we are not a military power and our alliance is sought for its naval not its military advantage'* † This was said even as his seniors were sniffing

---

* Letter to Esher, 5 May 1908
† TNA WO 106 /44 7 Decemeber 1906

out a new mission for the army in continental Europe.

Of course, the generals were no more inclined than the admirals to take any notice of dilettantes and busybodies on some Whitehall committee telling them how to march in step, but that didn't stop the soldiers using the CID to steal a march on the sailors. For Viscount Esher, though, the Committee of Imperial Defence had always been 'the coping stone of the Edifice' that would 'eclipse' the Cabinet,* but prime ministers were doing that anyway, preferring to closet themselves with a few favourites in what was known as 'sofa government.'

Esher too had a private sofa for *his* cronies – a sort of hot line to Sir Francis Knollys, the King's private secretary, and another to John Sandars, the man at the elbow of his lethargic master (Balfour). Allowing for Esher's creature Clarke, there was space in this virtual chat room for the viscount's other son Oliver (now in a Cabinet Minister's private office), *and* Arthur John Bigge, who'd been Queen Victoria's personal secretary in her final years. Bigge was now grooming one of her grandsons, writing his speeches, giving him lessons in deportment and telling him to smile at his future subjects. One day Mister Bigge would be Lord Stamfordham, Private Secretary to King George the Fifth.

There is something distasteful about a conceited, self-important snob attaching himself limpet-like to a pleasure-seeking monarch, encouraging him to intervene more in government, but Reginald Balliol Brett's job description was admirably concise – he was to write to the King 'fully and confidentially' on 'anything that you think will interest me' † and he did just that when he wasn't actually staying with his Majesty at Balmoral, gossiping with everyone and shooting the stags. The second Viscount Esher was 'not exactly a public servant' said his master, but '*the* most valuable public servant,' whereupon the most valuable public servant squeezed the royal hand and kissed it 'as I sometimes do.' ‡

Outsiders might question the constitutional propriety of all this in a supposedly democratic society, but Esher haughtily brushed that aside. 'Any "influence" which it is assumed I have,' he told Knollys, 'is only what we all have, and is every Englishman's right, i.e., to express his opinions to whomever he pleases.' There were matters of state every day, he boasted, 'where I can have my say, and can sway a decision.'§ He made much of his place on the Committee of Imperial Defence but notwithstanding his 'influence'—or perhaps because of his

---
* Journals 30 December 1903
† 14 April 1906
‡ Esher to Maurice Brett 5 March 1906
§ Esher to Knollys 19 March 1907

capricious slithering from one opinion to another as the fancy took him—the CID never did formulate a coherent 'grand strategy.' Instead, the generals took control, and it was the posturing self-admiring Brett who would be 'eclipsed' by events. But at least he kept a detailed diary to record his own profound self-esteem.

Lower down the food chain, the man driving the machine when Clarke departed was Captain Charles Langdale Ottley from Naval Intelligence, previously attaché in Paris, St Petersburg, Washington, Rome and Tokyo. After him came Captain Maurice Pascal Alers Hankey. This new broom—a Royal Marine by trade—might not be too happy about the CID's continental drift, but driving a desk in Whitehall was more agreeable to him than a life on the ocean wave. Hankey took command on the unexciting but all-important 'Home Front,' tying up the loose ends of administration for war. His diligent staff discovered an urgent need for joined-up thinking about the humdrum details of 'defence'—a task begun by Ottley—and the result of all this backroom labour was distilled into 'the War Book'; a bureaucrat's bible that became essential reading across Whitehall and beyond. So, if no one else had much idea of what had to be done on the outbreak of war with Germany—and how / by whom / at which department—then at least the civil servants would surely know.

But in August 1914 the Committee of Imperial Defence was 'suspended.' It was then instantly resurrected as 'the War Council' and 'the War Cabinet,' with the indispensable Hankey as Secretary to both. In turn these 'new' bureaucratic entities spawned a proliferation of 'cabinet subcommittees' whose task it was to mobilise, organise, control and coerce everyone and everything in the pursuit of victory. At the final count, there were a hundred and sixty five of these useful agencies; the sinews of war.

~ 9 ~

The Man Least Likely To

"A temporary leader.... a warming pan."
- *The Times 17 January 1899*

The new Prime Minister had other worries. He would soon be the wrong side of seventy, his health was failing, his wife was dying and no one expected him to last very long in Downing Street. Thirty-seven years in Parliament would soon make him 'Father' of the House of Commons, and he'd held half a dozen ministerial posts, mostly in that graveyard of reputations; the War Office. As *TheTimes* sneered, the 'warmimg pan' would do while the Liberals looked for 'a more commanding figure,' but Sir Henry Campbell-Bannerman had led the fractured Liberal Party through the wilderness of Opposition for seven long years – his only serious rival, the lawyer Asquith, having turned the job down to earn more at the Bar.

When the Right Honourable Arthur James Balfour, weary of the exertions of office, relinquished his burden in December 1905, King Edward VII asked the Leader of the Opposition to form a new government. This, on the very same day the official *London Gazette* announced that henceforth the Prime Minister would come *after* the Archbishop of York in the official pecking order.* With that important constitutional matter out of the way, His Majesty consented to the dissolution of a parliament that hadn't been sitting for the past four months anyway, and a writ was issued for the General Election that, conveniently, would *follow* the change of government.

It was a gamble. The Conservative majority was huge, and for the Liberals to accept office before the election was risky. Their party too was in disarray, they had no great confidence in Sir Henry's leadership and his brief stay in Whitehall would make failure at the polls even

---
* Hanham H J The Nineteenth Century Coinstitution 1815-1914 p 69

more humiliating. Perhaps Balfour hoped his own departure would entice the Liberals to self-destruction, for even if the Conservatives lost, they would still be a sizeable, and troublesome, minority. There was more to it. The elderly millionaire—'C-B' they called him—was a 'Little Englander' who denounced Kitchener's harsh treatment of the Boers and favoured 'Home Rule' for Ireland, but he was lumbered with three of his party comrades; the 'Liberal Imperialists' Asquith, Haldane and Grey, who were resolved that if the old man did become Prime Minister, he would sit in the House of Lords while they held the *real* power in the Commons. So, well before the long-expected change of government, the three conspirators joined the Conservative Prime Minister and the ever-present Esher at Balmoral, to play the Court Card against their own leader. Oddly, Edward VII didn't like Balfour that much and preferred the company of Campbell-Bannerman – both 'CB' and the King 'took the waters' at Marienbad Spa.

The spoils of office were parcelled out in advance, Haldane picking the War Department so Grey could have the Foreign Office. 'At Asquith's request,' Haldane artlessly recalled, 'I had communicated our agreement to the King and been summoned to Balmoral, where the King had indicated his warm approval.' Esher used the occasion to do a deal with Haldane, who promised that if he was in the next (Liberal) government he'd back the CID, and Sir John French would be another 'permanent member.'

Two months later the Right Honourable Herbert Henry Asquith, successful barrister of fifty-three and sometime Home Secretary, became Chancellor of the Exchequer, but Sir Edward Grey, ten years his junior, haughtily declined to join the Government should Campbell-Bannerman refuse to be bullied into a peerage. Grey's bluff was called and he went to the Foreign Office, as C-B's second choice. The third conspirator, Richard Burdon Haldane, fifty-year-old lawyer and German-educated intellectual, was dispatched to the War Office. 'We'll see how Schopenhauer gets on in the kailyard [cabbage patch]' said 'C-B,' but Haldane was now one of the three most powerful men in a cabinet of seven aristocrats and eleven 'middle class' men, plus one from 'the working class.' The royal mouthpiece, Private Secretary Sir Francis Knollys, had indicated the monarch's strong preference for men of 'moderate' views to balance the 'radicals and extremists' like David Lloyd George and Winston Churchill, but C-B defied his Sovereign and took both men into his administration. Lloyd George made an able President of the Board of Trade and Mr Churchill, a recent defector from the Conservative-Unionist cause, was found a junior place in the Colonial Office, with more power than usual as his boss the Earl of Elgin sat in the House of Lords. The young Winston had seen the writing on the wall. Faced with the prospect of prolonged unemployment he prudently announced his conversion to Liberalism and Free Trade, and crossed the floor of the House of Commons. It was a bet that paid him a dividend of twenty years in power, on and off.

In the General Election of 1906 the two great parties fought a noisy, messy campaign; 'Free Trade' versus 'Protection.' It took nearly a month for the five million six hundred and sixty six thousand votes to be cast and counted (one-day elections date from 1918). In a population of 43 million only six out of ten adult males over twenty one could vote for parliament, *and no women at all*, but when it was over more than eighty per cent of the seven and a quarter million of those entitled to vote had done so. The rest of Britain's 21-plus manhood had to wait until 1918 before they could vote, and 'property-owning' women, another ten years. Still, in the 1906 'landslide' two-and-three quarter million male votes—49 per cent of the electorate—gave the Liberals 400 seats in the new parliament, including two dozen 'lib-labs.' The Conservatives had to be content with 157 (they got 402 last time). It was a humiliating defeat, with 417 hopefuls rejected outright. Even their leader Balfour lost the East Manchester 'brewers' constituency' after twenty-one years – but he was promptly found a safer seat, the City of London. For the Liberals—who counted among their members the new member for Salford, Hilaire Belloc, author of *Cautionary Tales*—it was a great, and unexpected, victory. They had backing from the Labour Representation Committee's twenty nine MPs, some of whom were elected in a secret 'tactical voting' pact with the Liberals; secret because for many working men the Liberals were still the class enemy. Oddly, it took 330,000 votes to win those 29 seats for Labour, while the quirks of the electoral system meant the Irish Nationalists needed only 35,000 votes to get eighty-three MPs (74 unopposed) who would at least support 'Home Rule' for Ireland. Still, the Liberals and their allies got well over half the votes cast; 3,122,662 against 2,451,454 – a majority of 671,208.

Sir Henry Campbell-Bannerman was now undisputed leader of the world's greatest financial power with the world's biggest navy and the largest empire. He could expect trouble. Most of his supporters were impatient for 'social reform,' but to balance the 'extremists' in cabinet were those 'moderate men' Asquith, Haldane and Grey, who were to shape the nation's destiny in a way few of their countrymen could have imagined – even if they *had* been consulted.

As the new ministers fingered the contents of their red dispatch boxes, they contemplated their inheritance. There were some formidable challenges and much unfinished business. In Ireland the festering sore of nationalism must somehow be healed despite the stubborn hostility of the Protestant Unionists, and in South Africa the vanquished Boers had to be appeased with 'self-rule' – for whites only of course. Meanwhile at home, the emerging welfare state would have to be paid for somehow, and the labour unions had been promised legal protection during strikes.

Ominously, in the moment of electoral defeat the Conservative leader told his followers they had to save the nation 'from the consequences of its own folly' by using the House of Lords where they had a six-to-one majority, but the Viscount Esher consoled his King that the new regime would not survive long.* It lasted nine years.

Presumably, one consequence of the nation's folly would be the new regime's 'neglect' of the nation's defences, for many of the 400-strong Parliamentary Liberal Party were opposed to the use of armed force to settle international disputes. The Prime Minister understood their mood and even before the election assured his followers that he too was on the side of the angels. Now *they* were the majority, they wanted better schools, better health care, and pensions for old people who would otherwise be shut away in the workhouse. A welfare state, however modest, was what they expected to be voting for in parliament, not a 'warfare state.' They wanted the cheapest possible army, but the Cabinet was mostly content to leave defence and foreign policy to specialists. As a result Haldane and Grey had a degree of independence denied to other ministers whose jobs were more interesting to their colleagues round the table. Sir Edward Grey always took heed of homely concerns, but he disliked interference in his own bailiwick, for the Foreign Office handled 'highly sensitive' matters that were beyond the understanding of 'outsiders' (such as his very own supporters sitting behind him in the House of Commons).

Just how sensitive those matters were, they could scarcely guess – though just before the change of government Sir Edward had made his intentions pretty clear, declaring his 'support' for France in the latest international crisis. When Lord Lansdowne quit the Foreign Office, and Hugh Arnold-Forster vacated his chair for Sir Edward (the new man in the War Office) Mr Haldane and the generals were already taking the first steps in the shaping of Britain's future – well before the Election, and without even telling their chief, the new Prime Minister, what they were up to.

---

* Esher *Journal* 20 April 1906

~ 10 ~

What They Settled I Never Knew

"The General Election at this juncture is a misfortune. Nobody will think of anything else for weeks."

- Sir George Clarke to Lord Esher 3rd January 1906

".... this has advantages, for it leaves us free."

- Esher to Clarke 4th January 1906

There is a widespread belief that during an election campaign Britain is without a government. Ministers of the Crown however, are appointed by the Sovereign – on the Prime Minister's advice – and even amidst all the hurly-burly and ritual slanging-match of electioneering, they still have their departmental duty to perform. Ministers may be far from Whitehall, smiling, shaking hands, kissing babies and shouting themselves hoarse with fine words and firm pledges – but their dispatch-boxes are with them wherever they go.

When Mr Balfour and his colleagues relinquished their seals of office there was no interregnum – just a smooth transfer of power suavely and discreetly handled by civil servants and palace courtiers in accordance with protocol. The new Premier had to wait until the last day of January 1906 before he could hold a cabinet meeting but his government had functioned over Christmas and throughout the election campaign despite the strain on ministers travelling up and down the land to speak in support of Liberal candidates.

The new man in the War Office, Mr Haldane, lost no time in

getting acquainted with his portfolio. His diary for December was filled with engagements; departmental committees; meetings with the Prime Minister; with generals at the War Office; and with various 'experts' eager to thrust advice on him. He spent Christmas closeted with one of his principal counsellors, working on the blueprint for the New Model Army already taking shape in his mind, an idea he would have to sell to his own followers – without telling them its real purpose.*

Equally industrious was the new Foreign Secretary Sir Edward Grey, Northumbrian landowner and non-executive director of the North Eastern Railway Company. No stranger to the Foreign Office – Grey had been a junior minister there under Lord Rosebery, and his opposition portfolio was foreign affairs – Sir Edward took charge of his department without delay. In those hectic weeks of December, January and February he composes lengthy dispatches to ambassadors; receives foreign envoys; campaigns in his own constituency and stoically remains at his post despite his wife's tragic and fatal accident. And on one urgent matter he has already made up his mind; the Moroccan crisis, occasioned by France desiring to control that vast country and Germany's hostile reaction. If that meant war, should Britain should stay out, or fight on the side of France?

The charade that ended in August 1914 began nine years earlier when Mr Balfour had already left Downing Street, shortly before the nation could endorse the new (Liberal) government through the ballot box. In December 1905 The Director of Military Operations at the War Office, Major General James Moncrieff Grierson, had a 'chance encounter' with the French military attaché, Major Victoire Huguet. They met three times that week, and according to Grierson nothing of note was discussed, though the attaché said he was given details of British plans for war against Germany as well as Grierson's 'personal' view that Britain would not 'stand aside' should the Moroccan crisis lead to war between Germany and France.†

Six months earlier, under Balfour, a CID sub-committee had been set up by Esher to consider the 'possibilities' of military aid to France It never actually met,‡ but in December 1905 Esher really did 'eclipse' the Cabinet by arranging secret sessions of the Committee of Imperial Defence without informing the Chairman – the new prime minister. Four men including Charles Ottley, the Director of Naval Intelligence, Lieutenant-General Sir John French, sailor turned cavalryman, and Esher himself plus the Committee Secretary, Sir George Clarke, gathered to decide how the next war should be fought, against whom, *and*

---
* Spiers E M *Haldane – an Army Reformer* p 75
† Monger G *The End of Isolation: British Foreign Policy 1900-1907* p 236-256
‡ Searle G R *A New England? Peace and War 18886-1918* p 328

to commit Britain to a secret alliance with a foreign power.*

Two years before, Admiralty and War Office were at odds about how to handle a French invasion, but now it was Germany's turn to be the enemy, with Britain on the side of France. Such a seismic shift was foreseen by a Colonel William Robertson at the War Office, and Grierson himself had recently umpired a 'War Game' – an imaginary conflict between France and Germany – in which a very small British army had just tipped the balance so that the French won.†

At the same time, someone down the corridor was advising that this same army of 120,000 soldiers would be of 'immense assistance to our allies' if it was sent instead to occupy 'some limited tract' of north Germany. Grierson promptly smothered that one, but Clarke was all for the Navy to deposit the Army on the German coast, with a little extra help from the French who might have troops to spare, he fancied. He'd earlier suggested invading Germany through neutral Denmark – the German Navy had just scrapped its own plan to overrun that country and anyway, the German General Staff had started work on the 'Schlieffen Plan' to invade France through the Low Countries. This time, Clarke had to admit that Admiral Fisher's idea of landing the British army on a hostile shore wouldn't work, and when the War Office muscled in with *their* plan to send the soldiers straight across the Channel to France, he—and Esher—jumped ship. Fisher was furious and swore the Navy would have no more to do with the imperial defence committee, but it was a messy divorce and the soldiers would make the most of it, with Esher now playing the Continental Card, although he did nonchalantly warn Field Marshal Kitchener of the 'fatal trap into which we may fall, which is to depend upon foreign alliances.'

Meanwhile the freewheeling Lord Esher had developed an enterprising sideline when out to lunch. Conveniently, his table companion was an ambitious Frenchman; Georges Clemenceau the radical-republican-turned-hardliner. As Minister of the Interior and ruthless strikebreaker Clemenceau would soon show just how hard he was. By Esher's account the 'Tiger' – a future premier – wanted arrangements for immediate Anglo-French military and naval action against Germany should the Moroccan conference break down. Esher reported as much to his King but didn't think it worth mentioning to anyone else – not even the Foreign Office who remained unaware of this unofficial traffic outside the regular diplomatic channels. Meanwhile, another amateur initiative was imminent, in itself bizarre and scarcely credible.

---
* Conferences December 1905 – January 1906 TNA CAB18/24
† War Game April-May 1905 TNA, WO 33/364

Since his enforced retirement on half pay Colonel Charles à Court Repington had contrived to augment his pension by writing for the newspapers, and he was well suited to be military correspondent for the *Times*. The *Times* was widely regarded as a semi-official organ that reflected government thinking; a convenient back channel for diplomatic initiatives known as 'kite-flying.' This was the ideal platform for Repington, his passport to 'influence,' and his admission ticket to the minister's private office where he made full use of his privileged status.

Thus it was that Repington started a complex piece of legerdemain to create the legend that it was *he* who kick-started the Anglo-French military 'conversations.' He sent a personal letter to the Foreign Secretary, telling Grey of French 'anxiety' as to the intentions of the new government, and disquiet at its silence. Repington said he got his information from Major Huguet – whose ear was already bent by Grierson. The much-courted military attaché recalled that the man from the *Times* did all the talking, but Grey was not to know that and sent Repington a prompt and personal reply, an assurance that Grey hadn't 'receded' from anything Lansdowne had said, and he had 'no hesitation in affirming it.'

But what Henry Charles Keith Petty Fitzmaurice Lansdowne the fifth Marquess had said, was not what Sir Edward thought he might have said or indeed *should* have said, for, in conversation with the French ambassador in May 1905—when the French were being leaned upon by Germany—Lansdowne had merely suggested the two governments should 'keep in touch,' as agreed in the small print of the *Entente Cordiale*. Alas, the Third Republic's representative at the Court of St James understood little English and, seizing the wrong end of the diplomatic stick persuaded himself that the *Entente* was the alliance that neither Balfour nor his Foreign Secretary had intended. There was nothing to show *they* had begun 'military talks' with France, though when Grey asked Haldane about this early in the 1906 election campaign, his friend and colleague replied somewhat opaquely 'there had been before my time some general conversations.'[*] So, in Sir Edward's woolly logic, if Lord Lansdowne had thought fit to authorise 'some general conversations' there could surely be no harm in allowing them to continue, whatever they were about.

Delighted by Grey's response, Repington unblushingly touted his services, helpfully explaining how important it was to commence staff talks with the French military – and the Belgians – *before* the outbreak of war, and why he, Repington, was just the man to arrange this. He knew all the right people in Brussels, in the ministries and the Palace, and as military attaché there and at the Hague, he had urged his

[*] Haldane *Autobiography* pp 189-90

Belgian and Dutch hosts to join Britain in planning for war against Germany – stating 'Lord Lansdowne approved of my action.' He would need a badge of substance, so Clarke promptly invented the man from the *Times* as semi-official intermediary between London and Paris. 'I do believe we can trust him absolutely,' he gushed to Esher.* Since Repington was close to Huguet, the pair might as well continue talking – so much safer than going through the usual diplomatic hoops. It was 'very necessary to do nothing to alarm the government' and 'best that no one should know anything.' But Clarke couldn't help boasting to Esher how the Foreign Secretary had sent for him 'to ask if anything was being done....' and was much pleased to know that we are considering possibilities.....[Grey] 'thinks – as we agreed – that it is impossible to approach the French through official channels,' and the very next day when the French ambassador suggested that as 'some communications' had already been exchanged, they might as well continue, and Grey 'did not dissent,' according to Clarke.

Inside the Foreign Office they could hardly miss outsiders like Esher, Clarke and Repington trampling over the carpet, but conveniently the arrival of a Liberal government coincided with the departure of the old guard at the FO; those men who valued Germany as a bulwark against Imperial Russia. One senior diplomat now pushing for an alliance with republican France—in fact, if not in name—was Sir Francis Bertie, 'the Bull,' who, referring to the new government, was already urging the new Foreign Office head Sir Charles Hardinge to 'buck up these miserable creatures.' But Sir Charles already knew exactly what was going on. From his top posting at the Paris embassy Bertie could put his own gloss on official French thinking, and he did, encouraged by the up-and-coming new breed in the Foreign Office; Louis Mallet; Eyre Crowe; Francis Tyrell; all clever men, and all hostile to Germany. It was Mallet – Grey's private secretary – who advised Bertie to send Grey a 'very strong personal letter' which, like all Ambassadors' dispatches, would be seen by the King. It was also Mallet who cited 'public opinion' in support of his own fearless 'we will take our share of the fighting' pledge; but it was Grey who comforted the Paris envoy with the vague assurance 'we cannot stand aside, but must take part with France.' Writing to his ambassador in Berlin, the Foreign Secretary somewhat incautiously referred to 'our Alliance and Entente,' which rather gave the game away to those already in the know.†

Years later Repington would boast how the French military attaché was sent back to Paris with a shopping list of questions drawn

---
* Williamson S R *The Politics of Grand Strategy: Britain and France Prepare for War 1904-1914* pp 69-70
† Hinsley F H *British Foreign Policy under Sir Edward Grey* pp 426-7

up by Clarke, Esher – and Repington. Did the French General Staff understand that a German attack on France would involve Britain, so what help did France need? For officials in London to send a foreign diplomat home to ascertain his own country's secret plans for war was indeed pure farce, and in Repington's entertaining account the French staff officers were very much astonished, as *he* says they were at that very moment putting the finishing touches to plans for the invasion of England – and 'jaws dropped' *

Coming from Repington himself, this hardly constitutes the most reliable evidence and throws doubt on his own story of French anxiety lest Britain should abandon them. If their own military were as surprised as Repington says, it suggests they were hardly expecting a military alliance with their age-old foe, though they had of course shown a professional interest in the *possibility*, no more, of a foreign army – even a British one – coming to their aid. Hitherto their hardworking attaché had to make his own educated guess at the size of this hypothetical contribution. In November 1905, shortly before his 'chance encounter' with Grierson, he thought it would be 115,000 men.† For their part, the British could only speculate as to the French order of battle, and despite all those 'conversations' down the years, the War Office remained largely ignorant of French plans – as previously, with Balfour in Downing Street and Lansdowne in the Foreign Office, Major Huguet (soon to be Colonel Huguet) knew nothing of British intentions.

Long after the war *General* Huguet said his countrymen *were* somewhat surprised by the 'readiness' of the British government to authorise the military conversations or 'studies,' and while there was no military pact, no formal alliance, Huguet always believed it would never have happened if 'a considerable number of [British] officers had not been assigned to it' – so they would be obliged to 'come in on our side.'‡ They had even considered the possibility that a Liberal government would hesitate before declaring war, so the call-up of reservists would be delayed and the BEF would arrive too late. The unacceptable risk of civilian obstruction clearly required 'counter measures' as Huguet delicately put it, so the 'first stages' of mobilisation could proceed 'without waiting for this decision' and in 1914 the generals in the War Office did not wait.

In their memoirs Grey, Clarke and others preferred to give the Anglo-French military talks a much longer pedigree dating back to the previous, Conservative government, but it was a Liberal foreign secretary and a Liberal war minister who made all the running. As Huguet

---

* Repington *The First World War* Vol I pp 5-6
† Monger G The End of Isolation p 238
‡ Huguet p 6

observed afterwards, this pair and Asquith, who was also in on the secret, were 'too shrewd and wary' not to understand they had given France 'a moral undertaking to intervene.' *

It was several weeks before Sir Henry Campbell Bannerman found himself belatedly, and reluctantly, approving those 'conversations' – and thereby a virtual military alliance between Britain and France. Esher and the generals had 'eclipsed' the Cabinet, but Grey, Haldane and Asquith made sure most of their colleagues would remain ignorant of all this for several years, while Parliament was told nothing,

'It will be seen as an honourable undertaking' Sir Henry grumbled, 'and it will be known about on both sides of the Rhine.' But while *he* was the King's first minister, there would be no European entanglement, whatever his Foreign Secretary might say or do. Despite his own liking for France and its people he would soon make this embarrassingly plain on an official visit to Paris – he was fluent in French. After all, it was an article of faith set in stone fifteen years earlier and subscribed to by Liberal and Conservative governments alike, that such a thing could not, indeed would not happen. A 'progressive Whig' ever suspicious of the military, Campbell-Bannerman had done his best to make it a near-impossibility, for it was he as War minister in the eighteen-nineties who quashed the idea of a continental-style general staff, a 'brain' for the Army – he was afraid the generals would want a continental-style army as well. But now the generals did have a brain, of a sort, and soon they would have an army for a continental war. But after two years and four months in Downing Street, Sir Henry Campbell-Bannerman was dead.

Grey, Haldane, and Asquith the new prime minister were always careful though, never to give their ally a formal pledge that these 'conversations' could lead to something more – an army for France. Eight years before, when senior ministers were supposedly concentrating their thoughts on the election, Esher's cabal had sought to confront them with the accomplished fact of a secret military alliance that could plausibly—though disingenuously—be interpreted as a previous commitment entered into by the Conservatives; a commitment that must be honoured. But they were pushing at an open door. Haldane and Grey had already given their blessing to the secret staff talks, with the feeble escape clause that they were 'solely provisional and non-committal,' and of course, they could be stopped at any time, for they were purely 'technical.' Grey had made a facile comparison to arrangements between the London Fire Brigade and the Metropolitan Water Board. The fiddly details were not his concern, so with his 'bottomless capacity for self-deception' he could keep a proper distance

---
* Huguet p 26

and dismiss the matter from his mind. Asquith too seems to have forgotten all about it. Five years later, in another international crisis, Grey told him '..the rest of you were scattered for the Election. The military experts then convened. What they settled I never knew.'

~ 11 ~

Poisoned Wells, and Beatrice

"The future belongs to the nation that most resolutely picks over, educates, sterilises, exports, or poisons its People of the Abyss."

- *H G Wells 1901*

Strong words, but as the welfare state was slowly taking shape the Eugenics Society was concerned lest 'social sympathy and state aid' allow the 'intellectually and physically weaker' to breed as fast as the better sort of people. Roughly the same idea attracted Sydney and Beatrice Webb; George Bernard Shaw; Bertrand Russell; John Maynard Keynes; Sir George Clarke and Esher too. As Home Secretary Winston Churchill also worried about 'mental defectives' having a family,* though Wells led the pack, calling for sterilisation and euthanasia for criminals and the 'unfit' – adding that the lesser breeds, 'black, brown, dirty white, and yellow,' would 'have to go!' Genocide, or 'ethnic cleansing,' was an accepted feature of colonial settlement, mirrored in fiction. In one short story, biological weapons of mass destruction are unleashed on China – for 'hygienic ends' – by a united Europe using a novel delivery system; aircraft launched from warships, and with complete success; the entire Chinese population is exterminated.†

In the real world, Edwardian England was generously endowed with societies for the promotion of good behaviour and clean living among the lower orders. Hence, the National Anti-Gambling League;

---
* Cross C *The Liberals in Power 1905-14* p163
† Clarke I F (ed) *The Tale of the Next Great War 1871-1914* pp 257-270 "The Unparalleled Invasion"

the National Vigilance Association to put down immorality (one of Kitchener's pet causes); the churchgoers' White Cross League; or Mrs Ormiston Chant's Social Purity League – to regulate the music halls.

The twentieth century brought the Alliance of Honour to warn young men about venereal disease and the Snowdrop Bands to keep their sisters chaste, but there were 'pressure groups' too. The Fair Trade League; the Tariff Reform League; and the Passive Resisters' League for chapel-folk loath to subsidise Church-run state schools. Seven thousand were taken to court for not paying local taxes and one protester was jailed sixteen times. The unpleasant face of society, mirrored in the British Brothers' League and the Society for Preventing the Immigration of Destitute Aliens, was further disfigured by the Immigrant Reform Association, and one inglorious achievement of Parliament was the 1905 Aliens Act, harbinger of many more concessions to intolerance .

Those seeking wider horizons could choose the League of Frontiersmen, the League of Empire, or the Empire Day Movement whose stirring motto read, 'Responsibility, Sympathy, Duty and Self Sacrifice.' All these were courtesy of Reginald Brabazon, the Earl of Meath, a fairly recent aristocrat – the present line only dates from 1627, though one of his ancestors, Jacques le Brabancon the Great Warrior, arrived with William the Conqueror. The first 'Lord of Meath' was murdered in 1186. John Brabazon died on Bosworth Field in 1485 and the second 'Earl of Meath' drowned in the Irish Sea in 1675. With better luck and two extra peerages to his name (Baron of Ardee in Ireland *and* Lord Chaworth of Eaton Hall in England) Reginald Brabazon soon found himself in the upper House at Westminster. It was *this* Lord Meath, the Twelfth Earl, philanthropist, town planner and former diplomat impressed by Germany's apparent virility, who added the Duty and Discipline Movement; the British Girls' Patriotic League; the National Social Purity Crusade; and the National Council of Public Morals to his bulging portfolio of good causes. He would soon collect a few more.

And then the surge; the resounding defeat of the Conservative and Unionist Party in the electoral landslide of 1906 released a large number of unemployed politicians whose talent for publicity could usefully be employed in a welter of new causes. Most of those causes were tailored to suit 'Middle England,' such as the Income Tax Reduction Society; the British Constitution Association; or, the Coal Consumers' League—financed by the mine owners—with its torch-lit parades *against* an eight hour day for the miners. The Middle Class Defence Organisation deplored the extension of workmen's accident compensation and trades union exemption from liability in strikes. Hard-pressed householders who were compelled to pay the new National Insurance contribution for their domestic staff could now join the Servant Tax Resisters' Defence League whose members, in a commendable show of egalitarianism, took their maids and footmen along with them on demonstrations. There was an Anti-Socialist League too, a Non-Conformist Anti-Socialist Union and a Social Reform Committee to reach out to the 'non-socialist working class.' Predictably, organised labour behaved selfishly, and not just 'blue-collar' workers. When the British Medical Association told its members to boycott the state insurance scheme, Lloyd George offered the doctors more money, so they signed up and the BMA retired hurt.

The United Kingdom Alliance of temperance organisations backed the Liberal government's Licensing Bill, which was a piece of legislation successfully blocked by the brewers, the public house 'landlords' and His Majesty's loyal Opposition in the House of Lords. There was however cross-party support for a National Anti-Sweating League, and a Protest League for anyone upset by Lloyd George's 1909 'People's Budget' was matched by a Budget League for those who were not. The 'Marconi Scandal' with more than a hint of insider trading by Lloyd George and Attorney General Rufus Isaacs, was a gift to the National League for Clean Government, while twenty eight Conservative MPs, concerned about the close links between Liberal ministers and wealthy businessmen, set up the Radical Plutocrats Inquiry. There was a wholesome air to the National Hygienic League, and decent hard working citizens seeking the thrill of civil disobedience and an opportunity to flirt with treason would soon be invited to join the British League for the Support of Ulster.

Pressure to get votes for women produced an alphabet-soup of abbreviations. There was the Women's Labour League (WLL); the Women's Freedom League (WFL) – battle cry, *'don't pay the dog licence';* the Women's Liberal Federation (WLF); the People's Suffrage Federation (PSF); Millicent Fawcett's National Union for Women's Suffrage Societies (NUWSS); and Emmeline Pankhurst's Women's Social and Political Union (WSPU) – the movement's 'suffragette' militant tendency. Meanwhile, the Actresses' Franchise League wrote plays to spread the message and performed in them too, presumably when 'resting.' But not everyone applauded. Mrs Asquith shared her husband's distaste for female emancipation – he was afraid the women would all vote Conservative. Mrs Henry Wilson allowed her husband to escort her to meetings of the Women's National Anti-Suffrage League,* an organisation appropriately partnered by the Men's League

---
* Jeffery K Field Marshal Sir Henry Wilson p119

for Opposing Women's Suffrage. After a quarrelsome courtship the two bodies were joined in a brief marriage of convenience and mutual contempt.

The suffragettes came in for some pretty rough handling by the police, but Emmeline Pankhurst's lot were spearheaded by an 'Active Service League' which got headlines for 'symbolic' damage to public property, and a spell in jail for the activists, with hunger strikes and forced feeding. One of their more spectacular deeds was setting a small bomb set off outside Lloyd George's private residence. This brought Emmeline three years' penal servitude for 'incitement to violence' but the lady made a stirring speech from the dock and began her hunger strike as promised – but the war saved her and the women were set free. Fired by patriotism, they founded the Women's Party; rechristened their journal *Britannia;* condemned German beastliness, and denounced Asquith as a 'flunkey and toady of the Kaiser.' Women got the vote in 1918, but those under thirty had to wait another ten years.

Protesting against injustice abroad The Society of Friends of Russian Freedom and the Persian Committee vigorously lobbied the Foreign Office to sever relations with the Tsar, to the discomfiture of Sir Edward Grey. Meanwhile, Edmund Dene Morel's Congo Reform Association revealing the horrors perpetrated by King Leopold's 'secret society of murderers' aroused anger across Britain and the United States. The outcry contributed in no small measure to Belgian coolness towards Britain – occasioned also by the clumsy overtures of senior officers hoping to achieve a military 'understanding' with Brussels.

In an age of wars and rumours-of-wars, W T Stead, the crusading journalist who campaigned for a bigger navy in 1886, attended the Peace Conference at the Hague in 1907 where he called for better relations with Germany. In April 1912 he sailed for New York for yet another conference, this one on 'Great Men and Religions.' He was last seen helping women and children into the Titanic's lifeboats. But Lord Avebury's Anglo-German Friendship Society offered hope, as did the equally respectable Anglo-German Institute founded by Sir Ernest Cassel, a close friend of King Edward VII. There was also the Peace Society; the Workmen's Peace Association; the National Peace Council; and the League of Liberals against Aggression and Militarism (LAMBS) – Lloyd George was an early lamb. But all met with indifferent success, especially the British Neutrality Committee and Norman Angell's Neutrality League, both of which were hastily conceived in the last days of July 1914.. Years earlier, the socialists and some of the labour unions had earnestly debated with their comrades and fellow workers across Europe as to how war might be stopped by a spontaneous general strike in every one of the belligerent states. They never did agree on that one, and in the event, national identity prevailed over international class solidarity.

As always, religion offered consolation. One hopeful outcome of the 1907 Peace Conference had been a coming together of the British and German Protestant churches, a move led by a Quaker, J. Allen Baker, Liberal Member of Parliament. When a hundred and thirty German pastors arrived in 1908 for a week of prayer and communion with British clergy, even the Archbishop of Canterbury, Randall Davidson, Primate of all England, was obliged to grind the arch-episcopal teeth in a welcoming grimace. 'Outwardly we must put a brave face on it, vexatious as it is' he confided to a senior churchman. Some seed fell upon stony ground, but six years later an even more impressive feat of organisation deserved better luck when no fewer than eighty delegates representing thirty Christian denominations from twelve countries arranged to meet in the south German city of Constance – on the 3rd and 4th of August 1914. Not to be outdone, the Roman Catholics had fixed *their* international goodwill conference for the following week – in the Belgian fortress city of Liège.

It was not just a matter of timing, but presentation, for the message of peace and reconciliation was somehow harder to get across than the call for arms and military preparedness. With Lord Meath on the committee, The National Service League demanded 'compulsory military training' – conscription in all but name. A puny latecomer, the Voluntary Service League sat in the opposite corner, and the Independent Labour Party ran a 'No Conscription' campaign. The Navy League—with Lord Meath as vice-president—had been agitating for more battleships since 1895, and the breakaway Imperial Maritime League, inevitably dubbed 'the Navier League' wanted even more money for the Fleet, though the National Liberal Federation would give the sailors less. Viscount Esher's pet project 'The Islanders' could have been a children's adventure story, but for the verses penned by Rudyard Kipling just after the Boer War. Field-Marshal Lord Roberts had requested some 'stirring lines' now best remembered for the poet's lofty disdain for 'flannelled fools at the wicket' and 'muddied oafs at the goals.'

But while anyone could join the Navy League or the National Service League (and the *really* patriotic citizen belonged to both) only a few could gain admission to that very superior set; 'The Souls.' Membership of 'The Souls' clustered around Balfour and was strictly for the bright and the beautiful; for the rising stars in both ruling parties; and for the rich. At one such country house gathering the widower Asquith found his second, and wealthier, wife. In a less ethereal atmosphere, the dining and discussion clubs provided a sort of thinking man's Rotary for a cross section of 'the establishment' – academics, politicians, journalists and 'opinion-formers,' where the larger questions of Empire and 'National Efficiency' could be discussed.

They had a lot to talk about. Edwardian England was enjoying the fruits of Victorian labour and invention. It was an age of conspicuous consumption by the rich, and the lower middle classes prospered too, but too many people were living in poverty, and the figures for infant mortality, disease and premature death among the poor in town and countryside were sufficient reason for disquiet. These legions of slum dwellers with their poorly-fed rickety children were truly the 'people of the abyss.' Their rulers had long feared revolution. The young Frederick Engels confidently predicted it, and over the years both governing parties had sought to buy off unrest with sanitation, slum clearance and minor improvements in the lot of the poor. But at the close of Victoria's long reign this mass of human misery and stunted lives remained a lasting reproach to the rest of society. What William Beveridge would famously itemise forty years on; 'the evils of Want, Idleness, and Ignorance,' were all too evident in early 20th century England, so much so that by 1914 spending on 'welfare'; public health, housing, schools, old age pensions – was approaching the Navy's share.

There was more bad news for Britain, much of it 'Made in Germany.' Industrialists complaining of unfair competition from their best customer and principal trading partner wanted import duties on German goods and German steel. The cause of 'Tariff Reform' was championed by a Birmingham businessman and conservative politician, Joseph Chamberlain, who joined the 'Compatriots,' a small but influential dining club for Liberal Imperialists, the 'Limps' who had renounced the gospel of Free Trade.

One such Limp was the 'geopolitician' Halford Mackinder, soon to win fame for his 'Heartland' theory. A Rifle Volunteer with a law degree from Oxford, a lecturer at the London School of Economics and Political Science, and later its Director, MacKinder worshipped 'the Imperial idea'; a federation of self-governing colonies, unaware perhaps that the Mother's self-governing (white) children had their own ideas, But where Mackinder really went astray was in believing that salvation lay in high import duties to protect British industry from foreign competition. A busy man himself – a true 'workaholic' – he probably hadn't noticed that inside his own LSE the academic and journalist J. A. Hobson had a different explanation. As profit margins shrank, capital was exported to undeveloped countries to earn higher dividends for wealthy investors at home, while Britain's industrial plants were starved of cash – though he somewhat overstated the case.

Years later much the same point was argued by the economist John Maynard Keynes whose writings persuaded governments to spend their way out of slump. Earlier though, Hobson's *Imperialism* inspired an obscure and impoverished Russian exile living next door to a sausage factory in Zurich. Vladimir Ilyitch Ulyanov (later known as Lenin) turned out a prodigious quantity of pamphlets, including his own *Imperialism* (1916) in which he freely acknowledged his debt to Hobson.

Hobson was one of the Rainbow Circle, another Edwardian 'think-tank' – this one for just twenty-five talented, ambitious 'opinion formers' of whom ten got into parliament in the 1906 election. But the Top People's dining and discussion club was the 'Co-efficients' which was so exclusive it had only twelve members at first. This was the brain child of the 'political scientist' Sidney Webb and a young woman dismayed by the 'constantly decomposing mass of human beings' in London's East End. Her name (until Sydney entered her life) was Beatrice Potter – not to be confused with *Beatrix,* whose books are still in print.

Once a month 'a divine vocation' concerning 'the aims, policy and methods of Imperial Efficiency at home and abroad' (i.e. sweating more out of the colonies), was mulled over by future cabinet ministers Sir Edward Grey and Richard Burdon Haldane, as well as the Honourable William Pember Reeves, New Zealand's Agent-General in London. Halford Mackinder, who took the Conservative line on Protection and became one of their MPs, was also a Co-efficient, as was the far-right *National Review* editor Leo Maxse. The journalist Leo Amery was another; a disciple of Lord Alfred Milner the imperial pro-consul who was likewise a member. Milner was an admirer of Leo's sister Violet who was unhappily married to one of the Cecil family, the tribe that had been running England for more than three centuries, on and off. In the 1914 Ulster crisis, Amery and Milner would brazenly plot rebellion with Field-Marshal Roberts and Henry Wilson. The poet of muscular Christianity, Henry Newbolt, was another Co-efficient, and they even roped in Bertrand Russell, who decamped when Grey proposed an Anglo-French alliance – the philosopher feared that would lead to a European war.

Beatrice had high hopes of George Bernard Shaw, but he didn't like dinner-parties. She did manage to recruit the novelist and science fiction author HG Wells, who was hugely excited. But he soon quarrelled with his Co-efficient friends and departed, to avenge himself with a satire on Sidney and Beatrice, that earnest couple forever seeking to reform education, the Poor Law, and much else – Asquith found their books 'for the most part unreadable'* For good measure Wells contrived to seduce the Agent-General's daughter Amber Reeves – beautiful, clever and twenty years his junior. Ever tolerant, Mrs Wells stoically endured her husband's lengthy romance which he inserted, thinly disguised, into *The New Machiavelli*.

The soldiers were caught up in this too, marginally but with official blessing, as Beatrice spun her web even wider. Haldane, now at the War Office, brought along his Director of Staff Duties, Douglas Haig, and junior officers were sent to have their minds broadened at Mackinder's London School of Economics and Political Science where Haldane was a co-founder. They were also 'invited' to meet Beatrice and her Co-efficients over the tea table.

Prevailing middle class opinion was that 'National Efficiency' was not to be achieved just by slum clearance and 'welfare.' Too many young British males—though not their own sons of course—were physically, mentally and morally inadequate, undisciplined and unemployable, but that could be put right on the barrack square. To straighten the spine; 'thumbs in line with the seam of the trousers!' To mark time, 'form fours' and march in step must infallibly turn these feckless youngsters into useful citizens. Close-order drill would inculcate habits of punctuality, cleanliness and personal grooming, instant obedience and respect for authority – qualities that would take him off the street and render him industrious if unskilled. It was not a new idea, and nor was it confined to Britain, though a pamphlet †edited by George Bernard Shaw suggested military training of young men as well as technical education. Others in the business of social engineering were the Boys' Brigade and the Church Lads' Brigade. Commanded by Volunteer officers and drilled by regular army sergeants, the 'Lads' were required to attend church as a condition of being allowed to march behind the bugle, fife and drum. There was a Jewish Lads' Brigade too, and the irreligious were accommodated by the Lads' Drill Association under the Earl of Meath, who marched *his* lads straight into the National Service League. A relative late-comer to this sort of pressure group was the Boy Scouts Association founded by Robert Baden-Powell, cavalry officer and champion pig sticker. Determined not to be left out, Lord Meath (honorary member of the Much Wenlock Olympian Society) gained *his* Boy Scout proficiency badge at the age of eighty, and his fellow Irish peer Admiral Lord Charles Beresford was the very first Chief Sea Scout. The Scouts were quickly

---

* Jenkins R *Asquith* p 518
† Shaw GBS (ed) *Fabianism and the Empire* 1900

infiltrated by serving or retired army officers and National Service League 'conscriptionists,' but they faced stiff competition from the National Peace Scouts, the British Boy Scouts and the pacifist Boys' Life Brigade backed by the Cadbury and Rowntree dynasties.

A disciplined labour force (and military human resource) would have to be managed by lads of the 'right type.' Happily the so-called 'public' schools had turned out several generations of officer material. Young men steeped in the ethos of muscular Christianity comprised the essential tool for empire-building and the creation of 'a manly and high minded society' – a sentiment echoing George Gissing's disgust at 'the filth and insolence of a draggle-tailed, novelette-reading feminine democracy.' Life at 'public school' had become 'less hard and rough than 50 years ago.' Clearly, comfort and a 'general softness of manners' led to weakness and inefficiency. A feature of 'public' school and university life was the Officer Training Corps – now a recognised piece of the military establishment – and the middle and upper classes, who had always enjoyed the benefits of private welfare provision and their own job creation schemes (army and colonial service) cheerfully acquiesced in the militarisation of their children.

The bellicose approach to social problems might dismay the pacifist, but warfare was seen by some as 'that occasional tonic .... of which the body politic stands in need' and as *Morning Post* correspondent (and professor of military history) Spenser Wilkinson reminded his readers in 1909; 'a nation must ever be prepared for the martyrdom of war.' He favoured its 'nationalisation' and indeed, that would soon come to pass, but he was not alone. 'The warlike strength of the people,' wrote Harold Fraser Wyatt in 1899, 'is the true reflex of their moral and mental vigour.....war is the supreme test of national value.'*

Wyatt was another of those failed politicians – an unsuccessful 'Unionist' in the 1906 Election who found himself a berth in the breakaway Imperial Maritime League. There were many like him. They sent letters to the newspapers; they wrote articles, pamphlets and books; they made speeches and delivered lectures; they gave evidence to public inquiries; sat on committees, wrote reports and generally made themselves useful; and some even got into parliament. Pressure groups were now a thriving industry requiring managers to organise the mass rallies and the mail shots; produce the posters; target the politicians, the newspapers, the voters and the school children; to edit the campaign journals and write the leaflets; and drum up the membership subscriptions and the corporate donations.

But exactly how effective were all these pressure groups? Did they

---

* Wyatt H F in *Nineteenth Century* Vol XLIV February 1899 p 210

have any influence on the direction of public affairs, and where did the pressure come from – the membership, or the leadership? Social evils and vice were largely unchecked despite the National Council of Public Morals, and even the Navy League might seem to be losing ground to the National Service League – but both organisations had friends in Westminster, in Whitehall and in Fleet Street. Always a useful cheerleader, the Navy League was courted by the First Sea Lord Sir John Fisher, but he was already getting all the ships he wanted. In the War Office—where the generals were shaping a Continental strategy to fit the top secret 'alliance' with France—the need for a bigger army may have had more to do with professional ambition than anything Roberts might come up with, and for all the old Field Marshal's drum-beating over the years up to 1914, the Army did *not* get the men.

Both Navy and National Service Leagues, and others with similar aims, were valuable assets to goad, prod, influence, arm-twist, shame and 'destabilise' the new government, and to ensure that the Conservatives should 'still control—whether in power or in opposition—the destinies of this great Empire,' as Mr Balfour reminded his defeated legions. People like Wyatt and his fellow-traveller Graham Horton-Smith were going to be very busy in the next few years, but an earnest young man with a German mother and a law degree was already hard at work. His name was George Richard Francis Shee.

~ 12 ~

The Briton's First Duty

"No one imagines, even among the youngest of us, that he will ever see conscription adopted in this country."

- *The Marquess of Salisbury 30th January 1900* *

St.Valentine's is a day to remember. On the 14th of February 1902, when Kitchener's war of barbed wire, blockhouses and scorched earth had finally crushed the Boers, thirty-two year-old George Shee spoke at the Royal United Service Institution, the country's oldest military talking shop, and still the premier test-bed for strategic thought. Shee was a mere civilian with no experience of war, but he held the attention of senior army officers, academics, politicians and journalists, so much so that after his lecture the discussion ran out of time – so it was resumed a week later, and *again* a few days afterwards.

He was preaching conscription, not just for Britain but for the assortment of colonies, dominions, and protectorates amassed over centuries (all the bits coloured dark pink on the world map). Of course, Britain needed a powerful navy and a professional army, but that wasn't enough. There should be 'an immense reserve ... a pan-Britannic Militia of all able-bodied white men throughout the Empire.' Since all the white men in the Empire, able-bodied or not, were in a very small minority, this might be seen as a hint to His Majesty's subjects in the predominantly 'white' dominions of Canada, Australia and New Zealand, a reminder of their links with the Mother Country. A 'Limp' (Liberal Imperialist) like Mackinder, Asquith, Grey and Haldane – and a 'Co-efficient' as well, Shee thought the Mother could share the expense of imperial defence with her grown-up children, but

* Hanham H J *The Nineteenth Century Constitution 1815-1914* p 367

apparently, 'he children weren't all that keen. What Shee and those he spoke for really wanted, was to lay hands on all the 'able-bodied white men' in *mainland* Britain, since not every able-bodied Irishman might be that interested. Indeed, when conscription became law in 1916 it was never enforced in Ireland, and in 1939, on the eve of another conflict, the Northern Irish were exempt from 'national service.' Still, in the rest of the United Kingdom there was surely an abundance of able bodied white men to discharge 'the Briton's First Duty.'

Twelve days after Shee's Whitehall appearance half a dozen men turned up at the Duke of Wellington's imposing residence, Apsley House on Piccadilly – 'Number One, London' – and the National Service League was born. Some distinguished midwives were in attendance: Sir Charles Hardinge from the Foreign Office; *National Review* editor Leopold Maxse whose brother Ivor was to achieve distinction on the Western Front; Sir Clinton Dawkins the City banker whose team had condemned the War Office for its sloppy housekeeping; and Major JEB Seely DSO, Hampshire Carabineers (Yeomanry), a Conservative MP who would one day be Secretary of State for War – in a Liberal government. Lord Meath was there too. Their host, Arthur Wellesley the fourth Duke, graciously consented to be the League's President, and they made George Shee the Secretary. With such a head start the National Service League would soon become the best organised, and quite the noisiest pressure group Edwardian Britain could boast – and most certainly, the least effective.

Finances were precarious despite 'life' membership pitched at ten guineas – a sum well beyond the means of most dutiful Britons, though not too great a burden for the Earl of Derby or Lever Brothers, the soap makers. 'Ordinary' members paid one guinea a year, associate members 'not belonging to the working classes,' five shillings. For just one shilling (5p in New Money) *genuine* workers got a free badge (usual price sixpence), but 'supporters' from the working class need only pay one penny for an 'Adherent's Card.'

No pressure group can exist for long without its own newspaper, so after some delay the monthly *National Service Journal* appeared, price three pence, only to cease publication when its financial backer pulled out. Resurrection brought a snappier title, *The Nation in Arms,* and a respectable print run of 15,000. For just one penny, Essex Man could also read *The Patriot*, a glossy magazine with full-page cover pictures of local worthies, and reports of branch meetings.

Field-Marshals Wolseley and Roberts were first in the field along with Rudyard Kipling whose short story *Army of a Dream* featured an imaginary *volunteer* reserve of 'Guard,' 'Line' and 'Militia' with varying levels of commitment. The Bishop of Exeter, the novelist George Meredith and Moberly Bell of the *Times* all joined, as did that eminent busybody Sir George Sydenham Clarke, soon to be Secretary of the Committee of Imperial Defence, and there was even a Ladies' Auxiliary Section. Recruits came from the Navy League, and Vice-Admiral Lord Charles Beresford signed up, as did the old soldier Robert Blatchford, editor of *Clarion* magazine, and Hyndman the 'Marxist-Imperialist.' The maverick socialist Harry Quelch welcomed the idea of a 'citizen force' if that meant getting rid of the standing army *– which was not League policy, but no one knew exactly what League policy was until the first number of the *National Service Journal* appeared – eighteen months overdue – and Shee somewhat ambiguously defined the 'principle' of the National Service League as 'compulsory service for those who will not volunteer.'

To most people that sounded suspiciously like 'conscription' – a word that was almost an obscenity right across the political spectrum. As every politician and every constituency agent would tell you, there were no votes in making every young man waste a year or two peeling potatoes, polishing buttons and drilling on some dreary parade ground. The League originally wanted at least one year's military service but this was quickly scaled down to a modest 'four to six months' of compulsory training (though *not* in barracks), and annual drill thereafter – rather like the Militia of bygone times. As to how this might be achieved, Shee was rather vague, saying the idea was to create a citizen force 'somewhat on Swiss lines.'†

Since it was generally supposed they did these things better in Switzerland but the details thereof were not readily to hand in London (although a British officer, Colonel Gerald Ellison, had in fact published a study of it) the public-spirited Shee formed the 'British Committee of Enquiry into the Swiss Militia System,' packed it with twenty seven public figures including Liberal and Labour politicians, took them to Switzerland and duly reported their – or rather, his – findings.‡

The 'Swiss Model' was very much admired. Haig seemed to like it as did the veteran Volunteer Lloyd George, but however brave the Swiss might be—a virtue not tested for many years except in their civil war of 1860—it could be argued it was not so much her citizen army that kept Switzerland safe, but her situation, since little was to be gained by invading a mountainous country whose unique position, and neutrality, suited everyone. Besides, the Swiss had no colonies and no

---
* Letter, *National Service Journal* November 1903 Vol I No 1 p 12
† *Nation in Arms* March 1907 New Series Vol II No 13, p263
‡

navy, while Britain's frontier was supposedly on the North West Frontier of India.

Brusquely dismissing those Swiss militiamen, an anonymous writer in the *Daily Mail* ridiculed compulsory service as 'an unpractical dream' asserting 'the great mass of the males of this nation – especially the older ones – are in favour of everyone except themselves being compulsorily trained.' In the commotion no one heeded the 'carrot and stick' idea of one retired admiral speaking at the Royal United Service Instition; that 'no able bodied man in these islands' should draw the new old age pension – five shillings a week – 'unless he had qualified himself in youth to defend his home.'*

Would Shee's 'compulsory militiamen' be of more use than the Volunteers? Would they replace the Militia and the Yeomanry? And more importantly perhaps, would they be *cheaper*? Lord Curzon, still nursing his bruises from Kitchener's mailed fist, cited 'the old English principle already existing in the common law of the land that it is the duty of every able-bodied citizen to join in the defence of his country.' He was sadly out of date. Civilians carrying firearms could expect to be shot if captured. As one bemused patriot, the Sheffield industrialist Colonel Sir John Bingham plaintively told General Sir Ian Hamilton, 'Rifle Clubs and members would vastly increase in numbers and keenness were they protected from execution when fighting.' †

Compulsory military training—confusingly, without conscription —would give Britain an army to defend the homeland from invasion, but Shee had another argument to win over the doubters. 'National Efficiency,' the goal so dear to would-be social reformers, especially the Fabians and the Co-efficients with whom Shee had close ties. National Service would 'enormously improve the physique of our people' and give them 'a valuable training in methodic work, cleanliness, punctuality, order and discipline.' Just as important, it would 'bring all classes together' ‡

A seductive idea, it had its attractions not only for 'middle England' but elsewhere, notably in France and the United States.§ A simplistic but persuasive and timeless message, it would be echoed by successive generations of middle-aged men – 'bring back national service!' In another century, one war veteran – a *Guardian* reader! – bewailed the collapse of social standards, the indiscipline of young people, their indolent, sloppy appearance and bad manners. He thought they should have a choice between military service and 'a new

---

* *The Nation in Arms* March 1908 Vol III No 23 p49
† Hamilton MSS Liddell Hart Centre King's College London
‡ National Service Journal November 1903 Vol I No 1 p2, November 1904 p 4, and Hayes p 42
§

form of national service.'*

As in the Navy League, the top echelons of the National Service League were not short of rank and distinction, especially on the distaff side – the women's executive committee boasted six titled ladies, the women's general committee no fewer than thirteen. Branches were formed wherever a local worthy – often a leading employer – could be found to set an example, though too often his departure left a vacuum, as at St Helen's when the glass manufacturer Colonel Pilkington died. Little interest was shown by the landed gentry, and much of the organising and doorstep canvassing was done by retired officers like Major Beck in Norfolk, while in Essex a wealthy newcomer to country life, Major Frank Hilder, could usually be relied on for practical help.

Recruiting was sluggish at first with fewer than two thousand members and only nine branches, though numbers shot up with Roberts as President. Finding them all something to do, other than go to branch meetings and provide an audience for the Field Marshal's public speeches, was not easy. But whatever the Field Marshal might say (he sent Lord Esher 'the revised programme for the King to look over') the National Service League was never a genuinely popular organisation embracing all classes. His followers were 'Anglicans rather than Non Conformists; Unionists rather than Liberals; soldiers rather than civilians; Lords rather than Mps; employers rather than employees'; and as one branch secretary in Sussex lamented, 'It is so difficult to get at the lower-middle, and the labouring classes' – not many 'Penny Adherents' there.

When George Shee stepped down to undergo his sea change – running the Lifeboat Institution – much of the League's out-of-town business was done by paid organisers, usually retired army officers grateful for a £150- £200 annual top-up to the pension, and the fifty three 'sub' branches could keep half of what they managed to raise. Head Office looked hungrily at potential benefactors like the banker Rothschild and the press baron Northcliffe. – nor were they ashamed to add Major Hilder's name to their wish-list, confident at least of his generosity. Indeed this man seems to have given the League much of his personal fortune, though in one campaign to raise £10,000 he prudently made his own pledge of £1,000 conditional on matching sums from other donors – which did not materialise. Ever anxious to be of assistance, Lord Esher asked the American-born British newspaper magnate William Waldorf Astor for £100,000 to subsidise 'independent writers and lecturers' spreading the message of National Service – but no luck there, either. †

---

*

† Roberts to Esher 5 February 1906

Such was his stamina, Roberts would barnstorm the length and breadth of the nation almost to the end of his days, campaigning for 'compulsory universal military training.' But he had famously embarrassed a Conservative government with his strident call for 'the training of all boys and youths in drill and rifle shooting' followed by service 'in the home defence army.' Friendly newspapers tried to explain what he really meant – 'compulsion' was the *alternative* to conscription, but others saw it differently. 'Lord Roberts wants a conscript army, not for home defence, but for foreign and colonial war' cried the *Star:* 'Wrap it up as he may, that is the marrow of his scheme. Well, we say at once that the nation will not give him or any other soldier its youth to play with. Our militarists are always hankering after conscription. What is the good of our Navy if it does not save us from the blood tax?' *

Certainly, conscription was unthinkable, especially in *Liberal* Edwardian England, though not absolutely unthinkable. 'If in all our rough history we have never found conscription or even a large standing army necessary, what has happened to make it necessary now?' asked the *Manchester Guardian,* declaring itself with characteristic ambiguity 'against conscription for foreign service certainly and under all conditions, but against conscription for home defence not quite so unconditionally.'†

Roberts gave the League an image and authority it would otherwise have lacked. The Conservative leadership quietly resisted his efforts to put 'national service' in the party manifesto, but so long as he kept his distance he could usefully assist in embarrassing and upsetting the Liberal government, and this he did by his continual strictures on the administration of the army and his disparagement of the voluntary principle enshrined in Haldane's new 'Territorial Force.'

By 1909 the Field Marshal could flourish *his* Manifesto, declaring a membership of 35,000 including fifty two admirals and 50,000 'adherents.' Two years later he claimed 91,000, the admiral-count was now pushing seventy, someone had even managed to recruit the 'Tiger' Clemenceau, and by 1914 Roberts was boasting 270,000, counting all the penny 'adherents.'

The League's proselytising efforts were strenuous. In the first half of 1910 two hundred meetings *a month* were reported,‡ mostly quite small gatherings but clearly a message of sorts was being put across even if it was preaching to the converted. The London Stock Exchange pledged its members to raise £10,000 for the League (they managed

* Allison M *The National Service Issue 1899-1914* p 141
† Allison p 127
‡ July 1009 Vol IV No 39 p 270

£3,000). There was a branch in New Zealand and links had been forged with the Australian National Defence League – and by 1909 both countries had some kind of compulsory training.* In London's West End the more vocally patriotic actors formed their own Theatrical Branch, while A*n Englishman's Home,* Major Guy du Maurier's drama of a thinly-disguised German invasion, was playing to packed houses at Wyndham's Theatre. Lord Esher thought it 'most excitingly acted,' but *The Nation in Arms* reviewer found the play's popularity 'all the more remarkable' since there was 'practically no plot' and no sex.† With his jaundiced eye he may have noticed the Territorial Army recruiting booth doing a brisk trade in the foyer. The play had a mixed reception from a more discerning audience in Berlin – and a shorter run.

There *was* a plot, though. Marching behind the League was another much smaller outfit led by Colonel Repington who recalled 'some of us' took against Lord Robert's 'National Service' idea, and set up the 'National Defence Association' with the Right Honourable Sir George Dashwood Taubman Goldie, Knight Commander of the Order of St Michael and St George (and 'founder of Nigeria') as the NDA President. Goldie had been on a Royal Commission to assess the Army's performance in the Boer War, which made him the ideal front man for an organisation just big enough to contain Major Jack Seely, DSO, Hampshire Carabineers (Yeomanry); Alfred Milner; St. Looe Strachey of the *Spectator;* Charles Hardinge from the Foreign Office; and newspaper magnate Northcliffe. Attending their monthly dinners were Haldane, Balfour, and General Sir William Nicholson, Chief of the General Staff.

This was no ordinary debating society – it was Repington's 'Trojan Horse' that would back Haldane's Territorial Army until conscription seemed inevitable. The chairman was Roberts – ' a more useless person for the job no one could find,' he told a friend.‡ But 'old Bobs' deserved more than a minor walk-on part, and his next appearance would be in a piece of Whitehall theatre – directed by Colonel Repingon.

---

* Adams and Poirier p 17
† *The Times* 8 December 1911
‡ *Journal* 27 January 1909

~ 13 ~

Pussy in the Cabbage Patch

"In the end we shall have an army that we do not want where it can be used, and that could not be used where it is wanted."

– Pall Mall Gazette 12 December 1910

'Keep your hands off the regiment, ye iconoclastic civilian officials who meddle and muddle in army matters. Clever politicians you may be, but you are not soldiers and you do not understand them; they are not pawns on a chessboard' growled the venerable Field Marshal Viscount Wolseley,* this, shortly before Richard Burdon Haldane laid *his* hands on the War Office. Wolseley, 'the soldier's friend' who gave them the Maxim machine gun *and* the Egyptian Camel Corps, certainly knew about 'army matters,' but Generals and Field Marshals seldom miss a chance to bite the hand that feeds them.

Picking his cabinet ministers, Sir Henry Campbell-Bannerman might not have been too upset to see his old enemy 'Schopenhauer' sink in the treacherous mud of the 'kailyard' (cabbage patch). Haldane was a man with interesting ideas about higher education and a passion for German philosophy, but he knew nothing about the British Army, or its regiments. He was however, a career politician. This was his first job in government, and the War Office was an important post. As he explained in his memoirs, if he couldn't have the Colonial Office or be Lord Chancellor, the War Office was the one he really wanted. He'd been angling for it behind Campbell-Bannerman's back when the Liberals were still the opposition party and though 'C-B' was minded to make him Home Secretary or Attorney-General, the philosopher perversely preferred to sit in the proverbial Cabbage Patch.

* Wolseley *The Story of a Soldier's Life* Vol II p 376

13 - Pussy in the Cabbage Patch

Haldane's big idea: 'the Nation in Arms' was borrowed from General Wilhelm Leopold Colmar Freiherr von der Goltz, whose book *Das Volk in Waffen* (the people at war) had inspired him. Perhaps the National Service League, whose journal was rechristened *The Nation in Arms* also deserves some credit, but long before Haldane, another politician Henry Addington (Viscount Sidmouth) achieved a near-total mobilisation of Britain's manpower against Napoleon. As for the 'Expeditionary Force' that marched off to meet von Kluck's First Army at Mons in 1914; its size and shape had more to do with politics and economics than strategy, because the philosopher had to reorganise the standing army and reserves without spending more – he actually managed on slightly less. But he was careful not to let outsiders know the purpose of that Expeditionary Force. For Haldane and Grey, the Kailyard – the Cabbage Patch – was their secret garden.

A lawyer trained to master a complex brief, a bachelor with no domestic ties (although close to his mother) Richard Burdon Sanderson Haldane (aka 'Pussy') had an 'almost spherical' appearance, a high-pitched voice and an emollient, disarming manner. His speeches were often long and complicated however, and could be hard work for the listener. Indeed, when he reached the House of Lords one bemused peer confessed 'I never knew how incapable I was of understanding these things until I heard your argument.' His trump card though, was a firm grasp of Hegelian dialectic that few generals in the War Office could hope to match. But there he was fortunate to find at his elbow a most efficient and loyal 'military adviser,' Colonel Gerald Ellison – a posting quietly arranged by Esher, who also claimed to have got Haig *his* place on the General Staff. *

It was to Haldane's advantage that apart from his professed belief in a big navy – every Briton's theological birthright – he arrived in Whitehall with no declared opinions. To cabinet colleagues and supporters he was a bold reformer determined to eliminate incompetence and overspending, while the generals in the War Office saw him as a manager solely concerned to achieve efficiency. He brought comfort to the Profession, but most Liberals knew little about his job and cared less – if there *had* to be a standing army, and some of the party were not even sure of that, then it should take less from the public funds than it presently did.

In opposition Haldane had counselled frugality, resurrecting an idea of his that the Navy should pick up the bill for all that coast artillery – nine million pounds a year out of an army budget of thirty million – as the sailors could do it for half the price. Now an insider, he found ways to prune the estimates and please the faithful, for there

* Fraser pp 157-8

were many fiscal black holes and slugs among the cabbages. As his head of finance Charles Harris explained, the generals were spendthrifts. Clearly, the great purge had not reached every pigeonhole in the War Office.

Some of this weed-covered patch had been dug over by the previous government, and it must have been a comfort that he would see as many friendly faces opposite, as on his own side of the House of Commons – maybe even more. But he did have that Conservative-turned-Liberal, Major John Edward Bernard Seely, DSO, Hampshire Carabineers (Yeomanry) whose uncle won the Victoria Cross during the Indian Mutiny. Stanley Baldwin's 'fag' at Harrow School, Boer War hero and founder-member of the National Service League – and Navy League member too – 'Galloper Jack' was one of the few in his adopted party to show much interest in military affairs. His reward was a job as junior minister for the Colonies, and then a stint in the War Office, until at last *Colonel* Seely was sitting awkwardly in Haldane's old chair. Hopelessly lost in the Ulster crisis that sorely tested the Army's loyalty, this honest simpleton did the decent thing and departed ministerial life. Then the Great War came and *Brigadier-General* Seely galloped off to the front.

At the start of the twentieth century the Army existed – at least on paper – to defend the United Kingdom of Great Britain and Ireland from the French and the Russians. But its *real* chief task was to protect India from the Russians (and the ungrateful Indians); Canada from the Americans, Russians and Japanese; as well as the Scandinavian countries and the Netherlands (from anyone); and not least, to protect Belgium from everyone including the Belgians themselves should they forcibly object to British troops using their country as a battlefield – yet again. Thus the Army garrisoned remote outposts of empire, naval bases and coaling stations; it occupied the 'informal' colonies or 'protectorates' like Egypt and Cyprus – plus Crete and Corfu for a while – and it was always available to put a few more square miles under the Union flag whenever required – in punitive or acquisitive expeditions mounted from Britain or India – those 'little wars' that Wolseley and Roberts were so very good at. In the unlikely event of a European war the Army's task would be to relieve any hostile powers of *their* overseas possessions.*

This same army had to assist the police inside the United Kingdom, especially in Ireland, but it was India that really soaked up the manpower. Of the eighty-five battalions of British infantry – some of them Irish – guarding the empire to keep the foreigners out and the 'natives' in their place, most were in India, and while the rest had to

---
* Prime Minister's memorandum 11 November 1903 TNA CAB 38/3/71

stay at home in case someone should invade, formations overseas had to be fed with fresh drafts; youngsters shipped out to replace time-expired veterans. Just as important though, was the long term future of the army as an *organisation,* and the career prospects for its officers.

It seemed they didn't have much of a future. 'So long as the Navy is able to fulfil its mission,' that influential pair Sir Charles Dilke and Spenser Wilkinson pronounced back in 1891, 'there is little probable scope for the Army except on the Indian border, or in offensive operations elsewhere aiming at the protection of India.' So, any 'understanding' with Russia would remove the need for an army of any consequence on the North West Frontier – or anywhere else for that matter. In the same year that Dilke and Wilkinson pronounced the last rites for the Army, the Honourable Edward Stanhope, Secretary of State for War in a Conservative government, secured his niche in the hall of fame with the 'Stanhope Memorandum,' a policy document that ruled out all thoughts of employing even *one* army corps (two or three divisions comprising 40-50,000 men) in a European war.* The Liberals gratefully signed up to Stanhope, but his Memorandum became an article of faith for late Victorian and Edwardian governments of either party. The Army 'didn't do Europe,' though the recent *Entente* with France seemed to carry just a vague hint that a British army *might* be fighting on the Continent, some day in the distant future.

Meanwhile, how could any politician square the circle and fill the ranks of a home and colonial army? Two of Balfour's brightest, William St John Brodrick and Hugh Arnold-Forster, had been sacrificed in the attempt. The generals had dragged their feet, the King had interfered, and Arnold-Forster peevishly complained he had to deal with six armies including the regular Army at home as well as the British-officered 'Indian Army'; the Militia; the Volunteers; and all those retired officers 'entrenched' in the gentlemen's clubs – while his old crony the 'unauthorised and irresponsible' Viscount Esher, didn't help him this time. But the new man in the War Department was blessed with a tactful manner and a prodigious appetite for facts and figures. In just a few weeks he and the admirable Ellison had devised a scheme the generals and their king could understand.

They did it not by handing out redundancy notices but by increasing the time a soldier actually served in active service instead of serving on the Reserve, and by reshaping or rearranging battalions and regiments, and even losing a few. As always, amputation drew squeals of pain, especially when the knife came anywhere near the monarch's Household troops. Should the élite Guards Brigade be

---
* Beckett IFW 'Edward Stanhope and the War Office 1887 -92 *Journal of Strategic Studies* June 1982 pp 278-307

pruned of a couple of battalions, the rump could just about change the guard at Buckingham Palace but not much else. Others said redundant fortress gunners were no use in the field artillery. Fearful perhaps of old Field Marshal Wolseley, Haldane kept his hands off the one institution unique to the British Army – the Regiment.

Even the smallest professional army needs a reserve of trained men, but the Militia were no longer much use – if they ever were. So Pussy tackled the militia colonels head-on, scrapping this costly throwback with the highest desertion rate, and replacing it with a 'Special Reserve.' He was saving money by 'creative accounting.' Thus he kept the the treasury sweet, the prime minister informed and the King content – he reprieved one Guards battalion and tucked it out of sight in Egypt.

A professed Blue Water man – 'the Navy *is* the Nation' he once told his countrymen – Haldane reckoned that since the Royal Navy was bigger and better than anyone else's, an invasion of the British Isles was unlikely, so the Army was no longer needed for home defence. He might winkle a few battalions out of the colonies, the 'protectorates' or South Africa, but he could and did point eastward to a 'threat' the navy could do nothing about; a threat conveniently posed by the Tsar. Though ever since the 'Mutiny' British troops had been stationed in India not so much to keep the Russians out, but to keep the Indians down. As Haldane explained 'we have a certain number of white troops there' – about 75,000 – 'because we are a white government,' though of course that 'certain number' could be of more use for generals in search of a grand mission nearer home. Soon Haldane would have his 'go-anywhere, fight-anyone striking-force; but a field army that would gobble up men and money if he wasn't very careful.

But did Britain really *need* a "Striking Force"? Whom would it strike, and where? Winston Churchill didn't like the idea – 'dangerous and provocative'* – and nor did Lloyd George. They were reflecting a traditional sentiment – defence of the realm good; other people's wars bad! And in the Franco- Prussian war, Lord Derby wasn't the only one to think it was just as well Britain did *not* have a large army, for that might have been an inducement to intervene. Hadn't Queen Victoria said if Prince Albert had been alive she couldn't have stopped him joining the Prussians?† The *Economist* put it squarely: '*We* have learned from this war that we cannot be a great military nation. Now we see what first-rate war is; we know that we have not soldiers enough for it, and that without changing all our habits we cannot have them.' ‡

---

* Williamson *The Politics of Grand Strategy* p 99 and Searle *A New England?* p 488
† Esher *Journal* 5 March 1908

Decried thus by Walter Bagehot speaking to 'Middle England' in 1870; dismissed out of hand by Lord Stanhope in the nineties, and shunned by both ruling parties ever since, the idea of a 'continental' army was surely a non-starter. The Empire came first, and that was where the British Army should go – if indeed it had to go anywhere. It was naive to suppose a few long-service volunteers would be taken seriously by France or Germany, states with long frontiers to defend and huge armies of short-service conscripts, men discharged to the reserve after two or three years, so that mobilisation instantly put millions of trained soldiers into the field. Britain was different, and anyone running for parliament on the conscription ticket was wasting his time and his or someone else's money. To most people the 'C' word was politically incorrect, and the two great parties always closed ranks to stifle its utterance.

With a lawyer's caution, Haldane had not actually said his new model army was designed to fight on the continent of Europe. The Striking Force could be sent to 'any part of the world where it is required' which narrowed the choice to the Khyber Pass – or, just across the Channel perhaps? But because it could all be had for no additional expense the rest of the Cabinet were satisfied – his back benchers too – while the party faithful remained largely ignorant of those hole-and-corner military 'conversations' with the French, for only two or three ministers knew that Grey wanted a 'continental' army to give backbone to his diplomacy.

For all that, the notion of a 'striking force' had been in circulation a good thirty years, and though a 1901 plan for 120,000 men was dropped, the army corps at Aldershot was still earmarked for service overseas.* In the earliest days of the Liberal government, when the secret talks with the French began, Mr Haldane had assured the Foreign Secretary that Britain's new 'alignment' with France was underpinned by a hundred thousand soldiers – though it would take a while to assemble them.

The Committee of Imperial Defence spent the best part of a year ruminating on the merits of sending an army to the continent or relying on the Navy. They reckoned it would take three weeks to get the troops there, too late to help the Belgians, but Lord Esher thought the French might appreciate the 'moral support' of the Navy, plus twelve thousand soldiers – 'mounted brigades.' Remembering perhaps Colonel Huguet's warning that the French expected rather more than a token contribution, Esher mused, 'great difficulties would arise if this proposal was known in certain quarters,'† and the sages concluded

---
‡ *The Economist* 1 October 1870
* Williamson p 102, and Jeffery p 44

their deliberations with the usual Whitehall-speak about this being 'a matter of policy which can only be determined, when the occasion arises, by the government of the day.' Nevertheless they did oblige the War Office with the useful tip that the 'Striking Force' should be six full-strength divisions, plus the cavalry – about 160,000 men.

But where would these divisions come from? Recruiting figures usually matched the numbers of unemployed, often unemployable, young men, and for Campbell Bannerman, the army was more like a vast rehabilitation centre; a social service that took youngsters off the street and gave them a sense of purpose, echoing George Shee and others. But where else could men be found for the North West Frontier if not from the slums? Mr Haldane would soon be telling everyone a soldier's life was not so terribly hard and the Army was now attracting a better type, but as ever, the best recruiting sergeant was hunger.

Haldane's new reserve army could have been a throw back to the 'Nation in Arms' idea, but the 'Territorial Force' would be a volunteer army of 'weekend soldiers.' If that sounded pretty much like the old Volunteer Movement it wasn't meant to. Their colonels were invited to join, bringing their men behind them, and that was it. The territorials would be a replica of the regular standing army complete with majors, colonels and generals, battalions, brigades and divisions – fourteen divisions, each with its own cavalry, artillery and engineers, and recruited from its respective catchment area, the local County. To show how close they were to their roots, they would 'answer' to local dignitaries – the Chairman of the County of London Territorial Association was Haldane's ever ready 'adviser' Lord Esher.

No one expected the Territorials to take the field when war broke out. These patriots would need six months' hard training because their weekend drills and summer camps were not enough to turn them into credible Tommy Atkins look-alikes, and by the time they *were* ready for battle, the real soldiers, Haldane's 'Striking Force,' would most probably have fought and won the war on the North West frontier of India – or, perhaps somewhere much closer to home. *Their* reserve could have been this new lot, but the territorials were to stay behind for the invasion if that should ever happen, and because they were volunteers and weren't compelled to serve abroad, Lord Roberts would soon have his knife into them, and into Haldane too.

It would take the war minister a long time to cajole and convince everyone he'd got it right. Bargains had to be struck with Yeomanry and Volunteer colonels bristling at the thought of coming under local bigwigs, and deals had to be made with the 'militia wing' in Parliament

---

† Esher *Journal* 12 November 1908

so 'their' men could transfer to the new 'Special Reserve.' Tirelessly criss-crossing the Kingdom inspecting entire battalions, shaking hands with everyone in sight, making after-dinner speeches and smoothing ruffled feathers, he was fortunate to have two stout props to lean upon. King Edward deftly exploited snobbery by inviting the Lord Lieutenant of each county to hear His Majesty's endorsement of the Territorials. Haldane's other willing helper was Douglas Haig, now at the War Office, whose task it was to assure the civilians supposedly running the County 'Associations' that they would be listened to. And afterwards, the King told Viscount Esher 'you are a wonderful man, everything you touch succeeds.'*

When Haldane introduced his Territorial and Reserve Forces scheme† it was instantly condemned as 'dangerous...Voluntarism run mad.'‡ An invader 'would go through our Imitation Army as though the territorials were tissue,' sneered the *Observer,* but in the *Times* Colonel Repington advised readers to 'encourage' young men to join – and one big insurance firm made TA membership a condition of employment. The background noise grew louder, but the Vicar of Banbury (South) had got in first with his own somewhat fuzzy rules of engagement which could suit everybody, even Lord Roberts' National Service League: 'If the real women of the country will only let it be known that they will have nothing to do with the man who is too lazy or indifferent or is too great a coward to fit himself to defend his home' he told the *Pall Mall Gazette,* 'no woman should dance with him, ride with him, walk with him, be engaged to him or marry him...'

In parliament Mr Haldane cautioned against 'agitation for what may be unpopular.... an organised movement for compulsion,' but that organised movement was already in business and one of its supporters was another of Haldane's self-appointed 'advisers,' that same Colonel Repington. His old paper the *Westminster Gazette* did not agree. 'A great many soldiers appear to be living in a world of illusion on this subject, because they entirely fail to understand the objection which the average man takes to militarism...It is not, as they allege, degeneracy or moral cowardice, but a very proper reluctance to place the manhood of the country at the disposal of the small military caste which controls the Regular Army' §

To make sure everyone understood the problem, an old comrade of Lord Roberts was enlisted, Lord Raglan the third baron (all those Lord Raglan public houses and coat sleeves are named after his grandfather

---

* Esher *Journal* 3 March 1909
† 'The Military System of the Future in the British Empire' RUSI *Journal* September 1907 Vol LI
‡ *The Nation in Arms* Vol I New Series No 4 pp 35-36
§ *Westminster Gazette* 5 March 1907

who commanded the British Army in the Crimea). *This* Lord Raglan's enviable record of public service as Militia officer, Grenadier Guardsman, Afghan War veteran, sometime junior war minister and Governor of the Isle of Man, qualified him to pronounce that never in the country's history had its defences been in a worse state. The *Daily Express** recruited a 'Soldier' to make 'A Patriotic Appeal to the People' but the impact may have been lessened by his unflattering description of the same People as 'deaf, blind and listless' – qualities which might conceivably impede them in the performance of their military duty. Nevertheless this Soldier insisted they must be 'kicked into activity' – presumably to make them fall-in, behind Lord Roberts.

Roberts, the army's last 'Commander in Chief,' was not spared. 'He wants conscription, which is something for which the country is not prepared, and something which is not called for by the military situation.' The Field Marshal would spend much of his time and energy trying to explain that 'compulsion' did not mean 'conscription,' and vainly pestering a wary Conservative opposition to put 'compulsion' on their election ticket. He would also be very busy denigrating Haldane's administration of the Army, and disparaging the worth of the Territorials. Pussy could still have his Striking Force, his secret army for the Continent, but the Cabbage Patch was full of thistles.

---

* 17 November 1908

~ 14 ~

Last Post for Colonel Trench

> *"If people like Repington can succeed in persuading the country that the fleet is not a protection against invasion, then clearly we have no possible basis for military organisation except compulsion."*
>
> — Sir George Clarke to the Rt.Hon A J Balfour, 15 November 1906 *

With fresh fears troubling his mind, George Shee asked his readers 'are we absolutely safe against the risk of a surprise attack?' and clearly not expecting any assurance from them, forthwith opened his pages to Lord Roberts who obliged with a stark warning about 'the perils of Empire and the threat of invasion.' Another issue carried an 'eye witness account' of landing pontoons... each holding two companies of infantry' – as in that classic invasion thriller by Erskine Childers, *The Riddle of the Sands*.

The Field-Marshal would have been pleased to know that similar intelligence was reaching London from 'a reliable source' in Germany. A military attaché's job description specifically excluded anything so vulgar as espionage, but Colonel Frederick John Arthur Trench, D.S.O. could now inform his superiors that a surprise invasion of England was imminent. His dispatches went first to the Foreign Office, and then the War Office where they could hardly look with favour on anything that might keep a large part of the British Army permanently stationed at home to stop an invasion, when it could be sent to the continent. But for the author, Germany *was* the last post – Colonel Trench was not employed again. In retirement he promptly declared himself for Lord

---
* Ryan W *Repington* p 101

Roberts and National Service, so perhaps this military attaché had been leafing through a few back numbers of *The Nation in Arms*.

A surprise invasion, a 'bolt from the blue,' was generally reckoned a non-starter as long as the Navy controlled the waters around Britain. But George Shee had a populist editor's eye for a good story regardless of its source or accuracy, and, leaving no room for complacency, invited Colonel Repington to announce that the Navy was neither invincible nor infallible. The Field Marshal had three pages on the 'German Peril.'[*]

The stage was now set for another Whitehall farce – a top-level invasion inquiry. The previous Conservative government had assessed the likelihood of a French descent on the shores of England as 'not an eventuality which we need seriously consider,'[†] but a couple of years later Mr Balfour, now in opposition, was advised that a surprise invasion by Germany was not only possible, but probable.

Balfour, a statesman fondly remembered for his sage reflection 'nothing matters very much, and very few things matter at all,' seems to have thought this one *did* matter. Presumably, while keeping a very straight face, he promptly forwarded his visitors' 'intelligence' to Sir George Clarke at the Committee of Imperial Defence. Soon a team of heavyweights including Asquith, Haldane, Grey, Lloyd George, Admiralty First Lord Tweedmouth, Admiral Sir John Fisher (First Sea Lord), a quartet of generals and Lord Esher – assembled to hear 'evidence' presented by Field-Marshal Roberts – as composed by the obliging Repington. Neither man was appearing for the National Service League, or the Conservatives Party – their expenses were paid by a wealthy patron, Sir Samuel Scott.[‡]

It was in character for Repington to aim high. On his dream ticket were the Prince of Wales; Sir Frank Lascelles the ambassador in Berlin plus 'two other British diplomats and consular officials in German ports'; three previous Sea Lords; three former Directors of Naval Intelligence; plus a dozen serving admirals (including Beresford) *and* their chiefs of staff. His Army list was no less imposing, even without Henry Wilson.

Invitations, or summonses, to attend official inquiries not being in his gift, Repington had to get his old pals to do some research. Henry Rawlinson, who would command Haig's Fourth Army on the Somme, was asked about the size of an invasion force and the number of ships it would need. Lord Charles Beresford, commanding the Channel Fleet, was very helpful. Invasion was ' not only probable but possible,'

---

[*] Nation in Arms February 1908 Vol II No 22 pp 35-37
[†] Ryan p 102
[‡] Allison p 116

wrote the Admiral whose job it was to prevent that very thing, and he promised details of his fleet's disposition 'on the day that you give evidence.' Guessing that Beresford was giving Repington classified information, Sir John Fisher assured a Mansion House audience that they and everyone else could 'sleep comfortably in their beds,' but Viscount Esher consoled him, 'Invasion may be a bogey. Granted. But it is a most useful one.'

That high-powered Committee held sixteen sessions, and ruled that some of the regular army should stay at home to stop an invasion, though it must have been obvious that the German armada would have to be such a size that not even Beresford with his entire Channel Fleet could miss it. Haldane, who may well have assisted Repington, was quite relaxed about all this play-acting. It gave him a very good excuse to keep his 'Striking Force' at home – and ready to fight in France.

But the age-old invasion scare could not be allowed to go away. It was an essential part of the case for conscription or 'compulsion,' and to give his campaign credibility Roberts needed up-to-date information on the state of the Army, detail Repington could not readily obtain Conveniently. But someone else was happy to oblige – Henry Wilson, now commandant of the Staff College; but Henry would be back in the War Office one day, and be even more helpful.

~ 15 ~
Dreadnought Gap

"We see before us the towering strength of Germany...There is no pause in the German advance, and yet her interests on the sea are insignificant compared with our own."

– *The Navy League, October 1912*

If the young Alfred Thayer Mahan had gone to be a missionary in China like his uncle, instead of joining the US Navy, the world would have been spared that classic of special pleading, *The Influence of Seapower on History*, but even if Captain Mahan had preached a different faith, Germany would still have aspired to be a naval power. A nation of sixty million with thriving export industries and a sizeable mercantile marine, a people persuaded of their right to 'living space' – grabbing what remained of Africa and the far East – they surely deserved an ocean-going navy, even if that set them on a collision course with the one nation in Europe that measured its warlike power with a *maritime* yardstick.

Mahan argued that since the Royal Navy had made Britain a superpower, so America should build a large ocean-going fleet to fulfil her 'manifest destiny,' but when this reluctant seafarer, for whom a coal-fired steamship was such a noisy, dirty, unattractive place, stepped ashore in England he was warmly received by the Blue Water lobby. In Germany too, the Kaiser's admirals were lavish in their praise. Envious of Britain's global reach and the fleet that made it possible, the All Highest decreed that every officer in his navy should read *The Influence of Sea Power on History*.

In retirement a 'celebrity journalist' with marginal influence on his own country's navy and government, Mahan envied Britain's world-wide chain of naval bases, but he was really making the case for *American* sea power – and American imperialism. The doyen of British naval historians, John Knox Laughton, saw Mahan's aim was to 'encourage his countrymen to contest the supremacy of the sea with Britain,' but this foreigner could also be an impartial witness to justify even more spending on the Royal Navy.

The Kaiser would find battleships didn't come cheaply either. His armies belonged to Prussia, Bavaria, Saxony, Wurttemberg, but the imperial navy was a direct charge on all his subjects, and Germany's neighbours might hope that the more the Kaiser spent on his naval swings, the less would go on the army roundabouts. The French War Ministry could take comfort at the thought of all that heavy artillery from Krupp of Essen locked up miles away in Kiel and Wilhelmshaven. As one Admiralty First Lord observed, the German navy was 'a deduction from what might have been a still larger and still more powerful German army,' while in St Petersburg they might well ask 'how many *divisions* has the Kaiser? instead of how many battleships.

Only Edwardian England took fright at this new runner in the naval arms race. France was yesterday's foe, America and Japan were too distant and the Japanese had obligingly sunk a good part of the Russian navy, but the Kaiser's High Sea Fleet was less than a day's steaming across the German Ocean, as the map makers still named it, and that fleet could project German power beyond central Europe into the wide world, though that wasn't how the Kaiser's admirals saw it. They had no hope of winning a stand-up fight with the vastly superior Royal Navy, though they might make victory too costly for the British. Besides, their fleet was never quite ready and the Emperor was afraid he might lose some of his precious battleships in combat. Yet the mere fact of their existence spurred the British to spend even more on their own Fleet. For most Englishmen this was no bad thing, and pressure groups like the Navy League were really pushing at an open door – but for a handful of excitable malcontents it was more agreeable to kick the door down.

From 1906, the combination of a Liberal Government and a pugnacious First Sea Lord, Sir John Fisher (appointed by the Conservatives), was incitement to mutiny. Ringleaders claimed the new administration was about to repudiate its inherited undertaking (enshrined in the 'Cawdor Memorandum') that the outgoing First Lord of Admiralty (Cawdor) had bequeathed to his successor; an 'understanding' that four new battleships would be ordered every year. The new premier, Campbell-Bannerman, along with his 'radical-economist' ministers Lloyd

George and Winston Churchill – and even opposition leader Balfour – agreed with the Admiralty that the Navy had a comfortable edge over everyone else and could do without one of those extra ships, but that gave the Opposition a chance to embarrass the Government with yet another 'navy scare,' and the enemies of Admiral Fisher joined battle with a salvo from the 'Dear Sir' column of a friendly newspaper:

'If [the Navy League] is to be a lukewarm and complacent organisation, blindly and calmly approving the curtailment and depletion of our naval forces, and avoiding criticism...then I, for one, could not support its policy,' wrote one apparently dissatisfied member who thought the Navy itself had been in better shape 'until this present government came into power.'

The inevitable splinter group, the 'Imperial Maritime League' emerged in January 1908 'to fill the place left vacant by the paralysis of the Navy League.' Its purpose was crisply stated: 'To further the safety of the country and of the Empire; to foster, as the essential means to that end, the growth of the Fighting, the Patriotic, and the Imperial Spirit, and to Combat those Little England Ideas which are the Curse of our race.' All this could be had by 'Working Men and Women' for a shilling a year, so Life Membership at ten guineas was a snip – if you could be sure to live at least two centuries. The 'Junior Branch' charged infants a penny a month, which suggests the organisers ran a tight ship, but the Imperial Maritime League never got more than 1,500 recruits. Its *Weekly Notes* were to be found each Wednesday in *The Englishman,* price one penny, a journal standing for 'Sincerity, Simplicity, Sobriety, Patriotism, Civil and Religious Liberty,' with the catchy slogan 'Measures not Men.... At Home, England for the English. Abroad, the British Empire against the world.' *

Joint founders and guiding spirits of this latest crusade were the young barrister Lionel Graham Horton-Smith, a man quick to write to the newspapers from his club (the Athenaeum), to report sightings of German spies, and the 'Liberal Unionist' Harold Fraser Wyatt, another robust thinker – 'war is the supreme test of national value' – he was one of many whose hopes were dashed in the recent election. They made a colourful pair but their prize exhibit was undoubtedly the First Sea Lord's old rival, the ebullient Anglo-Irish Admiral and serial Member of Parliament Lord Charles Beresford, recently commanding the powerful Channel Fleet – the most senior job afloat. The Imperial Maritime League dutifully echoed his call for a 'Strategy Department' for the Navy, as defence analyst and *Morning Post* man Spenser Wilkinson had urged. Alas, when pressed to join, Wilkinson proved less than helpful. Though warning the London Chamber of Commerce that

* Wyatt H, Horton Smith L The Passing of the Great Fleet

the management of the Navy was now 'in dangerous hands' he would only confirm drily that he had indeed quit the Navy League when it lost interest in the idea of a naval 'General Staff.'

According to the gospel of Wyatt and Horton Smith, the government had 'laid party hands, for party ends, on the fighting strength of that Navy which is the Ark of the Covenant to the British peoples,' an interesting proposition couched in forthright, theologically inspirational language. The Liberals' massive majority in parliament included many like Winston Churchill who begrudged more spending on the Navy, but if the government was a fair target for abuse, so was Sir John Fisher – and Beresford probably thought so too. The two had long been at odds with each other, and neither was the most tactful of men.

It was Fisher who presided over a "revolution" in naval architecture. The conventional battleship carried an assortment of artillery, of different calibre, along each side, but HMS *Dreadnought*, launched in 1906, could bring most of her big guns to bear on *either* flank to deliver a much heavier broadside of armour-piercing shell – and soon, in another "revolution," those guns would be directed onto their moving target by mechanical computers. *Dreadnought* gave Britain an instant lead over all other navies, until they quickly caught up – and of course, the rest of the Royal Navy's battle fleet was instantly out of date. Fisher was slow to lay down more Dreadnoughts – he preferred the lightly armoured but swifter *'battle-cruiser,'* and, being a specialist in torpedoes instead of gunnery (as was usual in the higher ranks), he thought the submarine would dominate the North Sea.

Fisher had already played his other card – concentration of force. This idea was not new. In the eighteenth century the Western Squadron stood off Ushant ready to pounce on the French emerging from Brest, and the ships remained on station as long as masts and sails could withstand the buffeting squalls, while the sailors endured the misery of slippery rigging and cold, wet, mess decks. In another age Fisher identified Germany as the enemy, bringing home ships from remote stations and scrapping those 'too weak to fight, too slow to run away.' Distant outposts of empire were left unguarded and the Western Hemisphere was effectively abandoned to the United States, while in East Asian waters Japan had readily taken up the White Man's Burden. 'Far-called, our navies melt away' mused Rudyard Kipling, his finger on the weakening pulse of empire as early as 1897, the year of Queen Victoria's Diamond Jubilee and her Fleet Review at Portsmouth – an impressive thirty mile line-up of warships. But now the White Ensign was seen less in foreign parts, and even that hallowed sea the Mediterranean would cease to be a British lake.

The most disloyal of subordinates, and in retirement the noisiest of critics, Beresford had convinced himself that Fisher was fatally weakening the Fleet, and not surprisingly, conservative-leaning newspapers joined in the cry. The *Daily Express* had an 'exclusive' report from their man in Hamburg that a 'senior official' told him if the British Liberal government could be kept in power long enough 'the dearest wish of every German naval officer would be realised.' Then Viscount Esher mischievously brought the Kaiser into the fray.* Wilhelm complained to Fisher's political boss Tweedmouth, who tried appeasement, sending him the Naval Estimates *before* they were laid before Parliament. Repington seized on this to take revenge on the man who'd been so unkind to him and Roberts at the Invasion Inquiry, and the hapless Tweedmouth – already a sick man – was done for.

The British Liberal Government was not yet persuaded by talk of naval weakness, and even Balfour was doubtful until he remembered he was still the Leader of the Opposition, a job that required him to embarrass and upset the Government, and sea power was *political* power. The Navy had friends, though, like Julian Corbett, 'one of the half dozen doctrinaires,' Repington snarled, 'who are the curse of England,' as well as the big naval armaments firms and even his own paper the *Times*... 'I don't think Haldane quite realises yet the strength and guile of this confraternity.'† Since Mr Haldane was a regular recipient of Repington's gratuitous advice on all things military, the public-spirited colonel may have exerted rather less influence in high places than he liked everyone to think Even his own paper *The Times* could 'think of nothing but dreadnoughts.' Indeed they might, for there were fresh alarms to come. Edwardian England had discovered the Dreadnought Gap.

The 1909 'People's Budget' that so upset the House of Lords – that 'committee of landowners' the *Manchester Guardian* called them – was more of a navy-and-welfare package. But Sir John Fisher didn't quite trust the lawyer Reginald McKenna who, until he took over from Tweedmouth, was against spending more on the Navy. So the First Sea Lord fed his new master an intelligence 'dossier' which showed the Germans were secretly building more battleships than they admitted, and would soon have twenty-one modern 'dreadnoughts' to Britain's sixteen. The Dreadnought Gap was looking ominously wide.

Fisher made sure the story played well in Fleet Street, and his new boss dutifully stood up in Parliament to ask for a few 'Super-Dreadnoughts.' The 140-strong Liberal awkward squad behind him was duly outraged, and ignored – as was Churchill, still at the Board of Trade,

* Ryan p 109-110
† Letter to Roberts,14 April 1909

and Lloyd George, now Chancellor of the Exchequer who, along with four other ministers had earlier threatened to quit over increases in naval spending. In a wide-ranging, or rambling, speech addressed more to his own back benches, Sir Edward Grey deplored the international arms race which threatened to destroy civilisation, but Britain could hardly stay out of it, and as for the Germans, 'our navy is to us what their army is to them.' Next year he thought it wiser not to tell his countrymen the Germans were ready to discuss a slowdown of warship construction as part of an agreement which would include British neutrality in a continental war; a not unattractive idea to some of his Cabinet colleagues.

'Meanwhile we have been in the throes of a navy scare. Well engineered, it will bring us our 8 Dreadnoughts,' Esher smirked as the Conservatives, aided by Beresford, the Imperial Maritime League and the Navy League, orchestrated a noisy off-stage chorus of jingoism, best remembered for MP George Wyndham's music hall chant 'we want eight and we won't wait.' McKenna obliged, promising four big ships at once and another four to follow if deemed necessary – as of course they were. Australia and New Zealand raised the cash for a couple of extra battle cruisers, Malaya paid for a 'super-dreadnought' and the naval lobby was well pleased.

After that it scarcely mattered that Fisher's 'intelligence' dossier had been concocted by an armaments firm with an empty order book,* and that by 1912 it would be the Royal Navy that owned twenty one dreadnoughts while the Kaiser would have only thirteen. Oddly, it was the editor of the *Navy League Annual* no less who wryly recalled how Asquith, Grey and McKenna had 'vied one with the other in their endeavour to make our patriotic flesh creep.' †

Liberals might not like it, but the Navy League was now looking elsewhere for friends. Supporters were reminded that the 'Socialist Party,' as well as many in the Labour Party, should not be identified with the 'Little Navy Party,' those radical-pacifists and Liberal 'economists' (now bereft of Lloyd George and Winston Churchill). The industrial working class, so heavily dependent on naval construction and armaments, was always taken seriously. One Navy League speaker proudly reported 'an audience of over 250 men of Socialistic character' at Sowerby Bridge in Yorkshire, but didn't say how many converts he made – they'd each have to pay a guinea a year, though 'associates' could get off with five shillings, and for 'any less amount' they could still belong, but would have to manage 'without publications.'

---
* Searle, pp 488-9
† Alan Burgoyne, MP 'The Truth about the Dreadnought Controversy' *Oxford and Cambridge Review* October 1911 p 6

This was a real deprivation because the Navy League's *Journal* – good value for a penny – was full of accounts of bygone victories, accounts of the lives of famous admirals, and practical advice to young readers on how to join the Navy. The defence of the British Empire being 'The Duty of every British Boy' – the Navy was seen as the glamorous service. A continuous theme was German warship construction, shown in glossy cover pictures of 'the great gun-shop at Essen' with the caption 'How Germany prepares for war,' or intimidatory photos of the latest battlecruiser Seydlitz. Bizarrely, Herr Krupp's foundries also made the best quality armour plate for the Royal Navy, as the *Journal* freely acknowledged. The League's warning cry, 'there is no pause in the German advance, and yet her interests on the sea are insignificant compared with our own,' echoed by the Admiralty's new boss Winston Churchill with the zeal of a convert to the doctrine of naval prodigality. He replaced Reginald McKenna, scapegoat for the inept performance of Fisher's successor Admiral Arthur Wilson during the 1911 Agadir crisis, when brigadier-general Henry Wilson (no relation to the admiral) made a more convincing case for the Army.

McKenna was consigned to the Home Office in a straight swap for Churchill who—ever the good departmental minister and never much encumbered by principle—speedily transferred his loyalty. Conveniently forgetful now of prison reform or fiscal prudence, Churchill embraced the Sea Lords, the 'Band of Brothers,' with rather more vigour than they were accustomed to. His abrasive manner scarcely endeared him to the admirals, but he did preside over a surge of new construction and a further huge increase in the navy's budget – so much so that by 1914 it was nearly twice the army's share.

The sailors' willing hostage did more than browbeat the Treasury for extra Dreadnoughts. He pulled the fleet, or most of it, out of the Mediterranean, thereby completing the historic withdrawal Fisher had begun, and steered for a naval alliance with France – in fact if not in name – and under the cover of Sir Edward Grey's sophistry. Two centuries of maritime ascendancy ended as Britain's traditional enemy assumed control from Gibraltar to Malta, where only a token squadron remained. Such a weakening of the fleet meant Britain would 'forfeit the prestige attached to the power whose flag has floated on all the seas, and in particular has dominated the Mediterranean,' a senior Foreign Office 'Clerk' lamented in a lengthy and repetitive memorandum. 'The respect which English sea power commands, especially in oriental minds, is the measure of the attention with which her voice is listened to' wrote Sir Eyre Crowe. Warming to his theme he asserted, 'We hold Egypt and control her administration at present not by the actual number of bayonets assembled in the Nile valley, but in virtue

15 - Dreadnought Gap

of the political authority attaching to our position as commanding the sea.' Sir Edward Grey lamely agreed that the British pull-out would have 'bad consequences' – diminished 'to a certain extent' by the French navy filling the gap, whereupon Viscount Esher gave Balfour a lecture on naval strategy and told his son Maurice it meant an alliance with the French and 'conscription to cover Pussy's traces at the War Office.'*

Certainly the fortunes of the Fleet were of greater concern to Government, Opposition and the press, than the case for conscription that was being incessantly preached by Field Marshal Lord Roberts and his National Service League. In a straight fight the Blue Water team came out on top – the Imperial Maritime League, backed by a hundred admirals, and fifty generals shrieked for a £100 million 'Navy Loan, ' while the Navy League denounced as 'unsatisfactory' the 1911-12 construction programme of five large armoured ships – they wanted twelve. Even Repington joined the crew, sailing under false colours as 'Colonel Donner und Blitzen,' a newcomer to the *Times* staff who advised readers that an extra £60 million for the Navy, plus eight million to get Roberts' National Service scheme going, would be just enough to save the Empire.

Yet another pressure group, The Society of Islanders fathered by Lord Esher, was a bargain at only half a crown for membership card *and* badge (including postage), with 'no further liability.' Lady Islanders anxious to do their bit for the Empire could find useful tips in the Society's journal, where they could learn that 'two keels to one' was the basis of Britain's naval supremacy.† The Islanders claimed an improbable membership of seventy thousand, but delivered a strangely muted message – 'Our association is private and secret.'‡

The ingrained belief on the quarter-deck was that the next war would start and finish with a good old-fashioned sea fight, another Trafalgar with everything resting on the outcome. But it was a civilian, Julian Corbett, who spotted the fly in the ointment, the snag the admirals hadn't reckoned with. What if their enemy refused to come out and fight, and kept his battleships safe in harbour behind his minefields and forts? Victory would still be theirs if the Kaiser's fleet stayed there until it emerged to surrender – which is what the Imperial German Navy eventually did, save for a few forays and one large-scale outing, whereby the British Grand Fleet would have served its purpose without firing a shot or going anywhere.

Corbett believed in the traditional use of sea power – to 'select a

---
* Esher *Journal* 2 July 1912
† *The Islander* Vol I No. 1 December 1910
‡ *The Islander* Vol I No. 2 March 1911 p 15

theatre and thereby contain a force greater than its own,' he advised young officers at Greenwich Naval College. 'That is all that can be claimed for it, but it may be all that is required.' Admiral Fisher fancied the German coastline – even the Baltic – though he knew minefields made it risky for warships to venture close inshore, and railways made it easier to rush heavily-armed troops to any landing place. A maritime nation would always find it hard to get to grips with a continental power whose ideas of warfare were so different, but by the same token, any continental ally might reasonably expect something rather more substantial from its British partner than this unpredictable, and rather stand-offish, 'pick and choose' contribution. But when war came Fisher did send his submarines into the Baltic.

The sailors had another card up their sleeve; blockade. Seizing *all* seaborne cargo destined for Germany might well be Britain's most effective contribution to that unspoken 'alliance' in which the French and the Russians were expected to do the fighting on land; but the War Office thought otherwise. Helped by the Foreign Office, the generals commissioned their own 'research' to undermine the case with questionable 'evidence' of the enemy's staying power in time of war – they even assumed Russia would be neutral.* Of course, British cruisers could hardly patrol Germany's land frontiers to stop her trading with neighbouring countries, nor could they halt shipments of iron ore from Sweden since the Baltic was virtually a German lake, and the generals on both sides thought the war would be over in three months. The British Expeditionary Force was designed for a very brief encounter, and the Germans wouldn't have time to stockpile food, fuel and munitions anyway. Economic 'bread and butter' warfare might eventually prevail, but sea power was 'slow power' – much too slow for that sort of war.

Still, Naval intelligence chief Charles Ottley had predicted that 'grass would sooner or later be growing in the streets of Hamburg.' He doubtless remembered what Mahan had called that 'noiseless pressure on the vitals of France,' but a century later, 'close blockade' of the enemy coast was no longer feasible – the moored mine had seen to that – and besides, it was now illegal to seize cargo from ships of neutral states, even if it was for the enemy.

Thus it was in the Navy's interest to argue for 'stop and search' powers at the 1910 International Maritime Conference, and the brief went to a mine warfare specialist who took over the CID when Sir George Clarke quit in a huff – Charles Ottley. He'd been Fisher's man at the second Peace Conference at The Hague, but this time poor Ottley <u>had to stumble</u> through a legalistic thicket with little guidance from

* Offer *The First World War: An Agrarian Interpretation* pp 289, 292-293

his old chief.* He had to concede that blockade *would* be a violation of international law, but no one in Whitehall seemed to take the 'Declaration of London' seriously. One CID insider suspected Fisher had agreed to it 'with the deliberate intention of tearing it up in the event of war.' The Germans would infringe the agreement, 'then with great regret we tear it up – if they don't infringe it we must invent an infringement.'†
It would be a dirty war.

---

* Offer pp 276-7
† Major Adrian Grant Duff, Assistant Military Secretary CID 1910-13 *Diary* 24 Februarty 1911

~ 16 ~

Two Armies, Two Nations

"Do you imagine you can get a conscript army for foreign service?"
- Mr Haldane, Secretary of State for War, 24th November 1906

"Keep men hungry, just hungry enough, and they will swarm to the colours to end their misery.'"
- Colonel F N Maude War and the World's Life 1907

Nineteen Hundred and Ten was a bad year for Asquith – and Haldane too. It began as it would end, with a general election. In February the Liberals' huge lead over the Conservatives shrank to just two seats and by Christmas the two parties were level pegging. There was an armistice of sorts, a 'Constitutional Conference,' and with Asquith's connivance Lloyd George quietly sounded out the Opposition about the possibility of a coalition government, with Liberal concessions on 'Home Rule' for Ireland – and conscription.* Churchill was interested for a while, but Balfour had second thoughts and backed off, so that Asquith—who two years ago stepped into the shoes of a dying man—could remain in Downing Street at the pleasure of forty Labour MPs and eighty four Irish nationalists. Lloyd George's skulduggery, if successful, would have banished his own leader to the House of Lords – a replay of that shabby attempt to kick Campbell-Bannerman upstairs – but Lloyd George would have Asquith's job one day.

Between elections the King died. Already an old man at the start

---
* Blake R *The Conservative Party from Peel to Thatcher* pp 191-2

of his reign Edward VII had lived well and done his personal constitution no favours, but his war minister owed him a few. Royal approval of the Territorials gave poor Pussy much relief,* but he was feeling the strain, and in well-reported speeches, Field-Marshal Lord Roberts – now quietly 'managed' by the new Director of Military Operations at the War Office, Brigadier-General Wilson – ridiculed the Territorial Army for its deficiencies and disappointing recruitment figures.

Undeterred, Haldane persisted in his brave attempt to reach his target. Then he was stabbed in the back by Lord Esher of all people, though he should not have been surprised. It is difficult not to dislike Reginald Balliol Brett, the royal sycophant who famously landed the First Lord of the Admiralty in trouble with a cynical 'indiscretion,' and this time Esher informed his fellow peers that Territorial enrolment had already peaked. 'Your speech gave me great pleasure,' said Lord Roberts. But the rabbit punch – that Haldane would never get his 60,000 recruits a year – was proclaimed in the *National Review* by editor Leo Maxse – another founder member of the National Service League. The Secretary for War was not amused and neither was the new King, George V. Reginald Brett was definitely not a royal favourite. Always on the inner circle, member of the Royal Commission on the Boer War and leader of the razor gang that shredded the War Office, Esher had spurned offers to run that notoriously difficult department, 'preferring power to responsibility,'† so Balfour had let him loose on the Committee of Imperial Defence as a sort of statutory layman, a feature of the Whitehall landscape no one had the courage to remove. Esher didn't warn Asquith – the CID Chairman – and the damage was done. Haldane had been savaged by one of his closest allies, in broad daylight. As chairman of the County of London Territorial Association Esher was publicly identified with the idea of voluntary service and it was a gift to the headline writers. 'Indictment by Lord Esher' gloated the *Standard*, 'Striking Article…Failure of Voluntary System……Breakdown of a Great Project.'

Haldane took it badly, blaming a 'not too particular opposition' and Esher's 'inside knowledge.' Pussy was an unlikely prize-fighter to enter the ring against unscrupulous bullies like Roberts and his chums, but the Secretary for War was in a mood to tackle them head on, in print, but by proxy. With characteristic modesty he picked Sir Ian Hamilton, the outgoing Adjutant-General who was happy to oblige his old boss by writing a pamphlet with the confusing title *Compulsory Service*. He would soon be wishing he hadn't.

Compulsory Service was a collective effort by Sir Ian and his old

---

* Allison *The National Service Issue* p 110
† Beckett *Rifleemen Form* p 237

team, but in an *aide memoire** Haldane's Military Assistant Gerald Ellison – now a Major-General – wrote, 'We have to stake everything on command of the sea.' cautiously inserting in brackets and in his own handwriting, an escape clause: 'Sailors alone can say how far command of the sea guarantees us against invasion.' Given that assurance, he says 'we can deliberately organise our military strength for Imperial purposes......' and in obedience to his chief he plays down the need for conscription, or 'compulsion,' 'keeping it as far back in our military system as we possibly can.' He prefers a professional army backed by 'a well-organised citizen force of volunteers' – and a *third* line of defence, 'a great organisation which, for financial reasons, could be in peace very little more than a paper organisation.' Now the knife goes into the master's back, the master he has served so loyally – this third line organisation, 'might well be, and should be, based on conscription' – but he has his doubts. The Regular Army and the Territorials together have 'something like half a million men' and it is 'neither possible nor necessary to contemplate a larger force,' though 'if the Continental policy is to be the first consideration, nothing short of a complete upheaval in our military system would suffice. The danger in my mind is the giving to a purely defensive policy undue prominence, and ultimately letting this policy outweigh imperial considerations.' It is the age-old dilemma – are we to be a power in Europe and let our Empire go by default – must we lose India to save Belgium? Fifty three years after the Mutiny and a couple of centuries since William of Orange sent a British army to fight in Europe's wars, Ellison wasn't the only soldier to feel uneasy about a switch in priorities – while Mr Haldane would much prefer that nobody should enquire too closely into the purpose of his 'Striking Force.'

Compulsory Service was more than a restatement of the government's 'defence policy' of navy, standing army and territorials, every man a volunteer. Sir Ian makes a strong case for the professional long service soldier – cost-effective, cheaper than all those foreign conscripts despite their low pay and 'two or three years spent in barracks,' but the beauty of the British system is that the Army has always filled its ranks with unemployed, and unemployable, 'weedy youngsters.' In a hand-written note he estimates four fifths of them enlist 'because they cannot get a job even at 15 shillings a week.' One of his aides agrees; 'compulsory home service with continuous recruit training would deprive the regular army of many thousands of 18 to 19 year-old recruits,' or as Hamilton says, 'if hungry hobbledehoys knew that they would be called up for continuous housing and feeding during the winter, the Regular Army would shrivel up from the roots.' †

---
* 'Notes for Compulsory Servvice' Hamilton MSS 5/4/1 11 July 1910
† Hamilton MSS 5/4/1

Compulsory Service was published to confirm the faith professed by both great parties for many years, either through force of habit, or electoral prudence. In an innocuous foreword, rather like the Highway Code in a later age, Mr Haldane commended Sir Ian's 'memorandum' to 'all those interested in the question of National Defence' and indeed it caused quite a stir among the chattering classes. 'It bears a peculiar literary charm' wrote the anonymous *Times* reviewer, possibly with tongue in cheek; but the *Naval and Military Record* snorted, 'If this is all that can be said for the voluntary system ... the case against compulsion is weak indeed.' Meanwhile, Repington's pen pal 'Colonel Donner und Blitzen' sagely counselled *Times* readers that, 'Voluntary service is the secret of comfort. But national service is the secret of victory.'

Despite this mixed reception – or maybe because of it – *Compulsory Service* ran to a second edition so that the First Sea Lord Admiral Sir Arthur Knyvet Wilson could put *his* name to an appendix where he firmly scotched the threat of invasion, as one would expect of the efficient seaman known affectionately on the lower deck as 'Old 'ard 'eart' – a confirmed bachelor, he wouldn't even give them Christmas shore leave. He earned his Victoria Cross in the Sudan, wielding his broken sword to rally a broken square, even using his fists on the Mahdists as well as the machine guns he brought with him. A pioneer in torpedo and submarine warfare like Fisher, but a poor administrator and 'politically naïve,' *this* Wilson was way out of his depth in Whitehall, scoring below average in the basic skills of presentation – which became embarrassingly plain a year later when he followed the other Wilson, the man from the War Office. The sailor was quite outclassed by the soldier.

Meanwhile Sir Ian Hamilton was also embarrassed if not quite outclassed. The trouble began when supporters of the opposing team swarmed noisily onto the pitch. *Compulsory Service* was a political tract, and should have been written by a politician if it had to be written at all. It was no job for a simple soldier, a decent, harmless chap who should never have been dragged into the mire and really, Mr Haldane had turned the Army into a political football. Several bystanders joined in the barracking and some venerable old soldiers reached for their inkstands. Unused to the everyday knockabout of politics Hamilton began to wilt under pressure, but he could hardly plead that publication of *Compulsory Service* took him unawares. His – and Haldane's – mainstay was Charles Harris, the man in the back office who pulled everything together. 'The Magnum Opus has gone off to press' he reported 'and the Bomb should burst upon an astonished General Staff in less than a fortnight.'

The 'Bomb' duly burst – upon an astonished Hamilton, and Haldane too. They tried damage limitation, Hamilton explaining to Field-Marshal Sir Evelyn Wood he never expected his 'essay' to appear in book form – 'I wrote it to him [Haldane] in the shape of a personal letter.' Hamilton and his master were now at bay, fending off Field-Marshal Roberts himself and even more terrifying, Lady Roberts: 'Dear Mr Haldane' wrote the redoubtable Nora, 'How I wish you and Fred could see eye to eye on the question of national training....It is both unfair and disloyal to father the bogey [of conscription] on Fred and the National Service League, who have never thought of such a thing for England.' Bruised, poor Hamilton protested that 'the entire General Staff, with one, possibly two exceptions' were either in favour of National Service or Conscription.* He should know. Harris too had noted 'a tendency in certain quarters here to test very squarely all statements made, if they appear to be obstructions on the road that leadeth to conscription.'

Roberts was quick off the mark with his own blockbuster *Fallacies and Facts*, much of it ghost-written by Leo Amery – coyly described as 'a well-known writer on the problems of imperial defence' who would soon be the Honourable Member for Birmingham South, a safe Conservative seat. Anxious to avoid more trouble, Hamilton tried to mend fences and sit on them too. He told Lady Nora 'I lunched with Amery yesterday and he says he has regularly clubbed me to death.' As in any upper-class brawl, they remembered their table manners between bouts, for this debate was reserved for a select group of 'opinion formers' who moved in the same narrow circles and remained on good terms socially. The general was concerned about Mr Haldane – 'he looks very seedy.' Indeed, the War Secretary had diabetes, but he too was to be 'clubbed to death.'

Roberts, or Amery, recalled how the *Morning Post* defence pundit Spenser Wilkinson had wanted twelve months' compulsory training for everyone, but this time, they were recycling National Service League 'policy' – four to six months' continuous drill as the 'irreducible minimum' after *ten years* of 'cadet training' in school. Then they wandered off into geopolitical never-never land; 'The acquisition of a great Colonial Empire, and the vigorous defence of German trade interests' were the 'direct fruits' of the German military system whereas the geographical distribution of the British Empire had of late become 'a steadily increasing source of danger.' †

It was Amery who let slip the League's real purpose. 'It took ten years of struggle to make good our naval triumph at Trafalgar,' he

---
* Hamilton MSS 5/4/3
† Roberts *Fallacies and Facts* pp 59-65, 118-120

argued, while 'the burden of paying heavy subsidies to allies' was bringing England 'almost to the verge of ruin.' And then the clincher: 'What if we could have followed up Trafalgar with a large army?' Counterfactuals apart, this was the clearest indication of the meaning of a 'continental commitment' for Englishmen of military age.

Fallacies and Facts was hailed as, 'a crushing reply to Sir Ian Hamilton.' Amery even feigned ignorance of the probable size of the British Expeditionary Force, asking 'Can we supply France with ...at least 30,000 men?' and resurrecting another scarecrow – a recurring Foreign Office fright; 'Suppose France despairs of British help and throws in her lot with Germany?' Then with another swipe at Hamilton he challenged the assertion that only the hungry enlisted, asking snidely if the British Army existed merely as 'an appendix to Rowton House?'

In spite of *Compulsory Service*, agitation for that very thing was intensified by the noisy propaganda of the National Service League. From his Whitehall sentry box the faithful Harris lamented that many 'friends' of the Territorial Force were losing heart. 'The NS League is as active and as mischievous as ever' he told Hamilton. 'Moreover (be it whispered) the General Staff here, under the domination of Henry Wilson' – and a more senior general, Kenny-Kelly – 'is, if not actively hostile to the Force, at any rate developing that German quality of "schadenfreude".'

Harris the sympathetic civilian insider had put his finger on the generals' dilemma – and the politicians' predicament. Without conscription they had *two* separate armies, one of long service professionals and another for civilians, 'weekend soldiers' vaguely in support. Most regulars enlisted from necessity and on discharge to the reserve were unlikely to become skilled tradesmen, whereas Territorials were usually secure in their career of choice. Years in dismal barrack rooms in Aldershot or India were not for them. They joined for the novelty, the excitement and the social life – *at home*. It would always be hard to recruit men for a 'National Army' – and people like Esher had little faith in the 'fibre and patrictism' of the masses.

As Haldane's Territorial Force emerged in a welter of wrangling and bickering, an infantryman, Captain James Tulloch, came out in favour of the 'continental' strategy and an army to go with it – but what kind of army? A Staff College graduate, Tulloch could see beyond the barrack square. 'If we desire to form a National Army that the people can take an interest in, and "run" themselves,' he said 'we must not attempt to form rules and regulations for this Army in the same cast-iron way that prevails in the Regular Army.' But would such an army be taken seriously on the continent of Europe? Just as the size and shape of the BEF was fixed by economics rather than strategy, so too, Captain Tulloch's 'National Army' could never be larger than the number of civilians willing and able to join in time of peace – an argument for conscription, perhaps?

Two armies, two nations – a far cry from George Shee's dream of social mixing through compulsory service; duke and dustman learning from each other the secret of a classless society. Unconsciously echoing the Vicar of Banbury's blast at the shirkers in his own parish, Harris wrote despairingly, 'So we dig lower into the stratum of casual labour that recruits the Regulars and Special Reserve [while] the fellows who ought to be Terriers – the young men of that great middle class that provides neither officer nor man for the Regular Army are left to their smug tennis... It is a social disease and nothing but a social remedy will cure it. If only HM would give a strong lead!'*

If only, but the new monarch was not to be relied upon. Hamilton sadly replied, 'The King has been persuaded that compulsory service, which is the best known medium for the propagation of the Socialist microbe, would add to the stability of his throne. I have lost what little court favour I ever possessed in trying to open his eyes to his ghastly error.' Hamilton was not the only general to fear conscription. Gerald Ellison too was concerned that a militarised people – a 'nation in arms' – might use its new-found strength to create a socialist state. Did he know it, much the same thought was troubling the German General Staff.

---

* 'Is a National Army necessary for the British Isles?' RUSI *Journal* February 1907 Vol LI part 1 No 348 pp 185- 187

~ 17 ~

On The Brink

"Nothing will save us except the sight of red blood running pretty freely; but whether British and German blood, or only British, I don't know – nor do I think it much matters...Blood is the necessity."

- Fred Oliver to Alfred Milner 31 March 1911

He modestly described himself as an 'officious, mischievous and ignorant puller of wires.' Like Lord Esher, Fred Oliver knew everyone who mattered in Edwardian England and despised them for their indolence and selfish pursuit of material comfort, though somewhat oddly, he was managing director of Debenhams the London fashion store in London's West End. He had to earn a living after all, unlike the noble Viscount. Oliver shared, however, Esher's contempt for parliamentary democracy, preferring to remain on the fringe of politics, wielding influence but shunning responsibility – he was a formidable pamphleteer. As an active supporter of Lord Roberts and compulsory military training for boys, he was not alone in his thirst for blood.

In 1911 France and Germany were again at odds, this time about the future of Morocco, and the French had every expectation that should this crisis turn nasty their new friends would come to their aid. But the British, or some of them, were not sure if that meant naval warfare and the odd coastal raid, or the dispatch of an army to France, and some generals would still rather fight a separate war in Flanders – the 'Belgian Option' – a dream that faded as their clumsy, ill-judged wooing of Brussels came to naught,* and their secret 'conversations' with the French gained in substance .

So far, Sir Edward Grey had carefully distanced himself from all

---
* Williamson Politics of Grand Strategy pp 214-217

this, for officially there was no military alliance with France – though he and Haldane had authorised further 'conversations,' this time with the railway companies about how many trains it would take to move 160,000 men with their guns and stores, horses and fodder to the ports of embarkation. Food and fuel would have to be stockpiled, ships chartered and arrangements made for the French rail network to take the troops to their designated place on the battlefield – a considerable undertaking of which the new Director of Military Operations Henry Wilson was not the sole begetter, nor could be, given its complexity. It is said that true greatness wears a cloak, and it was not until well after the war that one of his disciples fondly recalled the 'ardent spirit' [of Henry Wilson], his 'tireless energy, wide vision and dauntless perseverance that got these conversations translated into definite practical arrangements – though the BEF's travel plans were slotted into the French railway timetables as early as 1908, a good two years before Henry reappeared in the War Office.* In that same year (1908) Haldane asked Esher to tell the King 'in three weeks or less' Britain could put 200,000 men 'on the line of the Meuse.' If the public knew, the courtier thought 'great difficulties would arise' – but a few weeks later he had 'a four hour meeting' with Sir John French and Major Huguet.†

But 1911, a year of crisis, was also Coronation Year, and all the Dominion prime ministers had come to pay homage to their new King – George the Fifth. It would have been ungracious to let them go home again without some idea of how they would be taken care of in time of war, so they were invited by the Committee of Imperial Defence‡ to hear the First Lord of Admiralty, Reginald McKenna, explain how the Navy would starve Germany into submission while protecting the Empire's maritime links with the Mother Country – and that was it. Then it was the turn of Sir Edward Grey who assured the esteemed gathering that there was no commitment to fight on the continent of Europe, no 'entanglement.' §The script had been written by Maurice Hankey, the marine from Naval Intelligence who rejoined his old boss Charles Ottley as the CID's 'naval assistant secretary' and would soon be the Committee Secretary. Hankey, a man with close personal links to the Dominions, was well pleased with his handiwork, but his Committee of Imperial Defence would now be the sounding board for a very different tune.

Not everyone was marching in step. From the Paris embassy, Sir Francis Bertie ('the Bull') radiated confidence, assuring his masters – a good seven years after the *Entente Cordiale* – that this had removed

---

*
† Huguet p 19
‡
§

the risk of a war with France that might give Germany 'her opportunity to attack us.' Then a fresh thought troubled the envoy's mind. 'I quite understand and appreciate the difficulty for His Majesty's government to anticipate events by a formal and binding agreement in furtherance of the entente with France' he wrote anxiously a couple of months later, 'but everything military and naval ought to be arranged to meet the contingency of British and French forces having to act together... Perhaps these arrangements have been made' he artlessly suggested.*

If the British ambassador to France was really so ill-informed, the British Cabinet and the British Parliament weren't doing much better, and the British Public knew nothing at all. They could read in the newspapers there was another row between Germany and France, the Kaiser had sent a gunboat to Agadir on the coast of Morocco, and their own Government had made appropriate noises with a well-publicised warning from Lloyd George who, like Churchill, privately thought it would be 'a great pity' if the crisis didn't end in war.

But Agadir was not the only distraction for a Prime Minister clinging to power by favour of forty two Labour members of parliament *and* the eighty four Irish Nationalists whose price for support was, unsurprisingly, 'Home Rule, while just down the road the House of Lords was being cut down to size by the Parliament Act. It was a long way from Morocco.

It would have been improper for any officer lower in rank than the Chief of the Imperial General Staff to dispense gratuitous advice on crisis management to Cabinet Ministers, but Brigadier-General Wilson probably forgot the niceties of protocol in his anxiety to give the Foreign Secretary and the Secretary for War a lunchtime lecture on grand strategy. By his own account, the schoolmaster inside him was 'profoundly dissatisfied' with his pupils' grasp of the situation, Grey being 'the most ignorant and careless of the two,' not knowing about war and 'not wanting to know' – a pretty accurate appraisal, though to call him 'ignorant, vain & weak,' unfit to be Foreign Minister of 'any country larger than Portugal' was less than kind to the small nation that seized vast tracts of Africa and South America when the British weren't looking. Asked about the Russian Army – the card Grey kept up his sleeve – Wilson brusquely dismissed its worth, but he could not have known about the Russian ambassador's reassuring visit to the Foreign Office that very morning.

While peers of the realm were sweating over their future at Westminster, the shape of things to come was revealed in another piece of

---

* Esher *Journal* 2 October, 12 November, 1908, and 14 January 1909

Whitehall theatre; an extended meeting of the Committee of Imperial Defence* – a conclave summoned to announce a new dimension to the British Way in Warfare. On the twenty third of August 1911 Asquith, Haldane and Grey, plus the 'trusties' – Lloyd George, Churchill and McKenna – were shown the Army's blueprint for the next war. Gesturing at a large map, Henry Wilson explained how the British Expeditionary Force, all six divisions, was going to France where its modest contribution would just tip the balance in favour of the defence. That is (as in that War Game long ago) if the Germans took the route Henry had assigned to them, avoiding the great fortresses guarding the heart of Belgium and marching along a narrow slice of territory instead. Henry had calculated the size of an invading German army by the amount of road space required for their boots, unless – (but he left out this bit)– unless they swept through Belgium to swing round on the other side of the river Meuse and fall upon the French Army's 'left flank' – the very place assigned to the BEF.

Wilson made a forceful sales pitch – it lasted an hour and three quarters – but it was the politicians, 'those ignorant men,' who asked the obvious question, what if our little army is overwhelmed? The Director of Military Operations had no answer, or none he could prudently give – conscription, perhaps? A few weeks ago, he'd hastened to Paris to sign an 'accord' with General Dubail on the destination of the BEF – and what might be its graveyard.† Lord Esher was ill in bed on the 23rd of August and so missed all the excitement, but he was sure Wilson was 'deep in the plans of the French General staff.' Henry knew next to nothing, but he could hardly plead ignorance of French military doctrine as taught by his hero Foch and other luminaries, especially their emphasis on 'the spirit of the offensive.' The faithful pilgrim riding his bicycle round the battlefields of the Franco-Prussian War may have dreamed that one day his mentors would avenge the defeat of 1870 and regain for France the lost provinces of Alsace and Loraine, this time with a little extra help from the British.

Sir Edward Grey had long since persuaded himself that whatever happened, the French – and especially the Russians – would do the serious fighting. For Britain, this would be a naval war, but that afternoon the sailors' case was so ineptly put by the First Sea Lord, Sir Arthur Wilson (no relation), with his blustering talk of landing troops on the German coast and attacking 'signal stations,' that after Henry's performance the admiral's turn was a flop – 'puerile' said Asquith, however sceptical he was of the Army's plan. Small wonder Haldane had always wanted the sailors to have a proper 'War Staff.'

---

* TNA FO 800/180, 186
† Callwell, Wilson *Diary* 9 August 1911 Vol I p 94

The Twenty Third of August signposted no strategic watershed, since everyone took from it only what he wanted to hear. Neither Sir Arthur nor his political chief McKenna showed the slightest inclination to assist the soldiers in a 'continental adventure' whose sole purpose, the previous First Sea Lord Sir John Fisher grumbled, was 'compulsory service and an increase in army estimates and military influence.'[*] The BEF's commitment to the French Order of Battle was 'suicidal idiocy,' and he was sure public opinion would not let a single British soldier fight in a war between Germany and France. But when Sir Arthur Wilson fell from grace and McKenna was dispatched to the Home Office in exchange for the more bellicose Churchill, the new Admiralty First Lord was quite taken with the soldiers' pipe dream of a separate war on the Continent, for the 'Belgian Option' was still favoured by Sir John French and a few other generals. Asquith thought it a safer bet than sending the BEF to France, and even Henry was briefly hooked – 'we ought to be able to snaffle these Belgians,' he scoffed, despite the rejection of his amateurish advances in the past. But 'these Belgians' were in no mood to be snaffled by anyone. The Army's Chief of Staff, Nicholson was not impressed and nor was Haldane. The 'new' strategy unveiled a few days before – by Henry Wilson – had been set in stone, long since.

It would be 'imprudent,' the War Office advised,[†] for Britain to stay out of a war between France and Germany because the BEF could just tip the balance – as shown in that War Game long ago. Hankey dismissed this as 'not even a gambler's throw,' and indeed, the soldiers may have thought it wiser not to draw too much attention to the 'new' strategy. In the aftermath of August 23rd the Chief of the Imperial General Staff was back-pedalling hard, earnestly assuring the CID that plans for the BEF to fight on the continent were 'secret, hypothetical, and non-committal.' In a prim disclaimer Sir William Nicholson said *he* had never spoken to 'any French officer, not even to Colonel Huguet'—the outgoing French military attaché who'd been so deeply involved in the 'talks'—heaven forbid. Fastidiously, the army's top general explained it had been 'unavoidable' for the Director of Military Operations to consult Colonel Huguet and his colleagues on ' technical matters' – at the attachés request.[‡] It was manifestly a distasteful business for a British officer to be obliged to speak to a Frenchman at all, except perhaps as a sanitary inspector might visit a house of ill repute, not for any immoral purpose but merely to inspect the drains in the line of duty.

---

[*] TNA CAB 2/2/2 CID 114th Meeting 23 August 1911
[†] Gooch *Plans of War* pp 290-291
[‡] Steiner *Britain and the Origins of the First World War* p 198, and Marder, *The Road to War* p 386

Fearful lest anyone should get the wrong impression, General Nicholson anxiously minuted; 'first and foremost, it is placed on record that these communications are devoid of any official significance, and are in no way binding on the British and French governments.' But not even the Prime Minister had known there *were* any 'communications' until Grey let him into the secret as late as 1911.... or so Mr Asquith would have everyone believe. Despite that, Sir Arthur Nicolson, the career diplomat and now Foreign Office head, was emboldened to comfort the British ambassador in Berlin with the welcome news that the French 'would not now flinch from war with Germany.' Rattling the departmental sabre, he boasted 'We also have been making preparations very quietly, and if need be, we shall be quite prepared to render efficient aid to the French troops.'*

The Cabinet was not so bullish – the Lord Chancellor, Loreburn, feared the country might be dragged into a 'purely French' quarrel with Germany. Even the Prime Minister affected concern that these staff conversations were 'rather dangerous' and the French shouldn't be given the wrong impression. Unmoved, Sir Edward Grey retorted it would 'cause consternation' if the soldiers were ordered to sever their contacts with the French. The 'conversations,' together with recent well-publicised speeches by himself and Lloyd George had undoubtedly led them to expect assistance, but 'I do not see how that can be helped,' he shrugged.†

Asquith sought to paper over the cracks in the wall of deception, only to shoot himself in the foot with a careless indiscretion. After a difficult session in Cabinet, he told the King that a minister had asked if it had been wise to allow the military to confer with their opposite numbers without Cabinet approval? Asquith had explained that 'conversations' began in 1906 and were sanctioned by Sir Henry Campbell Bannerman [thus, not by the previous, Conservative, premier], but he, Asquith, had assured his colleagues that 'questions of policy' were not for soldiers. 'Considerable discussion ensued,' he added, but the matter was 'adjourned for further deliberation later on.'‡

Barely two weeks 'later on,' those same ministers voted by an overwhelming majority – fifteen to five – to forbid any conversations which could lead to military 'intervention' unless the Cabinet had authorised them in advance. Esher called it 'a Cabinet Cabal v the Entente and the Defence Committee,' but it made no difference. As he told the Prime Minister, Britain was committed to fight, ' whether the Cabinet likes it or not,' though he agreed it *was* 'an extraordinary

---
* Williamson p 187
† TNA WO 106/47/E2/26 20 November 1911
‡ TNA FO 800/351 12 September 1911

thing' how those staff conversations could have gotten so far without the Cabinet ever having been consulted.*

But the Cabinet never was the smoothly-functioning collective instrument imagined by outsiders, and Asquith wasn't the first to exploit this structural weakness. Traditionally, Britain was run by a secret committee with no one to record its proceedings and circulate the minutes – a secretariat didn't exist until well into the war, though the premier composed his own handwritten account for the Sovereign's eye. It was not uncommon for a minister to leave Downing Street with only a hazy notion of what had been decided, and the preference for small 'cabinet committees' – the prime minister's cronies – would fragment and enfeeble any move to call the executive to account on anything of consequence, especially defence and foreign affairs. The system could have been expressly designed to suit Grey and Haldane who refused to share their thoughts with colleagues who were understandably dismayed when they did eventually find out.

Twenty years after the Agadir crisis, one of the famous five, Lloyd George, broke ranks, recalling 'a reticence and secrecy' that denied the majority a chance to debate what commitment, if any, had been made. It seems not even he—the man living next door to Number Ten—knew about things like military arrangements with another country. One of the most powerful men in government, Lloyd George only learned of these 'arrangements' in 1911, but even then he didn't share the news with the majority who hadn't been invited to Henry Wilson's briefing. *They* had to wait another twelve months and were understandably 'aghast' when Sir Edward Grey told them.†

The Lord Chancellor, Loreburn, would soon depart for good, to be replaced by Haldane, whose job at the War Office went to his second-in-command Colonel Seely aka 'Galloper Jack' of the Hampshire Carabineers (Yeomanry). There was still some fight left in the Cabinet, though it was too late to think about locking the stable door – the horse had bolted long ago.

---

* Williamson pp 97, 204, and Searle p 499
† TNA CAB 41/33/28, and Hanham, p 98

~ 18 ~

The French Connection

I was playing golf the day
That the Germans landed;
All our troops had run away,
All our ships were stranded;
And the thought of England's shame
Altogether spoilt my game

– Harry Graham *The Englishman's Home* 1901

How they managed to invade England unnoticed by the Royal Navy will forever be a mystery. For the enemy to have chosen the North Norfolk shoreline with its shifting sand banks and treacherous undercurrents is testimony to his skill in seamanship and his detailed local knowledge – doubtless gleaned by secret agents posing as waiters in the few hotels on this sparsely populated smugglers' coast. There were 50,000 German spies in England, said War Office intelligence, and Sir Edward Grey was concerned at the 'great number' of German officers spending their annual leave in England at the seaside, making 'strategical notes' instead of building sand castles – the Foreign Secretary may have read those warnings from Colonel Trench.

At daybreak on Monday 16th September 1912 no sign remained of the invasion fleet, but the enemy had secured a twenty mile stretch of coast from the Victorian holiday resort of Hunstanton overlooking The Wash, to Wells-next-the-Sea. Meeting no resistance, twenty three thousand men were marching through the Norfolk countryside (carefully skirting the royal estate of Sandringham) with a hundred heavy guns, six thousand horses, sixty-eight machine guns, a squadron of aeroplanes and an airship, all under the command of Sir Douglas Haig. His mission was to capture London, and his cavalry had already probed as far south as Bury St Edmunds in Suffolk.

The defence of the realm was entrusted to Sir James Grierson* commanding the "Blue" army, twenty five thousand men from various commands (all unused to working together) plus a brigade of the despised territorials; while the invading "Red" army was really the Aldershot Field Force, a regular formation with its own staff officers. The next few days would be critical as reputations were made and lost on a battleground spilling across six counties – Norfolk, Suffolk, Cambridgeshire, Bedfordshire, Hertfordshire and Essex. Did they but know it, officers leading battalions in the 1912 manoeuvres would soon be commanding divisions in France and Flanders.

After years of drought, the summer of 1912 was the wettest anyone could remember. But mid-September had brought ideal campaigning weather, the long columns of khaki-clad infantry trudged along dusty roads, mingling with horse-drawn artillery, supply carts and petrol-driven trucks, even ponderous steam traction lorries. Often they had to make way for mounted regiments, each trooper clutching the regulation lance that Haig insisted should remain their chief weapon rather than the Lee-Enfield rifle they handled so skilfully. War has exciting moments – a soldier 'captured' by Haig's cavalry in the village of Balsham tore up the documents he was carrying, but the troopers carefully pieced together the fragments to find they were reading secret orders for the defence.

With diplomatic punctilio, invitations to attend the manoeuvres had been sent months before to twenty six nations †– twenty-five when HM's Man in Beijing reminded the Foreign Office that revolutionary China ought not to have been asked. The Dutch were favoured with two places (one for their colonial army) but the Belgians were clearly embarrassed by the invitation to General Jungbluth, their Chief of Staff who had just 'resigned' over a 'difference of opinion' with his government. Possibly recalling ill-considered overtures made by Henry Wilson among others, and always anxious lest their neutrality be compromised, the Belgians made polite excuses for their man. The French got three invitations, though eight British officers had been at *their* manoeuvres. The Grand Duke Nicholas led a delegation from Imperial Russia, but very interestingly, the Germans could find no one

---
* Director of Military Operations in 1905, the man who met Major Huguet "by chance"
† TNA FO371/1559, 1561

to send.

Accredited military observers would make the most of this opportunity to study at close quarters the quality of the British army, its weapons, its equipment and the way formations were handled in the field. However remote the possibility that his own army might one day have to fight the British, even the Argentine's representative would have much to reflect upon and his superiors would expect a detailed report. Every effort was made to ensure the visitors did not waste a moment. Each day after breakfast they were collected from the Rutland Arms Hotel in Newmarket and driven to selected vantage points affording a good view of troop movements and mock attacks, and at tea time they had an official briefing on the course of the day's fighting.

This was a media war reported by 124 gentlemen of the press, national, local, foreign and of course, the military correspondents of the more serious newspapers. It was also a spectator war, and crowds of onlookers followed every movement, often parking so carelessly that the troops were seriously 'inconvenienced' – senior officers and privileged spectators were 'generally the worst offenders.'

At dawn on the third day of war 'the valleys of the Cam and Granta were dense with mist.' On the edge of Fenland the ancient university town of Cambridge was still held by the territorials, and Grierson's men were clinging to the outskirts of Steeple Bumpstead near Saffron Walden in Essex, but the invaders were perilously close to the capital – only fifty miles away. The fog of war was sometimes all too real, but Grierson made better use of his tiny air force, so he always knew what the enemy was doing, and *where*. His own formations were well concealed, they moved at night, they were skilfully handled, and the 'umpires' declared him to have won the war.

The armistice brought 450 officers from both sides to Trinity College Cambridge for the post-war conference. The universities were strongly supportive of militarism – by 1914 one in three undergraduates at Oxford was in the Officer Training Corps and Cambridge was debating whether OTC membership should be necessary to get a degree. Female students were exempt, of course, but anyway Oxford didn't let them graduate formally until 1920 and Cambridge held out much longer. The proceedings were graced by the presence of His Majesty King George V, and Grierson gave a detailed account of all his moves, but Haig, the court favourite who was expected to win, made an embarrassingly incoherent response.

The secret War Office report on the manoeuvres would not be

circulated for several weeks, but the delay was not that important since a surprisingly accurate account appeared a few days later in a foreign journal, the *Revue de Paris*. A remarkably well-informed piece of reporting that corresponded closely to the subsequent official version, it was quite a scoop given the editorial time constraints. But this brief 'war' had provided a useful peg on which to hang a message of the highest importance, to judge from its title. The sham battles are described in detail and with professional insight, and the author seems very well informed of the debates in Whitehall and Westminster about the reshaping of the army and its reserves, especially the Territorial Force which he finds wanting in many ways – a view reflected in the official narrative. The Frenchman even hints, gently, that the British Army's manpower shortage might be answered by ... conscription.

With an abrupt change of gear he then embarks upon a critical assessment of Britain's strategy, generally understood as 'the British Way in Warfare'—especially economic warfare—which he judges too slow to have any effect on a land campaign. As for using troops in amphibious operations on the coast of Germany or Denmark, he politely rules that out as impracticable. Scorning the idea of an independent mission for the BEF in Belgium, he flatly declares 'the place of the British is on our [French] left flank.' Those few words heavily underline the purpose of the BEF, as conceived by Messrs Haldane and Grey, and consummated by the War Office. The article is virtually an open letter to the British government, dictating what its strategy *should* be, and *will* be – it could have been written by Henry Wilson!

The real author, the one with the by-line, was an artillery officer, Captain Antoine de Tarlé. But he was not supposed to be at the manoeuvres. His country was represented by the renowned War College commandant Ferdinand Foch, now 'general of division,' accompanied by Colonel Reboul, 85th Infantry Regiment and a Captain Cochet of the General Staff. At the last minute the War Office specifically asked for an additional fourth officer, Chef d'escadron (cavalry major) Barbier. This formidable quartet was attended by the French Military Attaché (now Colonel de la Panouse) as protocol dictated, so why did they need a *sixth* man who hadn't been invited and would not have privileged observer status, nor even press accreditation? How did he manage to note everything of importance when his presence would be a breach of diplomatic etiquette? An enterprising officer on the General Staff and clearly on his way up in the highly politicised French army, Captain de Tarlé could have mingled incognito with the crowd of onlookers, he could have read newspapers like the *Times* or *Le Monde,* or just stayed at home – his service record shows him on 'sick leave.' His more exalted colleagues would have to stay up late in their shirtsleeves as they strove to meet the magazine's deadline for hard news, but the more leisurely addition, the all-important critique of Britain's grand strategy, was already set in type.

In this indirect manner the French General Staff could avoid embarrassment at the Quai d'Orsay or in Whitehall, and still dictate to their junior partner the terms of a military alliance that did not actually exist – well, not according to Sir Edward Grey, Viscount Haldane and Prime Minister Asquith. The French were saying in effect, "Englishmen! abandon your maritime delusions, concentrate your thoughts – and your absurdly small army – in the one place that matters, in *France*, to fight under our tutelage and under our command!"

The timing was opportune. By 1912 the French Army was still licking its bruises from the protracted Dreyfus affair, but the mood was changing. The Agadir crisis over Morocco a year before had persuaded left-wing anti-clerical politicians that the Third Republic was in more danger from the German Army than a home-grown military élite of catholics and closet monarchists.

France's top generals were scratching their heads trying to guess where the Germans would attack, and brooding over their own options. Ever since the debacle of 1870 * they had nervously looked eastward, but now it seemed the enemy's main thrust might be elsewhere. But if the conscripts who formed the bulk of the French Army were concentrated in the north, they would be thrown into a frontier battle before they were ready for combat. Meanwhile, the prospect of regaining the lost provinces of Alsace and Lorraine was a powerful incentive to go on the offensive eastward. It would play well with the public, it conformed to the doctrine of all-out attack as preached in the Staff College – and it would catch the enemy off balance, disrupting his advance through Belgium. A pre-emptive counter-strike northward was ruled out for another reason – the Belgians were wary of Anglo-French moves to draw them into war, and had put most of their army along the frontier facing France, not Germany. It was generally accepted that the Germans would not hesitate to use the south east of Belgium as a corridor, but no one, not even Henry Wilson, imagined a huge German army lunging right across the country – to descend upon a small British army.

Though of course, the Expeditionary Force would not be there. The British government had always denied there was any commitment, and to the very last moment the little BEF had no part in the order of

---

* The German Empire had annexed the French provinces of Alsace and Lorraine after their victory in the Franco-Prussian war of 1870.

battle, but French generals could hardly be ignorant of the detailed arrangements to make sure the BEF *could* arrive 'on the left flank.' Such a modest contribution would be of marginal use, but it would signal the end of Britain's traditional maritime posture *and* the beginning of an unconditional open-ended commitment to France, even in a war to regain France's lost provinces. As Foch quipped, they needed only *one* English soldier – 'but we would make sure he was killed' – for once the British were fighting *and* dying on French soil, there could be no turning back. The little 'Expeditionary Force' would swell in size as more young men were sucked in – with and without conscription – to fight for France, never mind Belgium. But in 1912, foreigners like Foch and that obscure French Captain could not imagine that the British Army was about to undergo its greatest test of loyalty in a corner of the United Kingdom that was England's 'oldest colony.'

~ 19 ~
# Agent Orange, and Mutiny on the Boyne

"The Army have done what the Opposition failed to do!"
— *Major-General Henry Wilson, 1914*

Henry Hughes Wilson hailed from Protestant Ireland, that seemingly-inexhaustible source of talent for the British Army wherefrom, either by birth or descent, the Army had historically swelled its upper ranks. Field Marshals Wolseley, Roberts, Kitchener and not a few generals were Irish Protestants, as were the Gough brothers; Johnnie, killed on the Western Front in 1915; Hubert whose Fifth Army was shattered in 1918; and the four 'Irish' generals, Dill, Brooke, Alexander and the bombastic Montgomery. Likewise their Commander-in-Chief General Lord Gort, whose Expeditionary Force was driven into the sea in 1940. There were others of note, not least Arthur Wellesley (Wellington, 1769–1852) who preferred to distance himself from his ethnic origins. But if the Anglo-Irish were over-represented in the officer corps when the Iron Duke flourished, their number had shrunk to a quarter by the mid-nineteenth century; just one in seven when Victoria died. By 1913 the tally of Irish-born 'other ranks' was less than a tenth of the Army's total strength, but Anglo-Irish *officers* were still thick on the ground: "Nor lack we still of heroes with Saxons to compete, While Roberts rules our Armies, and Beresford our Fleet" ...ran the jingle. *That* Field Marshal, so recently commander in chief in Ireland, did eventually rule all of the British Army, but he never hid his Protestant faith or his trenchant views on the Irish Question, while Charles Beresford, the Irish peer shuttling smoothly between the House of Commons and the Fleet he never ruled entirely, was no closet Unionist either.

Henry Wilson was born near Edgeworthstown in County Longford – Leinster Province – seventy miles west of Dublin. His father James, High Sheriff, deputy Lieutenant and local magistrate, inherited the Currygrane estate from *his* father, a Belfast shipping magnate. With such forbears it was natural that Henry should be faithful to the Protestant Church of Ireland and the Union with Great Britain – the touchstone for all 'Anglo-Irish' officers. They had watched with foreboding the rise of the Irish Republican Brotherhood and they were well acquainted with Fenian ways; the destruction of crops; the maiming of cattle and horses on the estates of Protestant gentry – and murder too – and they loathed the idea of Irish self-government. It was an ingrained reaction reaching back through centuries of mutual hostility, terror and bloody reprisal. To the Catholic majority, Ireland was England's oldest colony struggling to be free of absent landlords, poverty and Protestant vigilante bands. But to the Anglo-Irish landowners, and the smallholders, shopkeepers, businessmen and skilled craftsmen in the province of Ulster – all those respectable-looking men in bowler hats marching with drawn swords under the banners of the Orange Order chanting 'No surrender!' – the prospect of Home Rule, or 'Rome Rule,' for *all* of Ireland including Ulster, was unthinkable.

'Ulster will fight, and Ulster will be right!' cried the third son of the seventh Duke of Marlborough way back in 1886. Chafing under Lord Salisbury's leadership of the Conservatives, the ambitious Lord Randolph Churchill recanted his belief about 'those foul Ulster Tories' and played the Orange Card in a bid to win fame by overthrowing Gladstone's Liberal government. 'Please God it may turn out the ace of trumps and not the two' – he confided to a friend as he took the boat train to Belfast. Braving the scepticism and suspicion of those same foul Ulster Tories, Randolph acted the part of loyalist demagogue and his audience loved it.

Never a strong suit, Mr Gladstone's Bill for Irish Home Rule was thrown out along with its author and the 'Irish Question' perversely remained unanswered. It wasn't a big talking point in the 1906 election, nor with their huge majority did the Liberals show much interest until Lloyd George took on the House of Lords with his provocative 'People's Budget.' Two elections in 1910 wiped out that Liberal majority, and now Asquith was clinging to power courtesy of the Labour Party and 84 Irish Nationalists, who expected Home Rule as their reward. Thus the venerable 'Irish Question' now became 'the Ulster

Crisis' – a piece of theatre that threatened to split the British Army, and the United Kingdom too.

The curtain rose on Sir Edward Carson, sometime Conservative Solicitor-General, the lawyer whose skilful cross-examination brought down Oscar Wilde – another Dubliner. The oddly charismatic 'King Carson' his public face 'set permanently in a scowl of righteous defiance,' willingly ascended the Ulster Unionist throne despite being born in the wrong city, but his heart was in the right place. 'With the help of God you and I joined together ...will yet defeat the most nefarious conspiracy that has ever been hatched against a free people,' he promised a huge gathering, and he urged those same free people to prepare for the government of the 'Protestant Province of Ulster' should Home Rule for Ireland become law.*

An outsider might have wondered what all the fuss was about. Asquith had been 'blackmailed' by those Nationalists at Westminster who were keeping him in power, but that was to be expected in the rough game of politics, and the Bill grinding its way through the legislative machine promised a rather uneventful time for Irish politicians of either persuasion. They'd be responsible for 'good government' – but not finance; and they wouldn't be allowed to run the schools, Catholic or Protestant. It would years too before they got their hands on the police force, and because the land of saints and scholars would stay firmly inside the United Kingdom, they wouldn't need a Foreign Office – and they certainly wouldn't have their own Army. 'Home Rule' did *not* mean 'Rome Rule,' though Lord Esher said you couldn't trust those Catholics. But for Field-Marshal Roberts and his cronies, especially Henry Wilson, this small corner of the United Kingdom was to be the setting for a trial of strength between Government and Opposition, a cynical exercise in public relations – *and* the stage for mutiny and sedition, open rebellion and even civil war.

Meanwhile the Conservative Opposition at Westminster went head hunting for Balfour's replacement. They chose a Canadian-born Glasgow iron merchant with a solid Ulster-Presbyterian pedigree, the 'meekly ambitious' Andrew Bonar Law, who promptly re-affirmed his Party's colour preference, appearing in a Belfast spectacular with a troupe, or tableau, of seventy English, Scots and Welsh Conservative-Unionist parliamentarians shipped across the water for the occasion. Rudyard Kipling scribbled some appropriate verse for the *Morning Post,* and the Opposition Leader made an extravagant speech. Then, to mark that holy date in the Orange calendar, the Twelfth Day of July, marking the Battle of the Boyne,† Bonar Law – 'a good straight man'

---
* Stewart p 48
† (1st of July 1690 Old Style)

thought Esher – put on a grand performance at Blenheim, the Churchill family's ducal palace in Oxfordshire where Randolph's turncoat son Winston had forfeited his place in the Orange tabernacle when he'd changed his mind about Home Rule. Explaining how Mr Asquith's Liberal government (which included Winston) was a 'revolutionary commiittee' that had 'seized upon despotic power by fraud' the leader of His Majesty's loyal opposition could imagine 'no length of resistance to which Ulster can go in which I should not be prepared to support them' – with the backing of the 'overwhelming majority' of the British people.*

Greatly comforted and encouraged, close on half a million Ulstermen (and women) put their names to a 'Covenant' pledging themselves to civil disobedience or revolution should Home Rule for Ireland be enacted by the parliament of the United Kingdom. A British version of the Covenant collected two million signatures, claimed the Union Defence League, Field-Marshal Roberts affirmed his readiness to lay down his life in rebellion against the Crown, as did Rudyard Kipling and Sir Edward Elgar, while the British League for the Support of Ulster, backed by a hundred peers and 120 MPs, sought to enlist young Englishmen to fight for the cause across the water.† Carson's nine-county 'Protestant Province of Ulster' (actually, just the four counties where they had a majority, unlike the other five where the Catholics were more numerous) was now set on a collision course with His Britannic Majesty's Government.

But if it came to that, how would the Ulstermen fight? Touring his little kingdom Carson was escorted by followers 'with dummy rifles,' sneered the *Manchester Guardian,* but soon a hundred thousand Ulstermen were drilling openly, and legally, pledged to overthrow the State by force of arms if Home Rule became law, and form their own 'provisional' government – all very sensible, thought Henry Wilson.‡

Spirits were high but this band of brothers was still a stage army that would be swept away by the authorities – though not the local police. The British Army's Commander-in-Chief in Ireland, the Right Honourable Sir Arthur Paget whose grandfather Lord Uxbridge lost a leg at Waterloo – disposed of rather more firepower than Ireland's Chief Secretary Augustine Birrell, the politician responsible for the Royal Irish Constabulary, so it was the General, not the Cabinet minister, who would call the shots. In times of civil disorder the Army could be put onto the street as a giant riot squad acting 'in aid of the Civil Power,' all ranks supposedly impartial and blessedly ignorant of

---
* Stewart p 57
† Jeffery p 116
‡ Jeffery p 115

Irish history. Paget's men were not in Ireland to keep the Germans out, or ease overcrowding in mainland barrack rooms. They were there to keep *all* of 'John Bull's Other Island' inside the United Kingdom, not just the four mainly Protestant counties – though the Catholics might think the mission was to keep *them* in their place.

Civil War usually requires two sides, but the Ulster Volunteers and the catholic Irish Volunteers didn't seem very interested in fighting each other. This time the Protestants would be in open rebellion against the Crown to which they somehow still professed allegiance, and oddly, the battleground would be the one part of Ireland where British soldiers were generally accepted, though the enemy would be not the Catholic Irish, but the British Army.

The Ulstermen's rebel force was now taking shape under the guidance of serving British Army officers who happened to be 'on leave.' Their commander in chief was a retired general* selected by Lord Roberts who declined the honour for himself, being busy with his National Service League. That talented actor-manager in uniform Henry Wilson would have been the Field Marshal's 'Chief of Staff,' a commitment which might have clashed with his task of preparing the Expeditionary Force for the continental war he confidently expected, though this Director of Military Operations could always manage to slip away from his desk at the War Office to aid his former boss.

They made a good team. Wilson writing the speeches that the Field-Marshal delivered with apparent sincerity to enthusiastic audiences, calling for 'compulsory training' (though Henry wanted all-out conscription) while belittling Haldane's Territorials. As Roberts continued to make headlines with his ceaseless propaganda, the pair took more than a friendly interest in the growth of a sectarian force which, by a strange irony, embraced the very principle of voluntary service they were so keen to undermine in the rest of the United Kingdom. It seemed that Ulster was the exception, a special case, and Bonar Law had already given public encouragement to *these* volunteers, even 'reviewing' the rebels paraded for his inspection, and now this private army was to be traded in the futures market for sedition.

In one of his frequent, informal and quite improper counselling sessions with the Opposition Leader, Henry offered his client one of Mrs Wilson's bright ideas; that Carson should 'pledge the Ulster troops [the rebels] to fight for England if she was at war.' Such a generous inducement would surely prevent a Liberal government using the British Army to force Home Rule on loyal Ulster folk. As her grateful husband told his diary, Bonar Law was 'much pleased' with this artless

---

* Stewart pp 73-4, and see Jeffery pp115-6

notion, but Henry's 'old chief' Roberts would have gone further, advising the troops there were 'no ordinary rules' in Civil War – the soldier was a citizen and could choose sides. Bonar Law, and Carson too, had doubts as to the wisdom of this useful tip becoming public knowledge.*

Rebel headquarters were now in Belfast's Old Town Hall, where in a flattering burlesque of the institution that nurtured them, the captains, majors and colonels who yesterday were proud to wear the King's uniform – and would instantly recognise old friends in the Army they might soon be facing – now answered to a 'Revolutionary Military Council.' They had to organise communications, transport, a medical corps, and find armbands for fighting men without uniforms. Talent abounded – mechanics, railway staff, telegraphists, even code breakers, and there was no shortage of clerks, typists and motor cycle dispatch riders. The rebels had an edge over the real Army – private automobiles were still a luxury, but their owners would willingly drive 'volunteer' detachments on familiar roads at night, and besides, Carson's men were genuinely popular throughout the Protestant districts, so they could count on information or at least passive support from their compatriots in local government – and in the Royal Irish Constabulary.

The rebellion was carefully planned A 'flying column' – 5,000 strong – would block roads, occupy public buildings and 'requisition' arms. They were to seize heavy weapons by force, or by 'previous arrangement' with the British artillerymen. The police would be 'relieved of their duties,' trains would be stopped, telegraph, telephone and cable links cut, and Ulster would be sealed off from the rest of the United Kingdom.† Henry praised the 'discipline and spirit' of the rebels and promised his diary he'd come over to inspect them.‡

Meanwhile the legitimate authorities were just as determined. In a show of force to call King Carson's bluff, Seely in the War Office dispatched reinforcements and Churchill at the Admiralty sent warships. The rebel command was duly impressed, especially as it knew of every move, often before government forces did, thanks to its principal adviser in Whitehall, Henry Wilson.

The Ulster Crisis had now become the Army Question. If it came to a fight, would the British Army shoot back if shot at? Would it shoot first – or would it shoot at all? To be sure, the Army had ruthlessly put down the Protestant-led United Irishmen's rising in 1798, but that was long ago and these hard-working, reliable, friendly people were dif-

---
* Stewart p 137
† Stewart pp 125-128
‡ *Diary* January 1914 Calwell Vol I pp 137, 135-6

ferent. Besides, the Army never got involved in politics. Most officers, especially those of upper-middle class or aristocratic descent, held politicians in disdain, especially the sort that preached social equality and redistribution of wealth. They would describe themselves as Conservative with a small 'c' whenever they thought about it, and their sympathy lay with people who professed loyalty to the Crown and the established order – and of course, the Empire – for Army chiefs feared a rebellious nationalist Ireland might be the signal for another, and greater, uprising in India.* Yet in the matter of Ulster, the officer corps was dangerously gullible, and the British Army's senior management team was about to show itself as somewhat less than competent.

Unwilling to post more guards on military arsenals as instructed, the general across the water was called to London to be told things were more serious than he thought. But Sir Arthur was unwilling to upset the locals with a display of force. Like so many of his kind, he was convinced the Irish (Catholic) Nationalists were the threat, and they could be dealt with by 'loyal' Ulstermen. When War Secretary Colonel Seely, Hampshire Carabineers (Yeomanry), tried to explain the facts of military life – that soldiers had to obey orders – Paget got into a right old muddle. Seely had previously given him some woolly advice that if his soldiers thought they might be ordered to take some 'outrageous and illegal action, for instance, to massacre a demonstration of Orangemen who were causing no danger to the lives of their neighbours' then they – the troops – would be justified in 'contemplating' refusal to obey. 'Galloper Jack' further confused the general's mind with an escape clause for any officer whose home was in Ulster and who might suffer pangs of conscience if he had to put down a rebellion by the people living next door. Ever sparing of common sense, let alone tact, Sir Arthur firmly believed these instructions came from the King †– he never took orders from those 'swines of politicians.' Returning to his headquarters, he summoned his unit commanders and bleakly told them the country might be ablaze in twenty four hours. If they were ordered to impose Home Rule on Ulster by force, officers who actually lived in the Province would be allowed to 'disappear' for the duration of hostilities, but if the others refused to march north they would be instantly dismissed from the army – resignations would *not* be accepted. ‡

The spirited young gentlemen of the Third Cavalry Brigade stationed at the Curragh racecourse outside Dublin took offence at this implied slur on their honour and almost to a man demanded dismissal. They may not have seen themselves as the Army's militant tendency,

* Jeffery pp 120-121
† Srachan p 69
‡ Stewart p 155

but 'public opinion' was not entirely on their side. These officers had 'asserted the right to lay down the conditions under which they would continue to serve the King' declared the *Manchester Guardian*, and thus it was an act of 'contingent mutiny' – an opinion upheld by more recent legal authority – for which they should have faced a court-martial. 'They have not been so treated, first, because they were rich men; secondly because they had the prejudices of their class.'

It was now the turn of the brigade commander Hubert Gough to hurry over to London with two of his colonels, to 'negotiate' with the government on their behalf. These well-bred shop stewards, coached in the wings by the ever-present Henry Wilson, demanded a written assurance that the Army would *not* be used to 'crush' political opposition to the Home Rule Bill. The horse soldiers got their scrap of paper – composed by the top brass and improved on by the War Secretary and Viscount Morley, Lord President of the Council, but both statesmen forgot to tell the Prime Minister about this slap in the face for civilian authority. That night a jubilant Wilson persuaded himself it would bring down the government to which he, a serving officer, owed allegiance. In an exultant scribble to Roberts he reckoned 'poor fat Haldane' might have to resign, and the Cabinet too, perhaps, but he was wrong. Softer heads would roll. The Cabinet instantly repudiated the 'promise' so thoughtlessly given by those unworldly men in the War Office, whereupon Colonel Seely, General Sir Spencer Ewart and Sir John French the Army's Chief of Staff were greatly abashed, and being officers and gentlemen fell upon their swords.

At a stroke the British Army was headless in the nation's hour of need. Replacements were quickly found from the stock of spare generals, but such were the talents of the departing War Secretary that the Prime Minister could find no one with similar qualifications for the post, so Mr Asquith was obliged to assume that responsibility in addition to his own duties. As for 'poor fat Haldane,' *he* was not in the least minded to resign from anything. It was a good two years since he exchanged his War Office chair for the Lord Chancellor's more comfortable Woolsack, though he did make a clumsy attempt to reconcile that worm-eaten fable – 'the Army never interferes in politics' – with the real world.

The Cabinet of 'swines and robbers' Field Marshal Roberts called them (though he quickly denied it) had reasserted its lawful control over the Army, but in truth it was the Profession that prevailed over the politicians, as the soldiers smoothly closed ranks to draw a line beneath the Curragh 'Incident' and move on as if nothing had happened. Barely two months after the officers' mutiny, Brigadier-General

George Townshend Forestier-Walker was still tracing a near-invisible line between the use of troops 'for the purpose of Quelling Disorder' and their employment 'to coerce Ulster to accept the Home Rule Bill.' Presumably expecting a Protestant uprising and the emergence of a Unionist 'Orange Free State' this officer reminded his men which side they were on as far as he was concerned. 'No attempt must be made by the [British] authorities to seize the Post Office or Custom House, or otherwise prevent the establishment of a provisional government' he ordered. As the time approached for Home Rule to become the law of the land, a new 'Military Governor' Major General Sir Nevil Macready – himself no Orange sympathiser – brought instructions that if Carson did set up his 'Provisional Government' the Lord Mayor of Belfast would be responsible for public order, using the police – and the rebel Ulster Volunteer Force. The sizeable British garrison was to remain in barracks – the troops may have wondered why they were there at all.

Springtime for Carson, and Ulster too, had brought excitement and a conviction that the rebels had outfaced the King's ministers – with a little extra help from some of the King's men. It was a great victory, all the more remarkable since the Ulstermen did not have to fire a shot, which was just as well since most of them had nothing to shoot with. For months on end they'd been drilling and parading and marching about just like real soldiers, but it was hard for a volunteer to remain enthusiastic pretending his broomstick was a rifle. If shove came to shoot, these freedom fighters would look very foolish. Somehow, weapons must be found, and quickly. A few rifles had been smuggled from mainland Britain under the nose of customs officers who didn't ask what was inside those heavy crates labelled 'machinery,' but that wasn't enough. Screwing up his courage, the rebel commander, general Sir George Richardson – Lord Roberts' pet – gave his reluctant go-ahead to an ambitious escapade.

In a string of adventures that could be straight out of a yarn by Erskine Childers or John Buchan, twenty thousand rifles were purchased from an arms dealer in Hamburg. A few weeks later, and undetected by the Royal Navy, a small tramp steamer the *Mountjoy* began to unload her cargo at Larne one night in April 1914 – a month after the Curragh mutiny. Customs officials and police – surrounded by a large crowd of 'onlookers' – noticed nothing unusual as the rifles, with large quantities of ammunition, were removed and distributed by friendly motorists, while two more ships were on the way *The Times* ran excited accounts and Field-Marshal Roberts applauded.

There was no difficulty in paying for all this expensive hardware. The rebel war chest was topped up by some very respectable people –

Lord Milner raised £30,000 from Waldorf Astor. The Duke of Bedford, Lord Rothschild and Lord Iveagh gave £10,000 each and Rudyard Kipling sent a cheque for £30,000.* Four months after the *Mountjoy* broke Churchill's flimsy blockade, another arms shipment – this one partly organised by Erskine Childers – was unloaded in broad daylight at Howth near Dublin. The authorities had looked the other way in Ulster, but these weapons were for the Irish National Volunteers and this time the British Army *did* intervene, but clumsily, shooting into a hostile crowd. Three people were killed and thirty eight wounded.†

Home Rule was now law, though not in force and never would be. Nevertheless, King Carson's troops were parading the principal streets of Belfast with their new rifles and mounting guard outside the Ulster Hall for the inaugural meeting of the 'Provisional Government.' Henry Wilson now thought Ireland should be 'flooded with troops,' and with characteristic irresponsibility Esher advised the other king (George) that Carson should 'precipitate a crisis in the higher interests of the monarchy and empire,' and indeed by the end of July 1914 ninety thousand men were waiting for the signal to start a civil war that might spread far beyond Ireland. But Carson stayed his hand, and soon many of his rebels would enlist to fight in another war – serving the State they had so recently sworn to overthrow.

---

* Stewart p 136
† Stewart p 230

~ 20 ~

Conspiracy and Confusion

"How we can get out of the commitments of the General Staff with honour, I cannot understand. It seems all so shifty to me."

- Viscount Esher (Reginald Brett) 12th March 1913

Mutiny, rebellion and private armies were in fashion now, but Field Marshal Roberts had long been using his National Service League, and the House of Lords, to discredit Haldane's volunteer Territorial army. Citing its supposed 'inefficiency' to gain cross-party support for conscription – he was 'desperately keen' on the idea of a wholesale 'transfer' of the TA to a 'Union Defence Force.'* The Field Marshal's willing helpers included Amery, Milner and Fred Oliver; the latter being that shopkeeper who was so keen to see blood 'flowing freely' – all of them sharing Roberts,' and Henry Wilson's contempt for legality, parliament and constitution.

The Territorial 'army' was a magnet for mischief makers like the Viscount Esher, and Repington, who gave it his approval in *The Times*, while using his 'National Defence Association' with its tiny but influential membership to 'support' the TA until conscription became politically acceptable – whereupon he would 'raise Cain.' Lenin would have recognised the stratagem – to back the Territorials 'as the rope supports a hanged man.' Honest men were deceived – one battalion commander was proud to serve on the council of the NDA, 'an association which is very largely interested in promoting the interests of the Territorial force.' †

---

* Amery Diary 5 January 1914

But Repington would not be the hangman, for he had no monopoly of mischief. He was outranked and outclassed by his old friend and brother officer, the ever upwardly mobile Brigadier-General Henry Wilson – soon to be Major-General – whose self-righteous intrusion into Repington's private life had put an end to the man's army career. They held much in common, detesting all things German and holding the Orangemen's cause holy – though Repington had no link with Ireland. Both wanted conscription and both affected a patrician contempt for political institutions, especially civilian control of the military, but any trace of comradeship had long since vanished. Repington detested this 'arch-intriguer' and 'low class schemer' but Wilson shrugged off the insults. The man was 'a fool,' he told Roberts, 'though a charming writer.' Fool or knave, Repington was a man of straw whose only assets were his urbanity and his paper-thin reputation as 'military expert.' Whereas Wilson, by his devious exploitation of people and position, wielded far greater influence inside the War Office and beyond than his actual rank merited, and it was he who would raise Cain, not 'that lying brute' Repington

Meanwhile the National Service League, noisier than ever, claimed a large following in both Houses of Parliament, and in the Cabinet that one-time Volunteer Lloyd George was thought to be a closet 'compulsionist.' But as always, Government, Opposition and 'public opinion' too, shied away from conscription, and one zealot failed spectacularly in a by-election. A private member's bill for compulsory Territorial service, backed by Admiral Beresford (now retired), met the usual fate, as did a move in the House of Lords to compel 'public school boys, graduates and the professions' to join, *and* anyone earning £400 a year – 'the minimum for a gentleman.' Government and Opposition Whips quickly squashed that one. 'Pussy' had tried to appease the Field-Marshal with a meaningless title; 'Colonel-in-Chief of the Veterans' Reserve' – rechristened 'National Reserve' – but no one could take seriously a 'third army' of old soldiers without weapons, their 'uniform' a buttonhole badge because the quartermaster's issue did not allow for middle-age spread. Besides, this Colonel-in-Chief was not for turning.

As Haldane recalled, the generals advised him that conscription would produce 'a mob in place of an army,' and when his replacement Seely – a National Service League founder member – told the House of Commons that the General Staff was against 'compulsory service,' it was Henry Wilson who angrily tried to make Sir John French, the new Chief of Staff, resign in protest. What the generals really meant was

† Col R A Johnson, RUSI *Journal* February1912 Vol LVI No 408 pp209- 37 – and see Allison p 117

that 'compulsion' was of no use if it only produced men for 'home defence.' Wilson's leisure hours were spent in furthering the cause of conscription and fostering revolt in Ulster, but his day job was to prepare a small army of professional soldiers – volunteers all – to fight just across the English Channel in a war that would be over long before any conscripts could arrive.

The picture was distorted by a topic that never quite lost its allure, the 'invasion threat,' and another CID sub-committee duly gnawed at the same old bone, again at Repington's instigation – this time, it is said, in 'a circuitous attempt to handcuff the full-blown implementation of Wilson's continental strategy.' Oddly, it was Roberts who got Wilson and Repington into the same room to decide what the committee should be told. Roberts had testified in the 1907 Inquiry under Repington's direction. but now he took his cue from another impresario, the Director of Military Operations. Too late, Repington found his one-time friend and long-standing foe had not only captured the Field-Marshal but the War Office too. Now he saw what Wilson and the General Staff wanted – an army of conscripts for France in case the BEF was outnumbered and overwhelmed, as seemed all too likely.* Forgetting his earlier disdain for Blue Water – 'until we have put an end to all this damned nonsense that is written about sea power we shall never get our national army' – he now discerned in the Royal Navy a force equal to '500,000 bayonets' for France 'at the decisive point.'† Reading that, Wilson said the Fleet wasn't worth 500 bayonets – and not even one bayonet to the French.‡

The Defence Committee laboured to produce the inevitable mouse, a timid 'recommendation' that *one* regular army division should stay at home just in case someone invaded. Asquith however was promptly leaned upon by the War Office, for this Director of Military Operations was determined that the only military operations worth directing would be on the left flank of the French Army, where he had already committed the entire Expeditionary Force, all six divisions.

Realising this train had left the station without him, Viscount Esher studied the small print on the back of his ticket and began to fret. For this professed believer in Blue Water, the regular long-service army was a sort of outsize landing party, also available for 'Home Defence' since the Territorials were so useless, as he told a fellow peer. Therefore Britain's commitment to France 'by inference and assumption' was a futile gesture for a nation without a large army, and that 'honourable undertaking' old Campbell-Bannerman had grumbled

---

* Williamson p 306, Ryan p 134
† *The Times* 6th, 7th February 1913
‡ *Diary* 14 February 1913

about could only be fulfilled by conscription – otherwise, the Expeditionary Force would have 'no business on the Continent.' It was a remarkable statement by the man who in 1906 took it upon himself to 'authorise' the generals to prepare the army to fight in France, and had ever since been privy to discussions with the French military, as he constantly boasted.

It is difficult to imagine, though, what Wilson and his team were thinking as they fine-tuned the plan for the British Army to return to France after nearly a hundred years, for his vigorous presentation to the Committee of Imperial Defence in August 1911 could not hide the yawning gap between intention and reality. If he and his superiors in the War Office expected Britain's expeditionary force to make an appreciable difference in a struggle between two very large armies, how could they be so sure? The Kaiser was not persuaded, any more than the French. But to give the BEF sufficient numbers, mobility and firepower would require a huge slice of the Navy's budget, and such a reversal of priorities would be hard to explain, especially if the government came clean about its 'continental commitment.' Besides, doubling the size of the BEF would keep the entire British Army at home, abandoning the empire. And if Lord Roberts *had* managed to 'persuade' both Parties to agree on 'compulsory training' – conscription – in time of peace, would that have persuaded the Kaiser's generals to take Belgium off their plan for victory in the West?

Like that good General Nicholson in the War Office, the Foreign Secretary preferred to avert his gaze and hold a handkerchief to his nostrils at the merest hint of an alliance with a foreign power, despite his secret encouragement of the military. Having the Expeditionary Force as another card up his sleeve gave Sir Edward freedom of choice, or so he thought, but it was a tricky balancing act. A public commitment to France might provoke the Germans to launch a pre-emptive first strike, but if he kept the French guessing, *they* might think he wasn't serious and, in despair, turn to Germany – that perpetual Foreign Office bogey. You just couldn't be sure. 'How difficult it is to work with the French who never seem to act in a straightforward manner' grumbled one senior FO man, and Grey too deplored 'this aggressive spirit in France.'[*] In his department, the *entente* was merely a 'state of mind' – a friendly understanding, not an 'undertaking,' however honourable – and certainly no military alliance. And while his other achievement, the Anglo-Russian 'entente,' had taken the heat off the North West Frontier, this could only alarm the Germans who, ever fearful of a war on two fronts, had even more reason to strike a swift knock-out blow in North West Europe. Sir Edward was walking on a

---
[*] TNA FO 800/166 11 March 1913

tightrope — no wonder he fell off.

His faltering reach was still a global one. The FO's 'senior clerks' — a term that puzzled foreign envoys who thought they were talking to the office boy — were an expensively educated and socially exclusive élite with wide connections. Sir Eyre Crowe for instance, himself half-German, had a German wife, and though like Haldane he was wary of German intentions, he bore no enmity towards that country. (Crowe was also related to defence pundit Spenser Wilkinson, but nobody's perfect.) These desk diplomats spent their days reading telegrams and dispatches from British embassies and consulates, and dealing with the 'informal empire' — including Egypt, the 'Veiled Protectorate.' They handled Britain's commercial interests from China to Mexico, managing too, the affairs of Morocco where several European states had their say, where only the wishes of the Moroccan people themselves could safely be ignored. These 'senior clerks' — Grey's policy advisers — also shifted a prodigious amount of routine correspondence that could well have been left to the office boy. They also habitually strayed into the Colonial Office backyard where they rubbed shoulders with the Indian civil service — Foreign Office grandee Sir Charles Hardinge took the Viceroy's job in his stride — and they still found time to compose lengthy memoranda on the importance of Britain's maritime power; the value of the *Entente;* and much else. Yet however splendid the view from Whitehall, the steady decline of British influence since the days of Palmerston should have been plain to every foreign secretary, even Grey. Britain was a nation 'punching above its weight.'

Jealous of his own preserve and riled when the party faithful showed interest in the arcane world of foreign policy, Sir Edward still professed belief in the principle of collective cabinet responsibility. He willingly shared the burden of government with ministerial colleagues, using his forensic skills (a fourth class degree in jurisprudence) as arbiter between mineworkers and coal owners in the prolonged dispute of 1912. He might instead have led the mission to Berlin—that half-hearted bid to halt the naval arms race—but, like his King, this Foreign Secretary didn't do'abroad' leaving it instead to Haldane, who was badly briefed and hindered by 'amateur diplomatists,' although he *was* fluent in German.

Grey not only had to deal with his Cabinet colleagues, a no-longer 'silent majority' fretting about those 'secret conversations'; i.e. the staff talks they had only just heard about. Faced by growing suspicion and discontent in parliament and beyond, his response was to exchange letters with the French ambassador about 'joint consultations' should either side have 'grave reason to expect an unprovoked attack by a third Power' or, something that 'threatened the general peace' (meaning *the Entente*). There was no mention of any 'secret, hypothetical and non committal' arrangements the military people might have made – which, officially of course they hadn't. The French were not amused by this diplomatic waffle, and few in the House of Commons were impressed by the Prime Minister's habitual stone-walling of awkward questions. When Unionist Free-Trader Hugh Cecil, son of the Marquess of Salisbury, suggested the Government had 'given an assurance that, in the event of war, Britain must send a very large armed force to operate in Europe,' – Asquith denied the charge. The same MP helpfully proposed a 'co-ordination of foreign policy to see how far the military resources of the country were really sufficient to carry out the commitments of the nation.'

Of course, any politician wanting to know more had only to walk down the road to the Royal United Services Institution, that venerable strategic sounding-board where admirals and generals gathered to discuss the business of war, where Haig and Haldane spoke on the subject and George Shee called for a 'Pan-Britannic Militia.' There, the enquirer could thumb through recent numbers of the Institution's *Journal* for a translation of 'The British Army in a Continental War' to see what was arranged for his countrymen. The place of the British Expeditionary Force, he would discover, was indeed 'on the left flank of the French Army.' Staff Captain Antoine de Tarlé was not the only Frenchman to declare the 'British Way in Warfare' dead in the water.

It was business as usual in Fleet Street, where as always, tragedy and scandal sold newspapers; the *Titanic* disaster or hints of ministerial impropriety for instance, not to mention that reliable standby; the threat of a 'bolt from the blue' – invasion by an aggressive rival. This stuff of fiction for half a century was not entirely fanciful if you believed what old Field-Marshal 'Bobs' was saying – and he should know! You only had to read the *Daily Mail,* the *Daily Express* or the *Daily Telegraph*. On a 'thin' day for news a resourceful editor could usually find space for some 'Patriot' or 'Soldier' bearing urgent witness that the country was defenceless, the Liberals being responsible for this wretched state of affairs. Newspapers broadly supporting the government, the *Manchester Guardian,* the 'Cocoa Press' – papers owned by the Cadbury and Rowntree dynasties – and quite a few provincials too, all used equally robust language. The purpose of the National Service League was not defence, but 'an invasion of German territory' cried the *Daily News*.

Not surprisingly anyone who took the newspapers at face value might be confused, even to the point of mild hysteria. As one observer recalled, the 'militarist propaganda' of Field-Marshal Roberts's National Service League 'did more to increase neurotic moods, nervous impatience, ill deserved passion, than to gain acceptance for their nostrum, conscription, the nation in arms, and so on.' It was hard, of course, to measure the mood of a nation where two out of five adult men were denied a vote – as were *all* women. That magic 'public opinion' so important to Sir Edward Grey was – as in Palmerston's day – very much what the vigorous, confident, assertive middle classes gleaned from newspapers like the *Times*, (circulation 42,000), the *Manchester Guardian*, (not quite 50,000), or what the 'lower orders' could be induced to think by reading the *Daily Mail,* (circulation 750,000), and other 'family' papers. 'Public opinion' was shaped too, by a narrow educational system designed to produce army officers and colonial administrators, as well as a larger 'grammar school' group; the managers and book keepers of a mercantile nation. It was from this shapeless yet instantly recognisable class that the Navy League and the National Service League drew much of their support; and it was the same social group that gave Haldane volunteers for the territorial army so despised and undervalued by Roberts and his friends – that is, until *they* could lay their hands on it.

There may not have been a 'period of Utopian tranquillity about to descend upon the world' as Sir Edward's Man in Vienna reported,* but in his New Year's Message for 1914 Mr Asquith looked to a future 'no less glorious than the past.' Even Lloyd George radiated confidence and good will when, in May, Winston Churchill proposed a round of 'naval talks' with the Germans – an idea firmly sat upon by Grey.

Still, the beleaguered Asquith had to tread carefully, and not only in the Cabinet room where some of his colleagues might take fright – the more they learned about the preparations for continental war. There was the Army itself to worry about – for months he'd been nursing an officer corps distracted by mutiny and sedition while Ireland simmered on the brink of revolt. Sir Edward Grey said relations with Germany had much improved of late, which was just as well since his top official, Sir Arthur Nicolson, had warned the British ambassador in St Petersburg, 'I am afraid that should war break out the likelihood of our dispatching any expeditionary force is extremely remote; and it was on such an expeditionary force being sent that France at one time was basing her military measures. I believe that of late she has gradually abandoned the hope of ever receiving prompt and efficient military aid from us.' This was a sudden change of heart for Sir Arthur †

---

* *Tageblatt* 12 July 1912 TNA FO371/1111/561 doc 119 p 340

In the sultry days of July 1914 Sidney and Beatrice Webb were packing their bags for a six-month tour of Germany to study the trades unions, the professions, the co-operatives, and 'state action.' At home, the prime minister, his generals, and the opposition too, were still absorbed in the commotion across the Irish Sea, where the private army that Henry Wilson and Lord Roberts were so proud of, waited impatiently for Carson's order to start the civil war which Esher blithely advocated. Across the Channel, all of France was enthralled by two sensational murders – a socialist leader, and a newspaper editor slain by a cabinet minister's wife. Reports of an Austrian archduke assassinated somewhere in the Balkans was slower to sink in. It was quite possible this crisis in central Europe would go away, as such things usually did. In mid-July, Lloyd George thought the skies had seldom seemed so blue.

Sir Edward begged the French and the Russians to keep calm, and made all the appropriate diplomatic noises in an unworldly endeavour to persuade the Germans to restrain their cousins in Vienna. With his chief gone fishing in Hampshire, Sir Arthur Nicolson made a brave attempt to stop the conflict spreading beyond the Balkans by announcing a four-power conference to be held in London. It worked last year, but this time there were no takers. As Germany, France and Russia mobilised their huge armies, Henry Wilson was scurrying about excitedly, urging the French military attaché to make the ambassador, Cambon threaten Grey that if Britain did not declare war, he (Cambon) would 'break off relations' and go home.* In Paris meanwhile, General Castelnau was telling the British ambassador the French didn't really need the BEF.† Back in London, the Foreign Secretary bleakly reminded Cambon that Britain was under no obligation to help France – because of *France's* alliance with Russia!

The French were not at all pleased, claiming (wrongly) a continuing naval alliance with Britain, and arguing (rightly) they had dutifully sent their fleet to the Mediterranean leaving their Channel and Atlantic coast unguarded. As might be expected of a disjointed and secretive bureaucracy, the most senior man in the Foreign Office, Nicolson, seems not to have heard about this particular bit of Anglo-French cordiality. Aware that 'public opinion' was unhappy about involvement in a European war, but believing they could still choose their own strategy, Asquith and Grey raised fears of German activity in the English Channel. Sir Edward offered France the protection of the Royal Navy and Mr Churchill had mobilised the Fleet, with the approval of Asquith who didn't ask the Cabinet. The generals were

† TNA FO 800/373 7 April 1914
* Diary 30 July 1914
† Ambassador Bertie to Grey 3 August 1914 TNA FO 800/55

better informed – they had already called up the army reservists. The British Army was going to France.

Faced by a three-to-one Cabinet majority for staying out of the war altogether (on the Liberal backbenches too, as Asquith confided to his young friend Venetia Stanley)* the Prime Minister and his Foreign Secretary persuaded their doubting colleagues that if the Germans violated Belgian neutrality, Britain would be morally and legally justified in entering the conflict. This, even if the Belgians joined the invader, for the Belgians were just as wary of the French, because in their July manoeuvres an attack by *either* great power was envisaged.† In Brussels, the government was agonisingly slow to commit itself – the debate lasted all night. In London, two ministers resigned from a Cabinet that never had a choice.

---

* Searle p 522
† Kennedy PM *A nglo- German Antagonism* pp 461-2, and Searle p 522

~ 21 ~

The Wrong Kind of War?

"..this glorious delicious war.."

- Winston Churchill , 4 August 1914 *

'A noble cause, a crusade against the Devil,' said the Poet Laureate. Reminding his fellow Britons about the 'forgotten peaks' of honour, duty and patriotism, Lloyd George drew their attention to 'the great pinnacle of Sacrifice pointing like a rugged finger to Heaven' – they would soon understand that last bit.†

In August 1914 Henry Wilson nearly missed the boat and a job had to be invented for him. He was sent to France as the 'Sub-Chief of Staff,' a supernumerary post at BEF headquarters where his gift of tongues might help him explain to bemused French generals why the English had to bring their own 'sous-chef.' A useful stand-in when the real Chief of Staff had a nervous breakdown, Henry gave full rein to his carefree spirits, writing home after the BEF's first encounter with an enemy four times its size, 'I am afraid we are in for a disaster,'‡ and during the hasty retreat from Mons chanting 'we shall never get there!' When asked 'where?' Henry answered 'the sea, the sea,' – the destination preferred by the BEF's commander, though Henry didn't agree. Nor did Kitchener, who hastened to Paris in Field-Marshal's uniform where he put Sir John French on the British Embassy carpet, and told him to keep his men in France!§

---
* Searle p 663
† Grigg J *Lloyd George: from peace to war 1912-16* p 166
‡ Letter to Mrs Wilson 26 August 1914
§ Callwell vol I p 170, Bonham-Carter V *Soldier True:The Life and Times of Sir William Robertson* p 94

In the beginning it really *was* the war Henry wanted. The Expeditionary Force—only four divisions at first—was square on the French left flank just as Captain de Tarlé had said, for a brisk campaign of marching and counter-marching across Northern France lasting a few weeks at most. This was supposed to end in victory for the French (with the assistance of the BEF of course), as in that War Game long ago. But Henry had staked everything on the Germans playing by the same rules. Instead, the Germans pushed through Belgium and wheeled round in very great strength to fall upon the much smaller BEF – as Kitchener had guessed they would. Even so, it was a march too far for the horde of weary footsloggers who nearly reached the gates of Paris. The French and the badly bruised BEF rallied on the river Marne, and now it was *their* turn to advance. Henry reckoned they'd be on the German frontier in a month.*

This little war was soon over, and the Germans lost. In planning their grand encircling sweep, the Kaiser's renowned General Staff had substituted ponderous incompetence for plain common sense. The invaders had to trudge all the way round on foot, while their enemy could use the railways radiating from the French capital, and it really *was* quicker to take the train. Moreover, the stiff-necked German army commanders hardly spoke to each other and their communications verged on the primitive – the BEF had more telephone wire.

But the war was not going to end with a peace treaty and the exchange of a mere province or two. Joffre's foolhardy offensive in north-eastern France had met with a bloody repulse and the Germans had overrun all but a tiny scrap of Belgium plus a huge slice of French territory. They had dug themselves in and they wouldn't go home. Undaunted, Henry told his wife 'I still think the war will be over by February or March,'† but others weren't so sure as a swift-moving campaign turned into a mutual siege and the remnant of the BEF was stuck in Flanders mud. This little war had already 'transcended all limits of thought, imagination and reason,' thought one shaken observer [Repington], and Viscount Esher, who'd given it three months 'if everything goes well,' wasn't too happy either. 'We are going to lose this war,' he told a friend. 'It would end in a stalemate, and peace that is only a truce.' ‡

Henry Wilson was now complaining about Kitchener's 'ridiculous and preposterous army'; the thousands enlisting to fight for King and Country—volunteers all—'for shadow campaigns and at unknown and distant dates.' Viscount Esher agreed. 'If he persists in raising this new

---
* Callwell vol I p 177
† Callwell I p 181
‡ Letter to Williamson 16 January 1915

army,' he told himself, 'he will destroy the morale of the Territorial Force' *– the very organisation he'd so recently condemned as 'not only useless, but beyond remedy.'† Henry's old mentor Foch insisted, 'You English must not invite a long war by dilatory action; we French cannot go on for years, so send everyone you can as fast as you can.' ‡

Which is exactly what happened. The remains of the BEF were hastily reinforced by a Canadian army corps, a few colonial garrisons and some of those 'native' (Indian) troops that Lord Roberts considered 'undesirable' for European war – and even the despised Territorials whom Kitchener rated no better than the ones he'd seen in France during the Franco-Prussian War in 1870. Fresh from Egypt, Britain's new warlord had no idea what Pussy had been up to in the Cabbage Patch, but Sir John French would soon have another little army for his well-intentioned but ill-judged and costly 'offensives' of 1915.

Odd Men Out

On Day Three of the war, when the Cabinet timidly 'authorised' the dispatch of the BEF to France, Esher was complaining they'd got it all wrong, for by the 'precipitate alignment of our army to that of the French' they had forfeited the advantage of sea power.§ Repington was soon urging Field Marshal Roberts to assume command of an imaginary amphibious descent upon the Low Countries, and a year later, Esher thought the Dutch could be persuaded to come in with the Allies, but no one listened to him any more. By his own account, he'd spent 'years' vainly trying to prevent a continental commitment. ¶

Esher did take himself to France though, setting up shop as his country's unofficial emissary and self-appointed adviser to both armies. Incongruously attired in a semblance of military uniform suggesting high rank, he was a frequent visitor at the French Headquarters. Here, he renewed his acquaintance with that 'extraordinarily able Frenchman' General Foch 'who used to come to the Defence Committee,' and the 'charming and brilliant' Henry Wilson – who didn't speak French nearly as well as he did.

Esher spent a good deal of his time with the BEF too, 'advising' Sir John French and 'smoothing out those constantly recurring difficulties' with Lord Kitchener – but he wasn't the only one getting under the feet of the harassed Commander-in-Chief. Churchill's visits were 'a deep seated cause of trouble' he noted, though the Viscount was himself well

---

* Esher *Journal* 12 August 1914
† Esher to Percy 27 October 1913
‡ Callwell vol I p 206
§ *Journal* 6 August 1914
¶ Esher to Oliver Brett 5 September 1914

out of touch with reality. He did eventually find someone whose boots were firmly on the ground – William Robertson, 'probably the son of poor peasants' ...who married 'a highly intelligent and cultured woman...' He made a good chief of staff too, Esher decided.

Comrades in Arms

Forgetful now of Repington, who – briefed by Sir John French – made public the shortage of ammunition as his excuse for failure, Henry Wilson had one more reason to dislike another old comrade who was never his friend – the BEF's highly efficient Quarter Master General, William Robertson. For a dozen years he and Wilson had brushed against each other, leapfrogging upwards through the senior ranks. Staff College commandant when his hero Ferdinand Foch held the equivalent post across the Channel, Henry was followed by Robertson who later recalled how long ago, *he* had identified Germany as Britain's 'most persistent, deliberate and formidable rival.' For Henry Wilson however, *his* most persistent, deliberate and formidable rival was 'Wully' Robertson, and the passage of time had not lessened his distaste for this low-class fellow who'd come up the hard way.

When Wully stepped into the shoes, or boots, of the ailing Chief of Staff of the Expeditionary Force, it was to the dismay of Henry who thought the job should have gone to him. As the BEF's 'Principal Liaison Officer' between Joffre and Sir John French, the erstwhile sous-chef was little more than a suave interpreter good-humouredly smoothing over their differences, making sure the more disagreeable of Joffre's deliberate insults were lost in translation – although he still shared the Frenchman's childlike faith in early victory.

Henry Wilson found Wully's promotion hard to bear. The new chief of staff was 'secretive, & like all underbreds, suspicious,' and his manners were 'somewhat repugnant.' But the Principal Liaison Officer was himself not short of enemies – even his knighthood was slow to arrive. Grumbling to his diary, 'as nobody ever takes my advice it is obviously no good my staying on,' so he decided to resign on half pay. That was enough to concentrate the mind of every other general, for ever since the Ulster crisis Henry was considered much too dangerous to be left at large amid the swirl of intrigue and high-level backbiting in Whitehall. The established custom was to export trouble-makers, so Mr Asquith gave the "poisonous tho' clever ruffian Wilson"* a generous consolation prize; command of an army corps on the Western Front where he could be kept away from London and out of mischief. †

---
* Asquith to Venetia Stanley 20 December 1914
† Jeffery p 153

King and Country

Kitchener would rather wait until everyone else was exhausted on the battlefield, leaving Britain the strongest military power in Europe,* but barely a year later his 'ridiculous and preposterous army' – eager but inexperienced – *was* the Expeditionary Force. The Expedition was taking longer than expected, and many lives had been lost, but soon Britain would have a continental-size army, with the approval of the British public – after all, it was a crusade against the anti-Christ, or so they'd been told. Large crowds listened to self-appointed recruiting sergeants like the fraudster Horatio Bottomley, though a more respectable soapbox orator was George Shee, one of the founding fathers of the National Service League and now Honorary Secretary of the Central Committee for National Patriotic Associations. Declared medically unfit and thus denied the opportunity to serve his country in the field, he could at least remind his fellow Britons of *their* First Duty, and soon any man not in khaki could expect a white feather from some public spirited lady.

The initial excitement of a million eager volunteers had yielded to a more sober reflection that mere patriotism was not enough. As early as November 1914 a cross-party Parliamentary Recruiting Committee sponsored a 'census' of near-biblical proportions; a National Householders' Return that would seek out every male old enough to fight, whereby more than a million were found not to have heeded the call to arms. The politicians had always said there were no votes in conscription, but now they were cautiously edging to embrace the creature whose advances they had hitherto spurned, and even in good Liberal homes where the 'c' word dared not speak its name, the idea was becoming almost acceptable.

Almost, but not quite. Speaking for the government, Lord Crewe didn't see 'compulsion'—that old weasel word for conscription—'within the landscape, as we now see it.'† In the same debate Viscount Haldane—still in the government but only just—now exhumed the old chestnut that 'it was the duty of every subject to assist the sovereign in repelling invasion.' Yes, invasion – and 'defence of the realm,' and this from the same man who famously crossed swords with Field Marshal Roberts over voluntary service versus 'conscription.' So, conscription was 'not foreign to the Constitution' after all, and he could now imagine it happening. The Lord Chancellor's timid eleventh-hour conversion earned him few admirers, Liberal or Conservative, but as the victim of a particularly nasty press campaign, 'Schopenhauer' wasn't expecting a place in the expected coalition government. Still,

---
* French D *British Strategy and War Aims* p 20
† 8 January 1915

three months later even Lloyd George was telling everyone the war would not necessarily be run better with 'conscription.' He would shortly perform a nimble U-turn – and he did get into the coalition cabinet.

The new regime quickly discovered the existence of five million men of military age not yet in uniform. Allowing for the lame and the halt and the munitions workers, that left about two million whose country needed them. Kitchener wanted a quota for each district, so the freshly-minted Director of Recruiting, Edward Stanley, Seventeenth Earl of Derby and veteran standard bearer for 'compulsion,' urged all men between eighteen and forty one to 'attest' by pledging to enlist when summoned – bachelors first. The King made an appeal to 'his People' – composed by Esher. But for a million of the People, and especially the unmarried ones, the prospect of a soldier's life (and possibly a very short one) had little appeal even if it came with a red crown on a smart grey armband to show that although unwed, they weren't dodging their martial duty.

Threats to resign from the coalition were fobbed off with an inquiry into 'the optimum size' of the army, but the Attorney General Sir John Simon nevertheless quit just as party comrade Lloyd George was explaining why conscription wasn't such a bad idea. The Greeks had a word for it, 'Washington won independence for America by compulsory measures' (a questionable claim) and anyway, conscription was about Freedom and Democracy.* Field Marshal Wolseley, himself no lover of democracy, did not agree. In France, he was told, conscription was less useful for 'procuring men' than for 'control,' and over there, 'agitators, strike leaders and so on' were sent into the trenches

In Britain, George Shee and his old cronies in the National Service League could at last rejoice when on March the First 1916 every bachelor between eighteen and fifty not yet in the army was assumed to have enlisted anyway, although in fact some two and a half million, volunteers all, had taken the King's shilling *without* conscription. Many came from Ireland, north and south. The Nationalists in Parliament lost interest when they learned conscription would not be enforced in 'John Bull's Other Island' – though the Ministry of National Service tried to catch men seeking sanctuary across the water. That other Irishman, Henry Wilson, still thought conscription was 'a vital necessity.'†

Some did not, pleading hardship or ill health when called to the colours. Others explained their work was 'a vital necessity,' as did the

---
* Lloyd George *War Memoirs* vol I p 439
† Jeffery p 222

economist and wartime treasury official John Maynard Keynes, at length and with success. A few managed to convince the authorities that their objection to shedding human blood rested on genuine 'religious or moral convictions,' but of 16,000 'conscientious objectors' only 300 gained complete exemption despite an elaborate appeals system. The eighteen hundred local 'military service panels' were mostly staffed by an older age group – Charles a Court Repington sat on the Hampstead tribunal, in colonel's uniform. 'Friendly aliens' were exempt, but 30,000 Russian Jews of military age could have been an embarrassment to the leaders of British Jewry, so it was arranged that these men could either enlist in the British Army, as some already had, or go back to Russia.

'Conchies' got scant sympathy, and the *No Conscription Fellowship*, the *National Council against Conscription* and the *Independent Labour Party* all had their offices ransacked by the police. Most objectors got 'conditional exemption' and were put to work on farms; three and a half thousand were drafted into the Army's newest regiment, the Non-Combatant Corps; but six thousand stubbornly declared they would not fight their fellow men with whom they had no quarrel. Refusal to wear uniform guaranteed a court-martial and two years in prison; and fifty hard cases – 'absolutists' – were shipped to France where at least thirty were sentenced to death (commuted to ten years' penal servitude); but everyone was out of jail by August 1919, except a few who died in captivity.

The Nation in Arms

No one expected so many would volunteer when the war began. A million men had to be housed, fed and shod, clad in khaki and shown how to use a rifle – but there weren't enough rifles, and it would take more than a year to equip such a huge citizen force, not least because so many skilled blue-collar workers had heeded the voice of the demagogue. Ministers and generals alike were slow to realise that these men, rather than the white-collar pen pushers, were of more use at home. The peacetime British Army was never designed for a long war. The artillery soon ran out of shells and Henry was fuming 'six months after war breaks out we have only twelve divisions...and can't attack for 3 months... someone ought to hang..' He was too modest to offer himself as the scapegoat. In peacetime he'd complained about the inferior quality of army-issue rifles and machine guns, compared to those of possible enemies, but in 1912 a committee of senior officers headed by a Brigadier-General H. H. Wilson considered four different makes of automatic rifle and rejected every one.* The British soldier's

* TNA WO 242/7 p 143 -162

single shot magazine Lee-Enfield was arguably the best of its kind and used with a skill unrivalled by other armies, yet barely six months into the war, when the infantry's need for extra firepower became obvious, the hasty solution was a light machine gun designed by an American, Colonel Lewis – the Belgians had bought some a couple of years earlier.

The rush to enlist in 1914 suggests that 'joining up' offered excitement and a welcome change from tedious employment, though many had been thrown out of work as an immediate consequence of the war. Young men of the middle classes who believed in Duty, Empire, King and Country were certainly fired by enthusiasm, as were all those 'dispensable clerks' who joined the New Army battalions. They might also have joined the Territorials in peacetime, when Haldane's reserve force was still in the making and Captain Tulloch was urging that a 'national' army ought not to be a replica of regular formations with their rigidly-enforced discipline. The New Army had a high proportion of intelligent, educated men whose approach to soldiering was different – they only joined to fight in this particular war. The memoirs of 'Terriers' and New Army men alike reflect a general acceptance of rules that seemed to make sense, where a cheerful readiness to undergo hardship and plenty of personal initiative prevailed. But the informal relationship between officers and men, especially in Territorial units, bothered many of 'the old school.'

In peacetime, generals like Haig had helped formulate the Army's tactical doctrine, but by 1916, as the Somme offensive began to falter, Haig was complaining 'our system is at fault' (uncannily echoing Admiral Beatty's petulant remark during the Battle of Jutland: 'there is something wrong with our bloody ships' – adding next day 'and with our system'). Haig's armies did learn, however, and quickly. By 1916 the military art was becoming a science as fresh ideas and civilian technology began to shape the Expeditionary Force into the skilfully directed machine that two years later would defeat the most powerful army in Europe. No end of a lesson, to be sure – but Tulloch, a mere captain in 1907, was one of those skilled directors.

Corps Commander

Henry Wilson returned to a very different Western Front. It was now a huge industrial estate for making war, with a fast-expanding work force distributed among three, soon to be four very large organisations—'armies'—each headed by a chief executive, or 'General' who delegated the management of his dozen or so 'divisions' to three or four 'corps commanders.' Henry's IV Corps had its own headquarters staff and a few specialist units like aviation and heavy artillery, but everything else was what 1st Army HQ chose to shuttle in and out of his sector. Only the Canadians and the Australians kept their independence, but with up to four divisions under his command totalling 60,000 men, Henry was still an important link in the chain.

The troops spent much of their time not actually in the trenches, but 'resting'; i.e. labouring with pick and shovel; carrying ammunition, tins of bully beef and jam; and unravelling coils of barbed wire, often at night. The war had spawned a variety of special devices such as the trench mortar, hand grenade, poison gas, and very soon, the tank. Each weapons-system was championed by zealots asserting the primacy of their own 'decisive weapon' jealously guarding their exclusive preserve, and disputing rival claims of 'ownership.' Senior commanders were excited by such 'novelties,' but their more thoughtful staff officers had seen that the real tactical unit was the platoon, or, a few rifle-grenadiers with a 'light' machine gun—a miniature army—and how victory would be achieved by an intelligent combination of all arms.*

Alas, this corps commander didn't seem that interested, and nor did he impress his fellow generals overmuch. Henry complained about the quality of the troops he was given – though his ever-loyal diary shows how popular *he* was with junior officers. The fact was that until now he had never commanded anything larger than a battalion, at home, for more than twelve months. Undismayed by his indifferent performance, Henry noted approvingly that someone else was doing better – the maritime blockade was getting results. They were 'feeling the pinch' in Germany and the Boche was 'losing his head.' †

Like many senior commanders he had a touching faith in the credibility of information obtained from the usual source; prisoners of war. The Profession had always valued 'intelligence' supporting its case for greater resources – or to bolster confidence – and if Henry couldn't explain why the sailors were doing better than the soldiers, it was still a generous compliment from a man who so recently dismissed the Fleet as not worth even 500 bayonets. But hunger in Germany was what the British public wanted to know about – and hunger would give German generals a convenient excuse for failure and eventual defeat

Coming back to earth for a briefing on the 'Big Push' (the neighbouring Fourth Army's July offensive on the Somme) Henry reckoned 'we run a serious chance of doing something considerable here.' Alas, Sir Aylmer Hunter-Weston's VIII Corps suffered such grievous losses on the first of July that he would not be entrusted with an 'offensive'

---
* See Griffith P Battle Tactics of the Western Front : The British Army's Art of Attack 1916-18
† Diary 22 June 1916, Caallwell volI p 286

for another two years. Brave and resourceful in the Boer War, Master of Drag Hounds at the Staff College, 'Hunter-Bunter' managed to slip away from the Somme to fight in a parliamentary by-election at home – he soundly defeated his pacifist opponent.

Homecoming

By October 1916 Henry was restless and seeking wider horizons. The problem was Asquith's coalition Cabinet: 'They will talk of our losses being unbearable, of the enormous expense,' he scribbled, 'not beating the Boche to the ground, as we shall want him against the Russians...' – an idea Lloyd George would soon be toying with. If the generals didn't get more men, the ex-corps commander told himself, they wouldn't be able to 'take punishment of at least a million between April and October of next year' and still keep their divisions 'full up to the brim...' and that, said Henry, meant deadlock on the Western Front – 'in which case the war is lost.' *

It was not the best of times for the Prime Minister. His colleagues were annoyed by his feeble objection to the conscription of married men, and his dismay at the harsh suppression of the 'Easter Rising' in Dublin – while everyone was exasperated by his ambiguous answers to the Irish Question. His generals wanted to conscript every available man under fifty five for munitions work– and the new War Minister, Lloyd George, raised the age limit to sixty. The ill-assorted coalition was losing its palsied grip. They talked of armistice, and Lloyd George was intent on a three-man 'inner cabinet' – including himself. Asquith, who'd weakened his own peacetime cabinets in much the same way, saw the trap but could not escape.

Henry was not minded to sit twiddling his thumbs while lesser men were losing the war. Having done his bit at the front, he threw himself into the campaign waged by Carson's Unionist 'War Committee' to remove Asquith in favour of a leader who really would get the BEF's divisions 'full to the brim.' A dinner party in November 1916 was an impressive gathering of conspirators: Milner, Carson, Robinson and Leo Amery. Also there was Fred Oliver the shopkeeper and pamphleteer, political dilettante and peacetime firebrand who yearned to see blood 'running freely' (though his own indifferent health kept him out of the army) and Waldorf Astor, member of parliament, whose father bought him a newspaper, the *Observer*. Now a wartime major, his weak heart did not prevent him inspecting munitions plants. Henry Wilson was there, of course, and recalled their 'unanimous advice' that Carson should make Lloyd George 'smash' the Government, using

---
* *Diary* 10 October 1916

21 - The Wrong Kind of War

Bonar Law's Conservative Party machine to fight an election. 'If we manage things properly, we have Asquith dead,' Wilson reckoned, but 'we' were too slow, for the Prime Minister had quit Downing Street that very day, stoical to the end. His wife, still grieving for Asquith's eldest son Raymond so recently killed on the Somme, took it badly. At dinner that evening her tears dripped into the soup.

More efficient assassins were Lloyd George and Wully – the latter having already secured the Army's top job, Chief of the Imperial General Staff *and* on his own terms: Kitchener the overbearing warrior-minister had been cut down to size and dispatched on a mission to keep Russia in the war. Kitchener never got there – the cruiser *Hampshire* with him on board struck a mine off the Orkneys; but his travelling companion Lloyd George had better luck – delayed by the Easter Rising in Dublin, he missed the sailing.

~ 22 ~

The Chief
– and the Commander in Chief

"As a whole the French Commanders and Staff are a peculiar lot . The great thing to remember...is that they are Frenchmen and not Englishmen...I suppose they think we are queer people."

- General Robertson to General Haig, 5 January 1916

By 1916 the million and a half strong BEF (it would peak at two million) was the centre of gravity and the real power base of the military establishment. Commanding the greatest field army in Britain's history, it was inevitable that Sir Douglas Haig should loom larger in the public eye than his actual superior the Chief of the Imperial General Staff in Whitehall. But Haig needed Robertson. Wully didn't believe it was possible to break through a succession of strong defence works to allow the cavalry to break out into open country – as Haig expected. Wully's way was not to capture ground, but to pin down the enemy and wear him out– a grim task requiring yet more men for the BEF. Observing sarcastically that loss of life was politically acceptable in defence, but not when the troops were attacking, Wully wrote to Haig suggesting improvements in tactics, though he didn't always understand the technical difficulties. Unsure of Haig's methods, yet anxious to defend him from Lloyd George's tongue-lashing, Robertson dared not hint at any disagreement between himself and the commander in chief, for that would imperil the Western Front strategy. Pained that Haig was so unforthcoming, Wully plaintively urged him to have more care for his soldiers' lives, and begged for more information so he could put a stronger case to the Cabinet, 'the swines' he called them.* 'Charity begins at home,' said the C-in-C confiding to Lady Haig how distasteful it was having to deal with an ill-bred fellow like Robertson. Wully's task was made no easier when at the height of the battle of the Somme, the King made his favourite general a Field Marshal. So Robertson, supposedly 'the boss,' was now Haig's junior in rank.†

Wully was routinely fencing off ministers dismayed by the steady loss of life on the Western Front, but some, including Lloyd George and Churchill, were gazing further afield for new allies – Italians, Romanians, Serbs and Greeks, a coalition of the willing. Churchill dreamed the Navy would force the Dardanelles Straits unaided, knock Turkey out of the war and get supplies into Russia. The sailors did not succeed and failure was reinforced by the soldiers, in a hastily conceived landing at Gallipoli.

It was the fashion to talk of 'kicking away the props' of Germany and Austria – Wully called it 'fireworks strategy. He saw no point in sending British soldiers to 'kill Bulgars' when they could be killing Germans in France, and all too soon, the 'props' themselves would need propping up. But he was outflanked by French ambition in the Balkans – coalition warfare is always difficult. Ordered to 'consult' Joffre over the joint expedition to Salonika, Wully threatened to resign, but Northcliffe stepped in and the government backed off – Wully had friends in Fleet Street. He managed to close down the Gallipoli misadventure, and he clawed back troops from the Near and Middle East, but Lloyd George, who was War Secretary from July 1916 – and Prime Minister by Christmas – was not best pleased with his Chief of Staff.

Henry Wilson was not best pleased with *his* lot either. He knew he was out of the loop altogether when he – not Wully – was packed off on that pointless errand to St Petersburg. Fooled by window dressing – a smartly groomed frontline detachment – he assured his superiors, *in March 1917,* that Russia's 'profound' loyalty might be counted upon for the rest of the war.‡

He did however gain the ear of the Prime Minister. Ignoring objections by other generals – 'he [Wilson] talks but he can't act' snarled Hubert Gough in a private letter to the Palace.§ Lloyd George subsequently reinvented Henry as Chief of the British Mission to the

---
* Robertson to Haig 7 August 1916 p 65 and Woodwartd p 79
† Robertson to Lord Stamfordham 10 August 1916 *Military Correspondence* p 81
‡ TNA CAB17/197, Jeffery p187,Lloyd George *War Memoirs* p vol I p p 938-940
§ Jeffery pp 188-9

French Army, the link between Haig and Robert Georges Nivelle, the man replacing Joffre who'd recently fallen from grace. A sprightly artilleryman of sixty, Nivelle was having a good war – so far. The mirror-image of Henry Wilson, he was a hit with Lloyd George – who may have been one of 'les cochons de politiciens' (the pig-politicians) that so upset this bilingual Frenchman (his mother was English). Lloyd George's idea – which upset the King no end – was to put the BEF directly under Nivelle, who didn't think much of Haig, whereas Wilson was 'the only man in England who could save a most dangerous situation' as Henry modestly noted. As might be expected, an essential part of the deal was that Robertson—who as Chief of Staff was the government's sole adviser on military matters—would be bypassed and only permitted to communicate with Haig through a liaison officer at Nivelle's headquarters; namely, Henry Wilson.

Henry's new soulmate did not doubt his own talent. Disregarding the new French War Minister Painlevé and the new Premier Ribot, Generalissimo Nivelle confidently announced (in French) that he had a "formula for victory" on the Western Front. His hopes rested on the Russian army that Henry now thought so highly of, and more realistically, on friends nearer home. The Canadians seized Vimy Ridge for him, but the Russians were distracted by the 1917 March Revolution, and the 'formula' proved to be a recipe for disaster. The French Army was demoralised and entire regiments mutinied.

The discredited Nivelle was replaced by the more cautious Philippe Petain, who promptly put Henry's nose out of joint by talking directly to Haig. Now Robertson insisted that Wilson report to *him,* but Wully's authority as the government's sole military adviser was being steadily undermined. The failure of Nivelle, and the temporary discomfiture of Lloyd George, put Robertson and Haig in a stronger position but 1917 was a year of mixed fortune for the BEF: Vimy, Cambrai, Messines, 'Third Ypres,' and Wully's unfailing support of the Western Front had merely stiffened the Prime Minister's resolve to be rid of him.

Meanwhile England's 'Chief of Mission' began to feel he too had outstayed his welcome, despite his own profound sense of worth. When not invited to a high-level conference about the BEF taking over more of the front line, Henry spluttered 'here is another of those cursed misunderstandings..... Haig and Robertson think they understand the French – they don't and never will.' But neither did Henry understand – and there were many unemployed generals like him.

In the summer of 1917 the BEF was assembling for 'Third Ypres,' a series of carefully planned battles. Haig's not unreasonable aim was to relieve Admiral Jellicoe's anxiety by seizing the U-boat bases on the

Belgian coast and cut the Germans' east-west rail link, bringing comfort to the French whose confidence had taken such a knock. A further consideration was that a success of this magnitude would show the world that Britain could win the war before the Americans arrived in large numbers. Henry called on Haig in a vain search for employment, then returned home to advise the four-man War Policy Commitee that Sir Douglas should go on attacking, 'up to the mud time.'*

The 'mud time' arrived early with the heaviest rainfall in 30 years, and the prolonged artillery bombardment – a feature of all Haig's offensives – pulverised the Flanders field-drainage system. Wading waist deep in the 'wrong kind of mud' his soldiers duly captured what remained of the village of Paschendaele, but by November seventy thousand of them were dead and a hundred and seventy thousand wounded in pursuit of his sadly unattained 'strategic' goal. German losses were nearly as great. From a safe distance, Viscount Esher observed the start of 'Third Ypres.' Feeling cold, he went home next day and spent September in Biarritz.†

The Changing of the Guard

Rebuffed by Haig, Petain and Foch too – 'he does not want me – and he really is my friend,' Henry Wilson was kicking his heels, languishing on half pay and eyeing a safe parliamentary seat in Ulster. He thought of quitting the army altogether (as in 1915 *and* in 1916) and this time 'no one tried to dissuade him' says his latest biographer.‡ But at last he found a congenial billet, 'Eastern Command,' a one-day-a-week job guarding the shores of England against invasion, and a holding-pen for redundant top brass. With headquarters at Number 50 Pall Mall, it was a convenient location which afforded him ample opportunity to engineer Wully's downfall – 'a small group in the House of Commons' said they wanted him (Wilson) as CIGS, but Henry wouldn't help them get rid of Robertson, who'd 'done some really useful work.' It was a compliment Wully could have done without.

No one could escape a lecture from Henry. He pinned down Winston Churchill—who had recently been rehabilitated after the Dardanelles fiasco and was now the junior munitions minister—and counselled him to 'fix his eyes on the long view... the vital issues' – Turkey and the Balkans. Henry had seen the light in Lloyd George's eye and prudently renounced his faith in the Western Front in favour of little wars on the other side of Europe, the 'fireworks strategy' that Wully disdained.

It was no secret Mr. Lloyd George had become disenchanted by the

---
* Collier B *Brass Hat: A Biography of Sir Henry Wilson* p 289
† Fraser P *Lord Esher: A Political Biography* pp 367-8

performance of Sir Douglas Haig, and nor was he satisfied with the quality of advice tendered by Sir William Robertson. Desiring to be done with both men, the Prime Minister found willing allies in Sir Henry Wilson and Sir John French, the latter being the dispossessed commander of the BEF – victim of the 'Generals' Plot' hatched by Haig and Robertson with due assistance from Repington and the Northcliffe press. In written 'appreciations' Sir Douglas and Sir William asserted the primacy of the Western Front, as might be expected, while Sir John and Sir Henry entered the lists to win favour by casting doubt on its worth. With Jesuitical sophistry Henry insisted he was, and always would be, a 'Westerner,' but the time had not yet come for the decisive 'death grapple' with the foe*.

Henry was delighted when Lloyd George set up an Allied 'Supreme War Council' to run the entire war, with its own general staff at Versailles – with Henry as the British Government's principal military adviser instead of the task being assigned to the Chief of Staff in Whitehall. Wully could 'accompany' Henry to War Council meetings, but Henry 'and no one else' was to report back to the Prime Minister.† At a stroke, Wully was made redundant, but with a further twist of the knife Lloyd George, who'd convinced himself that Wully's ambition was to be a military dictator like his German counterpart,‡ decided to swap his Chief of General Staff for Henry. Henceforth Wully would report to his successor in the War Office, Henry Wilson, who had already promised his diary, 'If I'm to be CIGS, then the Military Representative at Versailles must be junior to me, and if he gives advice to [the] Supreme War Council, he must first submit it to the CIGS' – a neat reversal of his earlier position.§

A well-observed feature of every profession is that advancement may often be gained by self-advertisement rather than solid achievement, by style not substance. Politics being the art of the plausible as well as the possible, the successful practitioner who lives by the use of his tongue may himself be influenced more by the *form* of the advice he receives, than its content. Henry Wilson the 'political general' had paved his own road to power with specious eloquence, but he too thrived on flattery – 'the whole future of the war rests on your shoulders,' Lloyd George had told him,¶ and Churchill was impressed too. In their memoirs both statesmen rhapsodised about Wilson's advice– presumably what he guessed his listeners wanted to hear, though with

---

* TNA CAB WO 60 and 61 20 October 1917
† *Diary* 16, 22 November 1917, TNA CAB 23/23/4 WC 276, and Woodward *Lloyd George and the Generals* pp 226-8
‡ Lloyd George War Memoirs Vol II p 1684
§ *Dairy* 16 November, Calwell Vol II p 58
¶ *Diary* 2 November 1917, and Jeffery p 206

22 - The Chief, and the Commander-in-Chief

the benefit of hindsight perhaps, Lloyd George added that Henry could be 'frivolous' sometimes.

Fighting to keep his Whitehall job, Robertson played the Court card again – but this time in vain. That 'phenomenal little cad Lloyd George' (as Esher called him), curtly told the King to keep out of this one. In Court circles it was feared the Prime Minister was scheming to depose the King and set up a republic. 'I hope I may save Robertson' Henry scribbled piously,* but now it was Wully's turn to shuffle through the revolving door of Eastern Command. In his diary that night Wilson crowed over his fallen rival. 'The long duel between me and Robertson has ended in his complete defeat... I wonder will he resign?' He didn't, and not even Haig, who owed Wully so much, was inclined to rescue him from limbo.

Taking stock of his inheritance, the British Army's new Chief of Staff was confident that despite massive reinforcements from their Eastern Front after the Russian collapse, the Germans would not risk an attack in France. He was wrong. Few of the BEF's divisions were 'full to the brim,' and Hubert Gough's Fifth Army was shattered with the loss of 170,000 men and a thousand guns. The entire Expeditionary Force was threatened. The disaster gave fresh impetus to the idea of a 'general reserve' comprising French *and* British divisions, but neither Haig nor Petain would lend each other anything – spare divisions were harder to find than spare generals. All the same, Henry did 'advise' the Allies not to let the Germans drive a wedge between them, so Haig was spared the indignity of having to beat a hasty retreat to the Channel Ports.† But Wilson, the self-proclaimed architect of Anglo-French comradeship had lost what reputation he ever had as an honest broker. Lord Derby, 'the soldiers' friend' now War minister, noted, 'with what contempt apparently both Clemenceau and Foch regard him'‡ – questionable testimony perhaps from a man with 'the brains of a tomtit' but probably accurate enough. Henry complained to himself 'they [the French] mean to take us over body and soul,'§ but even the Viscount Esher didn't find them easy to get on with – 'I know these people and like them,' he told *his* journal,. 'but we are the born leaders of nations, not they.'¶

It was a dangerous time for the Allies – 'I find it difficult to realise that there is a possibility, perhaps a probability, of the French Army being beaten' Henry mused one night in June 1918.# 'What would this

---
* *Diary*, 30 December 1917
† Collier B *Brass Hat*
‡ French D *Strategy of the Lloyd George Coalition* p 221
§ Wilson *Diary* 12 May 1918
¶ Fraser p 356
# Wilson *Diary* 1 June 1918

mean? The destruction of our army in France? In Italy? In Salonika?' But in July, the French (reinforced by an American army now outnumbering Haig's) won a second Battle of the Marne; and in August a revived BEF rallied to complete the defeat of the German Army.

Wilson the 'political general' could hardly claim the credit. He'd shown little interest in the British Army's revolution in tactics and technology from 1916 onward, the renaissance that brought victory in the field, albeit at very great cost – the last 'hundred days' were just as bloody as the Somme or Paschendaele. He predicted the slaughter would continue well beyond 1918. But Henry was never much of a prophet. In 1901, as an intelligence officer pondering the future role of the British Army, he confidently advised his superiors 'the possibility of a European War may be ignored.'*

---

* Jeffery p 46

~ 23 ~

Never Again?

Britain is a world by itself;
and we will nothing pay for wearing our own noses.

- Cymbeline Act III, scene i

And when it was over nobody wanted to repeat the experience, except German generals crying 'foul,' stabbed in the back by their countrymen. Ludendorff's excuse for defeat was not having enough potatoes for soldiers already weakened by influenza – the scourge of friend and foe alike.* A senior British officer emerged from behind the barbed wire of his prison camp to announce that Germany was 'on the verge of starvation,' but grass did not grow in the streets of Hamburg as British naval intelligence confidently predicted. The Germans were defeated on the battlefield, not in the kitchen, and were never as famished as their rulers would later claim. They often went hungry, especially in the towns and cities, and they did have to eat a lot of turnips. Germans liked their meat, and as one nutritional scientist observed at the time, if they'd been vegetarians it wouldn't have mattered so much. The British didn't starve either, despite a vigorous 'counter-blockade' by the U-boats, though the admirals were sore afraid, for economic warfare was a card both sides could play, and did. But Britain was a global maritime power, and Germany was not.

Yes, Britain emerged victorious. The British Army was now the strongest in Europe, as Kitchener may have intended when he raised his New Armies, and the Empire was larger than ever, bulging with German colonies and Turkish fiefdoms, the 'mandated territories,'

---
* Offer A *The First World War: An Agrarian Interpretation* p 61

Palestine, Iraq, Jordan – while the French got Syria, the Lebanon and a bit of Turkey. It was an odd result since Britain had supposedly gone to war in defence of a small nation, not to seize more real estate. Twice as many Frenchmen died in the war, and Russia was racked by revolution, civil war and famine. Two million Germans had been killed in combat, the Kaiser was in exile and his Fleet lay captive, but his generals were taking careful note of how their enemy had defeated them – and quietly preparing for the next war.

The spoils of victory proved illusory. Deeply in debt to America, Britain was no longer the world's first and only super-power, and Sir Edward Grey's words in August 1914 'we shall suffer but little more.... whether we are in it or whether we stand aside,' would ring hollow in the years that followed.

For the Navy, it had been the *wrong* kind of war – they held the Kaiser's fleet at arm's length but never got their 'decisive' battle. They kept the Germans hungry and the troopships safe, but the admirals nearly lost the U-boat war and they certainly lost their nerve. Clinging to their battleships and ritually re-fighting Jutland at the naval war college while facing new threats from America and Japan, the sailors were elbowed aside by the aviators, brash newcomers who quickly found a mission to justify their existence as a separate institution. An expense—for the Profession was now split into three—which cost the taxpayer more.

The split also made it that much harder for Britain to wage war with anything like a coherent plan, for the airmen were determined to preserve their independence. They put in a lower bid to 'police' the unruly residents of Iraq – with poison gas at first – dropping high explosive on recalcitrant Afghans and Somalis too. 'Strategic' bombing, the declared reason for the existence of a separate air force, received rather less attention. Playing their war games, the air marshals selected 'targets' just across the English Channel, for France was no longer the staunch ally, so Paris could be bombed – on paper. Air power had taken the place of sea power in the public mind. Their prime minister (Baldwin) had said Britain's frontier was now on the Rhine, but he also warned 'the bomber will always get through' – as many had already discovered during the Great War.

Sensing that never again would 'public opinion' allow vast armies to be sent into battle, the generals quickly forgot what they had learned so recently and so painfully in France and Flanders. Stripped of their aviation, they found consolation in the Empire as if the Great War had never happened. It seemed the Western Front could teach them no lessons – it was now a graveyard for close on a million of their kinsmen. Next time, the soldiers would stay at home to man anti-aircraft guns and searchlights, and shoot looters on the streets of Britain's bombed cities, while the sailors waged 'economic warfare' to bring a Continental foe to his knees – if the airmen hadn't got in first and flattened his 'industrial targets.'

This might have been the time for a thoughtful restructuring of the peacetime British Army, inspired and directed by a Chief of Staff who would lead his fellow generals away from the traditional 'horse, foot and guns' model and the 'old boy' regimental snobbery. But Henry Wilson hadn't tried all that hard to save the army's Flying Corps, and besides, he had more immediate cares. His everyday hand-to-mouth task was finding troops to fight the Bolsheviks in Russia, though he did advise against invasion and occupation of the Caucasus region (Chechnya) as demanded by Churchill who now graced the War Office as well as the new Air Ministry. Henry was keeping an army of occupation in the Rhineland – and a much smaller one in Constantinople; he had to send troops to Iraq(Mesapotamia) and find men for a new Persian Expedition while sending four battalions of infantry to oversee a plebiscite in central Europe – Silesia. All this, and the enduring burden of empire – drafts for India, Egypt, Ireland – while the mighty British Army was shrinking fast as millions were demobilised and conscription would soon be ended. Henry would have liked to keep it though, for now he discerned those 'moral, physical and social benefits' that George Shee's National Service League had always claimed for 'compulsory service.'*

Wilson's method of raising an new army was certainly imaginative and innovative, and worthy of a military junta. Having first instructed his Prime Minister to 'crush out the poisonous part of Fleet Street,' Henry would launch a bold exercise in news management inserting "puffs" followed by an 'Army Order' whereupon 'the great adventure of compulsing a million men, in time of peace, to serve abroad, will have begun. There is not a moment to lose,' he raved.†

Indeed there was not, for many of the million 'compulsed' men would have to stay at home for another great adventure – Henry's crusade against home-grown Bolshevism. It was of course an ingrained habit in every senior officer to express a robust opinion on a wide range of social and political matters well outside his professional competence, and for a simple soldier like Henry an industrial dispute was 'mutiny and revolution' to be put down by the army – only 'as a last resort.' However, he would earn the distinction of being the first general, anywhere, to send tanks against his fellow countrymen.‡ They weren't

---
* Jeffery p 229
† 'Puffery' - the practice of using exaggerated statements to emphasise a subjective viewpoint.

used, which was just as well since police chiefs warned that the 'rioters' — ex-soldiers, many of them — would be better trained than the raw recruits they faced.

A gruelling campaign on the home front was beginning to tell on Britain's top soldier, who now felt an urgent need to bring an old acquaintance up to speed on recent events — Bonar Law, one of his old clients on the counselling couch who'd been in Lloyd George's Inner War Cabinet. 'I impressed Bonar a good deal... and was pleased with my morning's work.' He had another go at him a few weeks later, bursting in one morning when the poor man was still asleep in bed.

A good protestant like Henry did not intend to witness the break up of the Anglo-Irish Union in dignified silence. It was public knowledge that the Lord Lieutenant of Ireland, Field Marshal Sir John French, was the man who put down the 1916 'Easter Rising, but the public didn't know that in May 1918, when Haig's armies were so hard pressed by the German onslaught, Sir John was begging Henry for aeroplanes with bombs and machine guns 'to put the fear of God into these playful young Sinn Feiners.' *

They did know, of course, that the man now sending more troops into Ireland — sixty thousand were there in 1921 — was the same Henry Wilson who had aided and abetted the Ulster Rebels and in 1914 had commended the mutinous officers at the Curragh. Now he was all for martial law with a hard fist — reprisals against civilians and 'shooting by roster' in retaliation for Sinn Fein murders, though *not* a 'shoot to kill' policy,. He had no time for the infamous 'Black and Tans' however — a gendarmerie of sorts — but really an undisciplined rabble of ex-soldiers.† Henry would have nothing to do with 'peace talks' either — because if the Orange 'clubs' were given the weapons, 60,000 men 'could be put into the field very rapidly.' ‡

Quick to take offence — on one occasion displeased by 'a long and most impudent wire' from his namesake the United States President — Henry Wilson had become 'rather disgusted' with the government whose servant he was. 'They so rarely take my advice when I give it, and now they seldom ask it, so I suppose they no longer value it,' he sighed one night.§ Calling on Edwin Montagu, the minister responsible for India, he was told a 'strong course' was being taken by the Viceroy's military advisers in the third, and latest, Afghan war (not the one Mr Gladstone complained about, when villages were burned in

‡ Wilson *Diary* 21 October 1920
* Townshend C *The British Campaign in Ireland* p 170
† Jeffery p 263
‡ Callwell vol II p 228
§ *Diary* 27, 30 March 1920

reprisal for attacks on British troops). This time, Britain's top soldier discovered the Air Force was dropping bombs on Kabul and Kandahar. He thought 'this baby-bombing' had 'great limitations,' but the Cabinet took a year to reach the same conclusion.*

Rewarded with £10,000 and a baronetcy, Henry could at last enjoy his long-overdue metamorphosis from 'Brass Hat' into 'Frock,' with a safe seat in the Westminster parliament. Hired by the stripling Government of Northern Ireland to advise on 'security,' his new career ended all too soon in 1922 when a pair of Irish nationalists casually and callously murdered him on the doorstep of his London home. His widow consented to the publication of the diary, although his reputation was not necessarily enhanced by the revelation in their pages of a conversation between Wilson and the press baron Lord Riddell. Asked by Riddell what he should tell his three and a half million *News of the World* readers, Henry answered without hesitation, 'Let them hoist the flag of England, and rally England around them.' A truly generous sentiment from the Irishman of whom his Lordship declared, no one he had ever met had 'so clear a grasp of essentials, so wide an outlook, so far-seeing a gaze into the future' as ... Henry Wilson.†

His old foe Charles à Court Repington, 'The Playboy of the Western Front,' (and) 'one of the most unpleasant of the many unpleasant characters to flit across the scene of the First World War' (as one of Wilson's biographers described him),‡ would outlive Wilson by three years, dying in bed. Henry's 'chief,' Field-Marshal Frederick Sleigh Roberts, Earl of Kandahar, Pretoria and Waterford paid a visit in 1914 to his 'native' Indian troops shivering in Flanders where he caught a chill and died aged eighty two. Grierson the talented gourmet who nobbled the French military attaché in the first days of the Liberal government, and outwitted Haig in the 1912 manoeuvres, never got the chance to show what he could do against the Germans, for he died of apoplexy on his way to the front; but Ian Hamilton, author of Haldane's answer to conscription, was put in charge of the ill-fated Dardanelles expedition.

Field Marshal Sir John French, Earl of Ypres and High Lake, Colonel in Chief of the Royal Irish Regiment and Captain of Deal Castle, collected £50,000 and died in 1925, three years before Field Marshal Sir Douglas Haig (£100,000 plus Earldom). But Wully, snubbed by Haig who generously praised every other general except Robertson, usefully turned his hand to commerce with a directorship of the London General Omnibus Company. The only private soldier

---
* Townshend p 171
† Callwell vol II p 231
‡ Ash B *The Lost Dictator: A Biography of Field Marshal Sir Henry Wilson* p 32

ever to become Field Marshal, he survived until 1933 – his last recorded words; 'where's the bloody tea?'

Alas for Staff Captain de Tarlé, his brief venture into celebrity journalism did him no favours, and nor did war restore his fame. From base duties and the quiet Vosges sector he was banished to the Balkans under the staunchly republican General Sarrail, whose politics he may have shared. The Germans at least seem to have valued this Anglo-French bid to 'kick away the props' – as General Ludendorff sneered, Salonika was their 'largest internment camp.' And Major (soon to be Colonel, and then General) Victoire Huguet, sometime military attaché in London, duly published his recollection of the secret staff talks – adding for good measure his distaste for the British establishment, especially its 'Jewish financiers' – he disliked the French ones even more. And our man in Berlin, Colonel Trench who vainly warned of a German invasion, departed his ungrateful country for good, to die in Monte Carlo in 1942.

Of the three Liberal Imperialists who took Britain into a foreign war on a false prospectus, the Viscount Haldane of Cloan was soon forced out of government by 'popular feeling' – he was said to be 'pro-German.' Asquith, ousted from the premiership in 1916 became Earl of Oxford, dying ten years after the war. Haldane was Lord Chancellor once more, in the first, but short-lived minority Labour Government of 1924. He died five years later, but Sir Edward Grey, whose stay at the Foreign Office ended in 1916, lingered until 1933 as Viscount Grey of Fallodon. His sometime Permanent Secretary and mentor Sir Charles Hardinge survived to become Chairman of Battersea Dogs' Home, where in 1940 he cheerfully predicted *that* war would be over by Christmas. Had his old boss lived long enough, he would surely have welcomed what he long desired; the aid of a large Russian army – which effectively brought the *next* war to an end.

Haldane's successor at the War Office, John 'Galloper Jack' Seely, Hampshire Carabineers (Yeomanry), had a 'good war' riding into battle on his thoroughbred Warrior (the horse was intelligent); sadly, Seely's eldest son was killed on the Western Front. As the first Baron Mottistone – 'Lord Modest One' – Jack Seely was coxswain of the local lifeboat and an early admirer of Nazi Germany, but he was no match for Sir George Sydenham Clarke, the soldier-turned-bureaucrat despised by admirals and generals alike. First helmsman of the Committee of Imperial Defence, he was eased out of Whitehall and sent to govern the 'Bombay Presidency' where he managed to fall out with just about everyone in India, coming home as Lord Sydenham of Coombe to spend the years of retirement in a permanent sulk while composing his memoirs and crisply defining his world outlook. There was a long standing Jewish conspiracy to bring about the reign of the AntiChrist, he believed, *and* a global conspiracy of suffragettes, Sinn Feiners, Zionists, communists and the League of Nations. His helpmeet, Lady Sydenham, ran the British Fascists' children's club.

Those who followed him on the Committee of Imperial Defence seem to have been untroubled by such matters, though Sir Charles Ottley, perhaps the best chief of staff the Navy never had, played the Business Card to advantage by quitting the Navy for a more generous paymaster – the armaments giant Armstrong Whitworth, but he was said to be somewhat ashamed of his defection. Maurice Hankey remained in Whitehall, a seemingly indispensable functionary on and off, until he was dislodged by Mr Churchill, whose wartime leadership style he deprecated – it seems Lord Hankey wasn't the only one to feel that way. As for the ' slippery courtier' who always preferred power to responsibility, the Defence Committee's 'Permanent Associate Member' Viscount Esher, he became Governor of Windsor Castle, dying in 1930 aged seventy eight.

Of 'those two pirates' – as Neville Chamberlain called them – Lloyd George was the last prime minister the Liberals would have for a very long time, if ever, and Mr Churchill, now back in the Conservative fold, was still on probation, not quite forgiven for his apostasy. Thereafter both men took care to compose their wartime memoirs to their own satisfaction, and like any pair of ageing out-of-work senators, were always ready to oblige with a pithy but sometimes ill-considered comment on world affairs. In a crass display of gullibility Mr Lloyd George made a pilgrimage to Germany, hailing Adolf Hitler as 'the resurrection and the life' of the Fatherland. Mr Churchill demanded 'English jobs for English workers.' With a parting shot at the generals, Lloyd George observed there was 'no greater fatuity than a political judgement dressed in military uniform' – he might have added, '…or in top hat and frock coat!'

The Navy League sailed on to merge with The Marine Society (there was an Air League from 1909) but the National Service League was wound up in 1921, its £12,000 assets bequeathed to the Boy Scouts who were deemed to be teaching the NSL's 'ideals of citizenship.' Octogenarian Boy Scout' and keen conscriptionist Lord Meath the Twelfth Earl lasted until 1929, leaving his own memorial 'Empire Day' – May 25th. But George Shee, subsequently knighted for running the Lifeboat Institution, saw conscription – 'National Service' – brought back *in peacetime,* when on the eve of war in 1939 the 'National' Government decreed that Britain should once more have an army for the Continent. Twenty-five years after that first encounter at Mons, another BEF sailed for France, 'regular' troops, territorials and half-trained conscript 'militiamen.' It was fortunate for George Shee that he should die six months before the ignominy of Dunkirk – and fortunate for Britain too, that her army was spared four years of fighting on the Western Front, for modern war had become no less dangerous for the infantry.

But conscription, though not quite his 'Pan-Britannic militia of all able-bodied white men,' outlived him by twenty years and more. Where Henry Wilson failed, another Field Marshal – Montgomery – ensured that every able-bodied youth would have the choice of eighteen months in uniform (the Labour government made it two years), or three months in prison as a 'conscientious objector.' National Servicemen discharged the Briton's First Duty in Germany, India, Africa and even a tiny part of Japan. They faced Zionist terrorism in Palestine, they fought in Korea, they put down nationalist revolt in Malaya, Kenya and Cyprus. They were used to overthrow the elected government of Guyana, they garrisoned the Suez Canal and invaded Egypt, but in 1963 the last National Serviceman came home

Yet without conscription the generals could still keep a small but powerful 'Expeditionary Force' on the continent of Europe, again on the left flank of a larger army in a grand alliance facing their recent ally, the Russian Bear – in Germany instead of on the North West Frontier. Their soldiers would guard the last fragments of empire, 'keep the peace' inside the United Kingdom, and invade other countries to enforce 'regime change.'

Now thrive the armourers – Henry V, Act II prologue

These were good years for the 'military-industrial complex.' In 1914 Britain spent more per head on 'defence' than Germany or France, and after another ruinously expensive war, more than any of her European allies. Edwardian shipyards had turned out dreadnoughts by the dozen, but a century later nuclear-powered submarines, aircraft carriers and expensive warplanes were on order – with a healthy export trade too. The armaments industry continued to enjoy that special 'revolving door' relationship with its customers, so the Business Card was still the one to play. More than eighty years after his death, Colonel Repington would have been flattered by the birth of another 'National Defence Association,' this one aimed at 'the entire population of the United Kingdom' but especially the 'Chairmen of military related Big Business....and other Defence Industrial Giants.' With Winston Churchill's grandson as president, this NDA boasted an impressive array of generals, admirals, air marshals and statesmen too – all for just £12 a year, Life Members £100, Corporate Subscription 'variable.'

Jockeying among themselves for the principal and (often most expensive) role, the military seldom missed an opportunity to put a well-polished boot into their civilian paymasters should any of them doubt the 'threat'—supported by 'intelligence'—and reject the recommended response; the one favouring their own branch of the Profession of course. Conservative politicians were less afraid of the brass hats, but labour governments, anxious not to be labelled 'unpatriotic,' were usually a softer touch, keeping conscription—'National Service' nearly twenty years after the second world war; giving Britain nuclear weapons; and presiding over a massive increase in the defence budget. This perhaps reflected the fact that warships, aeroplanes and tanks were mostly built in 'Labour' constituencies – and it was a 'New Labour' government that sent the troops into Iraq and Afghanistan.

Field Marshals Woleseley, Roberts, Kitchener, Wully Robertson and Henry Wilson too, would have been at home in this brave new world. They would applaud the skill of their successors, who for almost half a century had used 'The Threat' to justify their sincerely-held belief that only *they* could save Western Civilisation. But their sometimes ferocious tribal squabbles as to which of them wielded the sharpest sword merely demonstrated that as always, the politics of the Profession had less to do with grand strategy and more with the need to preserve the Institution – or at least *their* part of it. Sagely delivering the platitude that 'victory' could not be achieved by force alone; whilst simultaneously advising that with one more 'surge' the enemy would be compelled to negotiate a lasting peace—(though it might take several years)—the guardians of the Profession managed to preserve the hoary fiction that their first loyalty was to the elected government rather than to the Institution; the Profession.

However unpopular a government might be when expectations proved illusory, one group has always stood high in public esteem – soldiers. Enduring the rigours of Britain's fourth and longest war in Afghanistan, British soldiers were informed by one visiting prime minister—without any hint of irony or shame—that a free press, and the vote, were won by soldiers, not by politicians or journalists.*

One wonders then what *real* value a 'free press' or hard-won democracy when those entrusted with the oversight of these institutions place such a premium on their own, secretive and undemocratic agendas?

---

* BBC Radio 4 *Today* 11 June 2010

Not every statesman nor his speech writer it seems, and not every general, would now remember, let alone heed Mr Gladstone's advice during the Second Afghan War – to 'avoid needless and entangling engagements.' *

Apparently, the Great War had taught them nothing.

---
* Third Midlothian Speech 26 November 1879

~ Conclusion ~

"I grew up in the shadow of that war. I listened to veterans of the Western Front, I lived through the second great war, and was old enough to play a small part in it; friends died in battle; one of my comrades fell beside me; I can still hear his dying screams..."

John Dekker, Middlesex, UK, 2013

If the 'war to end wars' has taught us anything, it is surely that History *does* repeat itself. The 'Great War' was a tragedy for Britain, but it was also a triumph – of sorts. A victorious Germany would certainly have imposed far harsher peace terms than the Treaty of Versailles – that's if the Treaty of Brest-Litovsk and the manner in which civilians were treated in occupied France and Belgium is anything to go by. But the horror of this 'Great War' still fascinates – and the question remains; could Britain have kept out of what was essentially a continental quarrel? Was there ever *really* a serious threat to England?

In 1914, the view from Berlin was clear enough. Confronted by two strong military powers—France and Russia—and taking into account Britain's huge navy (and possibly a smaller but powerful army as well) it was the Germans who might justifiably feel it was *they* who were threatened by hostile 'encirclement,' and maybe their generals were right to plan a 'pre-emptive strike'.

Perhaps the lesson of 1914 is that everywhere, agents of the state thrive on secret knowledge and 'disinformation.' Forever in need of a plausible mission, inscrutable officials feed ministers the sort of 'intelligence' their masters *want* to hear, though the 'source' of this information cannot usually be revealed 'for reasons of national security'. As one public servant argued in 1908; 'we have to suppress the truth and resort to subterfuge at times to meet hostile public opinion.'

In those troubled years of public hysteria and backstairs intrigue, the soldiers and the statesmen in Whitehall were doing just that, wilfully deceiving themselves and each other – and their countrymen too – as they blindly stumbled into 'the wrong kind of war.'

Yes, it was a clumsy, botched affair – but then, it *was* a very British conspiracy.

References & Further Reading

- Adams,RJQ, Poirier, PP: *The Conscription Controversy in Great Britain 1900-1918* London, MacMillan 1987

- Allison, M: *The National Service Issue 1899-1914* PhD Thesis Univ of London 1975

- Arnold-Forster, HO: *Military Needs and Military Policy* London Smith Elder 1909

- Ash, B: *The Lost Dictator: Field Marshal Sir Henry Wilson* London, Cassell 1968

- Beckett IFW: *Riflemen Form – a Study of the Rifle Volunteer Movement 1859- 1908* Aldershot Ogilvy Trust 1982

- Beckett IFW: *The Army and the Curragh Incident 1914* Bodley Head for Army Rcords Society 1986

- Beckett IFW: *The Amateur Military Tradition* Manchester University Press 1991

- Beresford, Admiral Lord Charles: *The Great Betrayal* London P S King 1912

- Blake R: *The Conservative Party from Peel to Thatcher* London Fontana Press 1985

- Bonham-Carter V: *Soldier True – The Life and Times of Field Marshal Sir William Robertson* London Frederick Muller 1963

- Callwell, Major General C E: *Field Marshal Sir Henry Wilson: His Life and Diaries* London Cassell 1927

- Clarke, Sir George (Lord Sydenham): *My Working Life* London John Murray 1927

- Clarke IF: *Voices Prophesying War* London Panther 1970

- Clarke IF (ed): *The Tale of the Next Great War 1871-1914* Liverpool Univ Press 1995

- Clausewitz C: *On War* Howard M, Paret P (ed, trans) Princeton University Press 1989

- Collier B: *Brass Hat A Biography of Sir Henry Wilson* London Secker & Warburg 1961

- Corbett Sir Julian S: *Some Principles of Maritime Strategy* (1911) London Conway Maritime Press 1972

- Corrigan G: *Mud, Blood and Poppycock- Britain and the First World War* London Cassel 1987
- Cross C: *The Liberals in Power 1905-14* London Pall Mall Press 1963
- Cunningham, Hugh: *The Volunteer Force: a Social & Political History 1859-1908* Archon Books Hamden Connecticut 1975
- Dilke, Sir Charles & Spenser Wilkinson: *Imperial Defence* London MacMillan 1892
- D'Ombrain, N: *War Machinery & High Policy: Defence Administration in Peacetime Britain 1902-1914* London OUP 1973
- Du Cane, Col Herbert (trans): *The German Official Account of the War in South Africa, the Great General Staff, Berlin* London John Murray 1906
- Earle M (ed): *Makers of Modern Strategy* Princeton U P 1943
- Esher, Reginald Brett, 2nd Viscount: *Letters and Journals* ed Maurice and Oliver Brett, London, Nicholson & Watson 1934-38
- Fergusson N: *The Pity of War* Penguin Books 1999
- Fraser, P: *Lord Esher: a Political Biography* London, Hart Davis, MacGibbon 1973
- French, D: *British Strategy & War Aims 1914-16* London Allen Unwin 1986
- French, D: *Strategy of the Lloyd George Coalition 1916-18* OUP 1995
- Gladstone W E: *Midlothian Speeches 1979* Leicester University Press 1971
- Gooch J: *The Plans of War: The General Staff and British Military Strategy, 1900-16* London, Routledge Kegan & Paul 1974
- Gooch J: *The Prospect of War – Studies in British Defence Policy 1847-1942* London, Frank Cass 1981
- Gordon A: *The Rules of the Game – Jutland and British Naval Command* Annapolis Maryland Naval Institute Press 2000
- Gough B M: 'The Royal Navy and the British Empire' in *Oxford History of the British Empire* OUP 1999 Vol V *Historiography* ed Wnks RW pp 327-341
- Grey Sir E: *Twenty Five Years* London Hodder & Stoughton 1928
- Griffith P: *Battle Tactics of the Western Front: The British Army's Art of Attack 1916-18* Yale University Press 1994

- Haldane, R B: *Before the War* London Cassell 1920
- Haldane, R B: *Autobiography* London Hodder & Stoughton 1929
- Hamilton, General Sir Ian: *Compulsory Service* London John Murray 1910 2nd edition
- Hanham, H J: *The Nineteenth Century Constitution 1815-1914* CUP 1968
- Hayes, D: *Conscription Conflict* London Sheppard 1949
- Hilton, Boyd: *A Mad, Bad and Dangerous People? England 1783-1846 The New Oxford History of England* OUP 2006
- Hinsley, F H (ed): *British Foreign Policy under Sir Edward Grey* Cambridge University Press 1977
- Hirst and Allen: *British War Budgets* OUP 1926
- Hogg, Ian V: *Coast Defences of England & Wales 1856-1956* David & Charles 1974
- Holden, Reid B: *Studies in British Military Thought* University of Nebraska Press, 1998
- Hoppen, KT *The Mid-Victorian Generation 1846- 1886 The New Oxford History of England* OUP 1998
- Horton Smith, LG, & Wyatt, HF: *The Passing of the Great Fleet* London Sampson Low 1909
- Howard, M (ed): *Soldiers and Governments* London, Eyre & Spottiswoode 1957
- Huntington, S P: *The Soldier & the State: The Theory & Politics of Civil Military Relations* Cambridge, Belknap/Harvard 1957
- Janowitz, M: *The Professional Soldier* New York, The Free Press 1964
- Jeffery, K: *Field Marshal Sir Henry Wilson A Political Soldier* OUP 2006
- Jenkins, Roy: *Asquith* London Collins 1964
- Kennedy, Paul M: *The Rise of the Anglo-German Antagonism 1860-1914* London Allen & Unwin 1980
- Kennedy, Paul M: *The Rise and Fall of British Naval Mastery* London Allen and Unwin 1976
- Koss, S E: *Lord Haldane, Scapegoat for Liberalism* Columbia University Press 1969
- Koss, S E: Asquith London Allen Lane 1976

- Kossmann, EH: *The Low Countries 1780-1940 Oxford History of Modern Europe* OUP 1978

- Lambert, A D: *The Foundations of Naval History: John Knox Laughton, the Royal Navy and the Historical Profession* London Chatham Publishing 1998

- Lambert, A D: *Admirals, the Naval Commanders who made Britain Great* London Faber & Faber 2008

- Lloyd George, D: *War Memoirs* London Odhams Press Ltd 1938 2 Vols

- Luvaas, J: *The Education of an Army: British Military Thought 1815-1940* London Cassell 1965

- McNeill, W H: *The Pursuit of Power: technology, armed force and society since AD 1000* University of Chicago Press 1982

- Marder, A J: *The Anatomy of British Sea Power: A History of British Naval Policy in the Pre-Dreadnought Era 1880-1905* London Frank Cass 1940

- Marder, A J: *From the Dreadnought to Scapa Flow: The Royal Navy in the Fisher Era 1904-1919 Vol 1 The Road to War* London OUP 1961

- Massie, R K: *Dreadnought* London Jonathan Cape 1992

- Maurice, F: *Haldane* London Faber 1937

- Monger, G: *The End of Isolation: British Foreign Policy 1900-1907* London Nelson 1963

- Morris, A J A: *The Scaremongers: war and rearmament 1896-1914* London, Routledge & Kegan Paul 1984

- Porter, A (ed): *Oxford History of the British Empire* Vol III OUP 1999

- Offer, A: *The First World War: An Agrarian Interpretation* Oxford, OUP 1989

- Repington, Charles à Court: *Vestigia* London Constable 1919

- Repington: *The First World War* Aldershot Gregg Revivals/King's College London

- Robbins, K G: *'Public Opinion. The Press and Pressure Groups'* in Hinsley, F H (Ed) *British Foreign Policy under Sir Edward Grey* London CUP 1977

- Roberts, Field Marshal Lord: *Fallacies & Facts: an Answer to "Compulsory Service"* London John Murray 1911

- Robertson, W: *From Private to Field Marshal* London Constable 1921

- Robertson, W: *Soldiers and Statesmen* London Constable 1928

- Robertson, W: *Military Correspondence of Field Marshal Sir William Robertson, Chief of the Imperial General Staff, December 1915 – February 1918* (ed. Woodward D) London Army Records Society & Bodley Head 1989

- Ryan, W M: *Lt Col Charles à Court Repington: a Study in the Interaction of Personality, the Press and Power* New York & London, Garland Publishing 1987

- Schurman, D: *The Education of a Navy* London Cassell 1965

- Searle, G R A: *New England? Peace and War 1886-1918 The New Oxford History of England* O U P 2004

- Spiers, E M: *Haldane – Army Reformer* Edinburgh University Press 1980

- Steiner, Z S: *Britain and the Origins of the First World War* London MacMillan Press 1977

- Stewart, A T Q: *The Ulster Crisis* London Faber & Faber 1967

- Strachan, H: *The Politics of the British Army* Oxford U P 1997

- Strachan, H: *The First World War* Vol I *To Arms* Oxford U P 2001

- Townshend, C: *The British Campaign in Ireland 1919-1921* OUP 1975

- Toye, R: *Lloyd George and Churchill* London Pan MacMillan 2007

- Tyler, J E: *The British Army and the Continent 1904 -14* London Edward Arnold 1938

- Webb, B: *Letters, Partnership 1892-1912* London CUP/LSE 1978

- Wilson, J: *C-B; a life of Sir Henry Campbell Bannerman* London Constable 1973

- Wilkinson, S: *Britain at Bay* London Constable 1909

- Williamson, S R: *The Politics of Grand Strategy: Britain & France Prepare for War 1904-14* Cambridge Harvard University Press 1969

- Woodward, D: *Field Marshal Sir William Robertson* Westport Praeger 1998

- Woodward, D: *Lloyd George and the Generals* London Associated University Press Ltd 1983

Papers and Journals

- De Tarlé, A: 'The British Army and a Continental War' RUSI *Journal* March 1913, Vol LVII Part 1, No 421, pp 384-401

- Hamilton. The Papers of Sir Ian Hamilton: Liddell Hart Centre for Military Archives, King's College London

- Low, Sidney: 'War, that occasional tonic of which the body politic stands in need' – *Nineteenth Century* October 1898 Vol XLIV p 523

- Milner. The Papers of Lord Milner belonging to New College, Oxford, deposited in the Bodliean Library, Oxford

- O'Domhnaill, Ruari: 'The Curragh Mutiny in Historical Perspective' RUSI *Journal* February 2004 Vol 149 No 1 pp 80-84

- Roberts. The Papers of Field Marshal Lord Roberts of Kandahar; National Army Museum, London

- Ropp, T: 'Conscription in Great Britain, 1900-1914: a Failure in Civil-Military Relations?' *Military Affairs*, No 20 1956 pp 71-76

- Seligman, M S: 'A View from Berlin: Colonel Frederick Trench and the Development of British Perceptions of German Aggressive Intent, 1906-1910' *Journal of Strategic Studies*, June 2000 Ilford, Frank Cass Vol 23 No 2 pp 114-147 Fabianism and the Empire (ed Shaw GB) London 1900

- Shee, G F: 'The Advantages of Compulsory Service for Home Defence, together with a consideration of some of the objectives which may be urged against it' - *RUSI Journal* May 1902 Vol XLVI No 291, pp 569-593

- Smith, S R B: 'Public Opinion, the Navy and the City of London: The Drive for British Naval Expansion in the Late 19th Century' *War and Society*, May 1991 University of New South Wales Vol 9, No 1 pp 29-50

- Tulloch, Capt J B G: 'Is a National Army necessary for the British Isles?' RUSI *Journal* February 1907 Vol LI Part 1 No 348 pp 184-192

- Wright, Col AJA: 'The Probable Effects of Compulsory Military Training on Recruiting for the Regular Army' RUSI *Journal* December 1911 Vol LV Part 2 No 406 pp 1589-1689

- Wyatt H F: 'War as the Supreme Test of National Value' *Nineteenth Century* February 1899 Vol XLIV

www.ingramcontent.com/pod-product-compliance
Lightning Source LLC
Chambersburg PA
CBHW061305110426
42742CB00012BA/2060